Solutions Manual

for use with

Investments

Fourth Edition

Zvi Bodie
Boston University

Alex Kane
University of California, San Diego

Alan J. Marcus
Boston College

Irwin
McGraw-Hill

Boston   Burr Ridge, IL   Dubuque, IA   Madison, WI   New York   San Francisco   St. Louis
Bangkok   Bogotá   Caracas   Lisbon   London   Madrid
Mexico City   Milan   New Delhi   Seoul   Singapore   Sydney   Taipei   Toronto

Irwin/McGraw-Hill

A Division of The McGraw-Hill Companies

Solutions Manual for use with
INVESTMENTS

1 2 3 4 5 6 7 8 9 0 BBC/BBC 9 3 2 1 0 9 8

ISBN 0-256-26191-1

http://www.mhhe.com

CHAPTER 1 :   THE INVESTMENT ENVIRONMENT

1. a. Cash is a financial asset because it is the liability of the government.

   b. No. The cash does not directly add to the productive capacity of the economy.

   c. Yes. You can buy more goods and services than previously.

   d. If the economy is already operating at full capacity, and you now command the extra purchasing power offered by the $10 billion, then your increased ability to purchase goods must be offset by a decline in the ability of others to purchase goods. Thus, the other individuals in the economy can be made worse off by your discovery.

2. a. The bank loan is a financial liability for Lanni; conversely, Lanni's IOU is the bank's financial asset. The cash Lanni receives is a financial asset. The new financial asset created is Lanni's note (that is, its IOU to the bank).

   b. Lanni transfers financial assets (cash) to its software developers. In return it gets a real asset, the completed software. No financial assets are created or destroyed; cash is simply transferred from one party to another.

   c. Lanni gives the real asset (the software) to Microsoft in exchange for a financial asset, shares in Microsoft . Since Microsoft issues new shares to pay Lanni, this represents the creation of new financial assets.

   d. Lanni exchanges one financial asset (1,500 shares of stock) for another ($120,000). It gives a financial asset ($50,000 cash) to the bank and gets back another financial asset (its IOU). The loan is "destroyed" in the transaction, since it is retired when paid off, and no longer exists.

3. a.

Assets		*Liabilities & shareholders' equity*	
Cash	$ 70,000	Bank loan	$ 50,000
Computers	30,000	Shareholders' equity	50,000
Total	$100,000	Total	$100,000

   Ratio of real to total assets = 30,000/100,000 = .30

   b.

Assets		*Liabilities & shareholders' equity*	
Software product*	$ 70,000	Bank loan	$ 50,000
Computers	30,000	Shareholders' equity	50,000
Total	$100,000	Total	$100,000

   *Valued at cost
   Ratio of real to total assets = 100,000/100,000 = 1.0

c.

Assets		Liabilities & shareholders' equity	
Microsoft shares	$120,000	Bank loan	$ 50,000
Computers	30,000	Shareholders' equity	100,000
Total	$150,000	Total	$150,000

Ratio of real to total assets = 30,000/150,000 = .20

Conclusion: when the firm starts up and raises working capital, it will be characterized by a low ratio of real to total assets. When it is in full production, it will have a high ratio of real assets. When the project "shuts down" and the firm sells it off for cash, financial assets once again replace real assets.

4. The ratio is 628/17,252 = .036 for financial institutions, and 5,230/8,097 = .646 for the non-financial business sector. The difference should be expected mainly because the bulk of the business of financial institutions is to make loans which are financial assets.

5. The tax increased the relative attractiveness of Eurobonds compared to dollar-denominated bonds issued in the U.S., contributing to the growth of that market. This provides a lesson on the potential efficacy or lack of efficacy of financial regulations in global markets where market participants can direct trades across national boundaries.

6. a. Primary-market transaction

   b. If we consider gold bullion to be the primary asset, then the certificate, which is a claim to gold, would be a derivative asset. Its value depends on the value of the primary asset.

   c. Investors who wish to own gold without the complication of physical storage.

7. Securitization requires access to a large number of potential investors. To attract them the capital market needs: 1) a safe system of business laws and low probability of confiscatory taxation/regulation, 2) a well-developed investment banking industry, 3) a well-developed system of brokerage and financial transactions, and 4) well-developed information systems, particularly for financial reporting. These are found in (indeed make for) a well-developed financial market.

8. a. No. Diversification calls for investing your savings in assets that do well when GM is doing poorly.

   b. No. Although Toyota is a competitor of GM, both are subject to fluctuations in the automobile market.

9.   Unlike fixed salary contracts, bonuses create better incentives for executives to enhance the performance of the firm.

10.   Securitization leads to disintermediation; that is, it provides a means for market participants to bypass intermediaries. For example, mortgage-backed securities channel funds to the housing market without requiring that banks or thrift institutions make loans from their own portfolios. As securitization progresses, financial intermediaries must increase other activities such as providing financial services or short-term liquidity to consumers and small business.

11.   The REIT manager pools the resources of many investors and uses these resources to buy a portfolio of real estate assets. Each investor in the REIT owns a fraction of the total portfolio according to his or her investment. The REIT gives the investor the ability to hold a diversified portfolio. Moreover, the investor has the ability to buy and sell shares in the REIT far more easily and cheaply than the underlying real estate itself could be bought or sold. Investors will be willing to pay the manager of a REIT a reasonable management fee for these benefits. Therefore, the profit motive will lead qualified firms to organize and sell REITs.

12.   Ultimately, real assets do determine the material well-being of an economy. Nevertheless, individuals can benefit when financial engineering creates new products that allow them to manage their portfolios of financial assets more efficiently. Because bundling and unbundling creates financial products with new properties and sensitivities to various sources of risk, it allows investors to allocate and hedge particular sources of risk more efficiently.

13.   Financial assets make it easy for large firms to raise capital to finance their investments in real assets. If General Motors, for example, could not issue stocks or bonds to the general public, it would have a far more difficult time raising capital. Contraction of the supply of financial assets would make financing more difficult, increasing the cost of capital. A higher cost of capital means less investment and lower real growth.

14.   In 19th-century America, with a largely agrarian economy, uncertainty in crop yields and prices was a major source of economy-wide risk. Therefore, there was a great incentive to create devices that would allow both producers and purchasers of agricultural commodities to hedge this risk. In contrast, the risk of paper or pencil prices was far smaller, and the need to hedge against such risk was minimal. There would be no demand for trading in securities that would allow investors to transfer risk in the prices of these goods.

CHAPTER 2 : MARKETS AND INSTRUMENTS

1. a. (iv)

   b. (ii)

   c. (i) Writing a call entails unlimited potential losses as the stock price rises.

2. a. $r_{BEY} = \dfrac{10,000 - P}{P} \times \dfrac{365}{n}$

   $= \dfrac{10,000 - 9600}{9600} \times \dfrac{365}{180} = .0845$, or 8.45%

   b. One reason is that the discount yield is computed by dividing the dollar discount from par by the par value, $10,000, rather than by the bill's price, $9,600. A second reason is that the discount yield is annualized by a 360-day year rather than 365.

3. $P = 10,000\,[1 - r_{BD}\,(n/360)]$ where r_{BD} is the discount yield.

   $P_{ask} = 10,000\,[1 - .0681\,(60/360)] = \$9,886.50$

   $P_{bid} = 10,000\,[1 - .0690\,(60/360)] = \$9,885.00$

4. $r_{BEY} = \dfrac{10,000 - P}{P} \times \dfrac{365}{n}$

   $= \dfrac{10,000 - 9886.50}{9886.50} \times \dfrac{365}{60} = 6.98\%,$

   which exceeds the discount yield, $r_{BD} = 6.81\%$.

   To obtain the effective annual yield, r_{EAY}, note that the 60-day growth factor for invested funds is $\dfrac{10,000}{9886.50} = 1.01148$. Annualizing this growth rate results in

   $1 + r_{EAY} = \left(\dfrac{10,000}{9886.50}\right)^{365/60} = 1.0719$ which implies that $r_{EAY} = 7.19\%$

5. a. i. $1 + r = (10,000/9,764)^4 = 1.1002$

   $r = 10.02\%$

   ii. $1 + r = (10,000/9,539)^2 = 1.0990$

   $r = 9.90\%$

   The three-month bill offers a higher effective annual yield.

b. i. $\quad r_{BD} = \dfrac{10,000 - 9764}{10,000} \times \dfrac{360}{91} = .0934$

ii. $\quad r_{BD} = \dfrac{10,000 - 9539}{10,000} \times \dfrac{360}{182} = .0912$

6. a. Price = $\$10,000 \times [1 - .03 \times \dfrac{90}{360}] = \$9,925$

b. 90-day return $= \dfrac{10,000 - 9,925}{9,925} = .007557 = .7557\%$

c. BEY $= .7557\% \times \dfrac{365}{90} = 3.065\%$

d. Effective annual yield $= (1.007557)^{365/90} - 1 = .0310 = 3.10\%$

7. The bill has a maturity of one-half year, and an annualized discount of 9.18%. Therefore, its actual percentage discount from par value is $9.18\% \times 1/2 = 4.59\%$. The bill will sell for $\$100,000 \times (1 - .0459) = \$95,410$.

8. The total before-tax income is $4, of which $.30 \times \$4 = \$1.20$ is taxable income (after the 70% exclusion). Taxes therefore are $.30 \times \$1.20 = \$.36$, for an after-tax income of $3.64, and a rate of return of 9.1%.

9. a. The index at $t = 0$ is $(90 + 50 + 100)/3 = 80$. At $t = 1$, it is $250/3 = 83.333$, for a rate of return of 4.167%.

b. In the absence of a split, stock C would sell for 110, and the index would be $250/3 = 83.33$. After the split, stock C sells at 55. Therefore, we need to set the divisor d such that $83.33 = (95 + 45 + 55)/d$, meaning that $d = 2.34$.

c. The return is zero. The index remains unchanged, as it should, since the return on each stock separately equals zero.

10. a. Total market value at $t = 0$ is $(9,000 + 10,000 + 20,000) = 39,000$. Market value at $t = 1$ is $(9,500 + 9,000 + 22,000) = 40,500$. Rate of return = $40,500/39,000 - 1 = 3.85\%$.

b. The return on each stock is as follows:

$r_A = 95/90 - 1 = .0556$

$r_B = 45/50 - 1 = -.10$

$r_C = 110/100 - 1 = .10$

The equally-weighted average is $.0185 = 1.85\%$

c. The geometric average return is $[(1.0556)(.90)(1.10)]^{1/3} - 1 = .0148 = 1.48\%$.

11.	The after-tax yield on the corporate bonds is .09 × (1 − .28) = .0648. Therefore, munis must pay at least 6.48%.

12.	a.	The taxable bond. With a zero tax bracket, its after-tax rate is the same as the before-tax rate, 5%, which is greater than the rate on the municipal bond.

	b.	The taxable bond. Its after-tax rate is 5 × (1 − .1) = 4.5%.

	c.	You are indifferent. The after-tax rate of the taxable bond is 5 × (1 − .2) = 4%, the same as that of the muni.

	d.	The muni offers the higher after-tax rate for investors in tax brackets above 20%.

13.	Equation (2.5) shows that the equivalent taxable yield is: $r = r_m/(1 − t)$.

	a.	4%
	b.	4.44%
	c.	5%
	d.	5.71%

14.	If the after-tax yields are equal, then 5.6% = 8% × (1 − t). This implies that t = .30, so the correct choice is (a).

15.	a.	The higher coupon bond.
	b.	The call with the lower exercise price.
	c.	The put on the lower priced stock.
	d.	The bill with the lower yield.

16.	There is always a chance that the option will be in the money at some point prior to expiration. Investors will pay something for this chance of a positive payoff.

17.

	Value of call at expiration	−	Initial Cost	=	Profit
a.	0		4		−4
b.	0		4		−4
c.	0		4		−4
d.	5		4		1
e.	10		4		6

	Value of put at expiration	−	Initial Cost	=	Profit
a.	10		6		4
b.	5		6		−1
c.	0		6		−6
d.	0		6		−6
e.	0		6		−6

18.   The put option conveys the *right* to sell the underlying asset at the exercise price. The short futures contract carries an *obligation* to sell the underlying asset for the futures price.

19.   The call option conveys the *right* to buy the underlying asset at the exercise price. The long futures contract carries an *obligation* to buy the underlying asset for the futures price.

20.   The spread will widen. A deterioration in the economy increases credit risk, that is, the likelihood of default. Investors will demand a greater premium on debt subject to default risk.

21.   On the day that we tried this experiment, 37 of the 50 stocks met this criterion, leading us to conclude that returns on stock investments can be quite volatile.

CHAPTER 3: HOW SECURITIES ARE TRADED

1. a. In addition to the explicit fees of $70,000, FBN appears to have paid an implicit price in underpricing of the IPO. The underpricing is $3/share or $300,000 total, implying total costs of $370,000.

   b. No. The underwriters do not capture the part of the costs corresponding to the underpricing. The underpricing may be a rational marketing strategy. Without it, the underwriters would need to spend more resources to place the issue with the public. They would then need to charge higher explicit fees to the issuing firm. The issuing firm may be just as well off paying the implicit issuance cost represented by the underpricing.

2. a. In principle, potential losses are unbounded, growing directly with increases in the price of IBX

   b. If the stop-buy order can be filled at $78, the maximum possible loss per share is $8. If IBX shares go above $78, the stop-buy order is executed, limiting the losses from the short sale.

3. The stop-loss order will be executed as soon as the stock price hits the limit price. If the stock price later rebounds, the investor does not participate in the gains because the stock has been sold. In contrast, the put option need not be exercised when the stock price falls below the exercise price. An investor who owns a share of stock and a put option can hold on to both securities. If the stock price never rebounds, the put can be exercised eventually, and the stock sold for the exercise price. This provides the same downside protection as the stop-loss order. If the price *does* rebound, however, the investor benefits because the stock is still held. This advantage of the put over the stop-loss order justifies the cost of the put.

4. Calls are options to purchase a stock at any time prior to expiration. Stop-buys require purchase as soon as the stock price hits the limit. The advantage of the call over the stop-buy is that the investor need not commit to buying until expiration. If the stock price later falls, the holder of the call can choose not to purchase.

5. The broker is to attempt to sell Marriott as soon as the stock is sold at a price of 38 or less. Here, the broker will attempt to execute if a sale takes place at the bid price, but may not be able to sell at 38, since the bid price is now 37 1/4.

6. Much of what the specialist does -- crossing orders and maintaining the limit order book -- can be accomplished by a computerized system. In fact, some exchanges use an automated system for night trading. A more difficult issue is whether the more discretionary activities of specialists that involve trading for their own accounts, such as maintaining an orderly market, can be replicated by a computer system.

7. a. The buy order will be filled at the best limit-sell order, $50.25.

   b. At the next-best price, $51.50.

   c. You should increase your position. There is considerable buy pressure at prices just below $50, meaning that downside risk is limited. In contrast, sell pressure is sparse, meaning that a moderate buy order could result in a substantial price increase.

8. The system expedites the flow of orders from exchange members to the specialists. It allows members to send computerized orders directly to the floor of the exchange, which allows the nearly simultaneous sale of each stock in a large portfolio. This capability is necessary for program trading.

9. The dealer. Spreads should be higher on inactive stocks and lower on active stocks.

10. Over short periods of time, membership price generally increases along with trading volume. This makes sense, since trading commissions depend on trading volume.

11. Cost of purchase is $80 \times 250 = \$20,000$. You borrow $5000 from your broker, and invest $15,000 of your own funds. Your margin account starts out with a net worth of $15,000.

   a. (i) Net worth rises by $2,000 from $15,000 to $88 \times 250 - \$5,000 = \$17,000$.

      Percentage gain = $2,000/$15,000 = .1333 = 13.33%

      (ii) With unchanged price, net worth remains unchanged.

      Percentage gain = zero

      (iii) Net worth falls to $72 \times 250 - \$5,000 = \$13,000$.

      Percentage gain $= \dfrac{-\$2,000}{\$15,000} = -.1333 = -13.33\%$

   The relationship between the percentage change in the price of the stock and the investor's percentage gain is given by:

   $$\% \text{ gain} = \% \text{ change in price} \times \frac{\text{Total investment}}{\text{investor's initial equity}} = \% \text{ change in price} \times 1.333$$

   For example, when the stock price rises from 80 to 88, the percentage change in price is 10%, while the percentage gain for the investor is 1.333 times as large, 13.33%:

$$\% \text{ gain} = 10\% \times \frac{\$20,000}{\$15,000} = 13.33\%$$

b. The value of the 250 shares is 250P. Equity is 250P – 5000. You will receive a margin call when

$$\frac{250P - 5,000}{250P} = .25 \quad \text{or when P} = \$26.67.$$

c. The value of the 250 shares is 250P. But now you have borrowed $10,000 instead of $5,000. Therefore, equity is only 250P – $10,000. You will receive a margin call when

$$\frac{250P - 10,000}{250P} = .25 \quad \text{or when P} = \$53.33.$$

With less equity in the account, you are far more vulnerable to a margin call.

d. The margin loan with accumulated interest after one year is $5,000 × 1.08 = $5,400. Therefore, equity in your account is 250P – $5,400. Initial equity was $15,000. Therefore, your rate of return after one year is as follows:

(i) $$\frac{(250 \times \$88 - \$5400) - \$15,000}{15,000} = .1067, \text{ or } 10.67\%.$$

(ii) $$\frac{(250 \times \$80 - \$5400) - \$15,000}{15,000} = -.0267, \text{ or } -2.67\%.$$

(iii) $$\frac{(250 \times \$72 - \$5400) - \$15,000}{15,000} = -.160, \text{ or } -16.0\%.$$

The relationship between the percentage change in the price of Intel and investor's percentage return is given by:

$$\% \text{ gain} = \frac{\% \text{ change}}{\text{in price}} \times \frac{\text{Total investment}}{\text{investor's initial equity}} - 8\% \times \frac{\text{Funds borrowed}}{\text{investor's initial equity}}$$

For example, when the stock price rises from 80 to 88, the percentage change in price is 10%, while the percentage gain for the investor is

$$10\% \times \frac{20,000}{15,000} - 8\% \times \frac{5000}{15,000} = 10.67\%$$

e. The value of the 250 shares is 250P. Equity is 250P – 5,400. You will receive a margin call when

$$\frac{250P - 5400}{250P} = .25 \quad \text{or when P} = \$28.80$$

3-3

12. a. The gain or loss on the short position is $-250 \times \Delta P$. Invested funds are $15,000. Therefore, rate of return = $(-250 \times \Delta P)/15,000$. The returns in each of the three scenarios are:

(i) rate of return = $(-250 \times 8)/15,000 = -.133 = -13.3\%$

(ii) rate of return = $(-250 \times 0)/15,000 = 0$

(iii) rate of return = $[-250 \times (-8)]/15,000 = +.133 = +13.3\%$

b. Total assets in the margin account are $20,000 (from the sale of the stock) + $15,000 (the initial margin) = $35,000; liabilities are 250P. A margin call will be issued when

$$\frac{35,000 - 250P}{250P} = .25, \quad \text{or when P} = \$112.$$

c. With a $2 dividend, the short position must also pay $2/share $\times$ 250 shares = $500 on the borrowed shares. Rate of return will be $(-250 \times \Delta P - 500)/15,000$.

(i) rate of return = $(-250 \times 8 - 500)/15,000 = -.167 = -16.7\%$

(ii) rate of return = $(-250 \times 0 - 500)/15,000 = -.033 = -3.33\%$

(iii) rate of return = $[-250 \times (-8) - 500]/15,000 = +.100 = +10.0\%$

Total assets (net of the dividend repayment) are $35,000 - 500$, and liabilities are 250P. A margin call will be issued when

$$\frac{35,000 - 500 - 250P}{250P} = .25, \quad \text{or when P} = \$110.40.$$

13. a. 55 1/2

b. 55 1/4

c. The trade will not be executed since the bid price is less than the price on the limit sell order.

d. The trade will not be executed since the asked price is greater than the price on the limit buy order.

14. a. There can be price improvement for the two market orders. Brokers for each of the market orders (i.e., the buy and the sell orders) can agree to do a trade inside the quoted spread. For example, they can trade at $55 3/8, thus improving the price for both customers by $1/8 relative to the quoted bid and ask prices. The buyer gets the stock for $1/8 less than the quoted ask price, and the seller receives $1/8 more for the stock than the quoted bid price.

b. Whereas the limit buy order at $55 3/8 would not be executed in a dealer market (since the ask price is $55 1/2), it could be executed in an exchange market. A broker for another customer with an order to sell at market would view the limit buy order as the best bid price; the two brokers could agree to the trade and bring it to the specialist, which would execute the trade.

15. a. You buy 200 shares of AT&T. These shares increase in value by 10%, or $1000. You pay interest of $.08 \times 5{,}000 = \$400$. The rate of return will be

$$\frac{1000 - 400}{5000} = .12, \text{ or } 12\%.$$

b. The value of the 200 shares is 200P. Equity is 200P – 5000. You will receive a margin call when

$$\frac{200P - 5000}{200P} = .30 \quad \text{or when P} = \$35.71.$$

16. a. You will not receive a margin call. You borrowed $20,000 and with another $20,000 of your own equity you bought 500 shares of Disney at $80 a share. At $75 a share the market value of the account is $37,500, your equity is $17,500, and the percentage margin is 47%, which is above the required maintenance margin.

b. A margin call will be issued when

$$\frac{500\ P - 20{,}000}{500P} = .35 \quad \text{or when P} = \$61.54.$$

17. a. Initial margin is 50% of $5000 or $2500.

b. Total assets are $7500, and liabilities are 100P. A margin call will be issued when

$$\frac{7500 - 100P}{100P} = .30 \quad \text{or when P} = \$57.69.$$

18. The proceeds from the short sale (net of commission) were $14 \times 100 - \$50 =$ $1,350. A dividend payment of $200 was withdrawn from the account. Coverage at $9 cost you (including commission) $900 + $50 = $950, leaving you with a profit of $1350 – $200 – $950 = $200.

Note that your profit, $200, equals 100 shares × profit per share of $2. Your net proceeds per share were:

$14	sales price of stock
–$ 9	repurchase price of stock
–$ 2	dividend per share
–$ 1	2 trades × $.50 commission per share on each trade.
$ 2	

20.   (d) The broker will attempt to sell after the first transaction at $55 or less.

21.   (b)

22.   (d)

CHAPTER 4: MUTUAL FUNDS AND OTHER INVESTMENT COMPANIES

1. The unit investment trust should have lower operating expenses. Because its portfolio is fixed once the trust is established, it does not have to pay portfolio managers to constantly monitor and rebalance the portfolio as perceived needs or opportunities change. Because its portfolio is fixed, the unit investment trust also incurs virtually no trading costs.

2. The offer price includes a 6% front-end load, or sales commission, meaning that every dollar paid results in only $.94 going toward purchase of shares. Therefore,

$$\text{Offer price} = \frac{\text{NAV}}{1 - \text{load}} = \frac{\$10.70}{1 - .06} = \$11.38$$

3. NAV = offer price $\times$ (1 – load) = $12.30 $\times$ .95 = $11.69

4.

Stock	Value
A	7,000,000
B	12,000,000
C	8,000,000
D	15,000,000
Total	42,000,000

$$\text{Net asset value} = \frac{\$42,000,000 - \$30,000}{4,000,000} = \$10.49$$

5. Value of stocks sold and replaced = $15,000,000

$$\text{Turnover rate} = \frac{\$15,000,000}{\$42,000,000} = .357 = 35.7\%$$

6. a. $$\text{NAV} = \frac{\$200,000,000 - \$3,000,000}{5,000,000} = \$39.40$$

    b. $$\text{Premium or discount} = \frac{\text{Price} - \text{NAV}}{\text{NAV}} = \frac{\$36 - \$39.40}{\$39.40} = -.086$$

    The fund sells at an 8.6% discount from NAV

7. Rate of return $= \dfrac{\Delta \text{NAV} + \text{distributions}}{\text{Starting NAV}} = \dfrac{-\$.40 + \$1.50}{\$12.50} = .088 = 8.8\%$

8. a. Start of year price $= \$12.00 \times 1.02 = \$12.24$

   End of year price $= \$12.10 \times 0.93 = \$11.25$

   Although NAV increased, the price of the fund fell by $0.99.

   Rate of return $= \dfrac{\text{Distributions} + \Delta(\text{Price})}{\text{Start of year price}} = \dfrac{\$1.50 - \$0.99}{\$12.24} = .042 = 4.2\%$

   b. An investor holding the same portfolio as the manager would have earned a rate of return based on the increase in the NAV of the portfolio:

   Rate of return $= \dfrac{\text{Distributions} + \Delta(\text{NAV})}{\text{Start of year NAV}} = \dfrac{\$1.50 + \$0.10}{\$12.00} = .133 = 13.3\%$

9. a. *Unit investment trusts*: diversification from large-scale investing, lower transaction costs associated with large-scale trading, low management fees, predictable portfolio composition, guaranteed low (or zero) portfolio turnover rate.

   b. *Open-end funds*: diversification from large-scale investing, lower transaction costs associated with large-scale trading, professional management that may be able to take advantage of buy or sell opportunities as they arise, record keeping services.

   c. *Individual stocks and bonds*: No management fee, realization of capital gains or losses can be coordinated with your personal tax situation, portfolio can be designed to your own specific risk profile.

10. Open-end funds are obligated to redeem investor's shares for net asset value, and thus must keep cash or cash-equivalent securities on hand in order to meet potential redemptions. Closed-end funds do not need the cash reserves because they do not have to worry about redemptions. Their investors instead sell their shares to other investors when they wish to cash out.

11. Balanced funds keep relatively stable proportions of funds invested in each asset class. They are meant as convenient instruments to provide participation in a range of asset classes. Asset allocation funds, in contrast, may vary the proportions invested in each asset class by large amounts as predictions of relative performance across classes vary. They therefore engage in more aggressive market timing.

12.   a.   Empirical research indicates that past performance is not highly predictive of future performance, especially for better-performing funds. While there *may* be some tendency for the fund to be a better-than-average performer next year, it is unlikely to once again be a top 10% performer.

      b.   On the other hand, the evidence is more suggestive of a tendency for bad performance to persist. This is probably related to fund costs and turnover rates. Thus if the fund is among the poorest performers, I would be concerned that its performance will persist.

13.   Start of year NAV = $20

      Dividends per share = $.20

      End of year NAV is based on the 8% price gain, less the one percent 12b-1 fee:

      End of year NAV = $20 × (1.08) × (1 − .01) = $21.384

      $$\text{Rate of return} = \frac{\$21.384 - \$20 + \$.20}{\$20} = .0792 = 7.92\%$$

14.   Suppose you have $1000 to invest. Class A funds will leave you with an initial investment of $940 net of the front-end load. After 4 years, your portfolio will be worth:

      $$\$940 \times (1.10)^4 = \$1,376.25$$

      Class B shares allow you to invest the full $1,000, but your investment performance net of 12b-1 fees will be only 9.5%, and you will pay a 1% exit fee if you sell after 4 years. Your portfolio value after 4 years will be:

      $$\$1000 \times (1.095)^4 = \$1,437.66,$$

      which after paying the exit fee will leave you with: $1,437.66 × .99 = 1423.28.

      Class B is better if your horizon is 4 years.

      With a 15-year horizon, the Class A portfolio will be worth:

      $$\$940 \times (1.10)^{15} = \$3926.61$$

      The Class B portfolio will be worth (there is no exit fee in this case since the horizon is greater than 5 years):

      $$\$1000 \times (1.095)^{15} = \$3901.32$$

      At this longer horizon, Class B is no longer the better choice. The effect of Class B's .5% 12b-1 fees accumulates over time and finally overwhelms the 6% load charged to Class A investors.

15. Suppose that finishing in the top half of all managers is purely luck and that the probability of doing so in any year is exactly 1/2. Then the probability that a particular manager would finish in the top half of the sample 5 years in a row is $(1/2)^5$ = 1/32. We would then expect to find that $350 \times (1/32) = 11$ managers finish in the top half for five consecutive years. This is precisely what we found. Thus, we should not conclude that the consistent performance after 5 years is proof of skill: we would expect to find 11 managers exhibiting precisely this level of "consistency" even if performance is due solely to luck.

16. a. After 2 years, each dollar invested in a fund with a 4% load and a portfolio return equal to r will grow to: $\$.96 \times (1 + r - .005)^2$. Each dollar invested in the CD will grow to $\$1 \times (1.06)^2$. If the mutual fund is to be the better investment, then the portfolio return, r, must satisfy:

$$.96 \times (1 + r - .005)^2 > (1.06)^2$$
$$.96 \times (1 + r - .005)^2 > 1.1236$$
$$(1 + r - .005)^2 > 1.1704$$
$$1 + r - .005 > 1.0819$$
$$1 + r > 1.0869$$

or $r > .0869 = 8.69\%$.

b. If you invest for 6 years, then the portfolio return must satisfy:

$$.96 \times (1 + r - .005)^6 > (1.06)^6 = 1.4185$$
$$(1 + r - .005)^6 > 1.4776$$
$$1 + r - .005 > 1.0672$$
$$1 + r > 1.0722$$
$$r > 7.22\%$$

The cutoff return is lower because the "fixed cost," i.e., the one-time front-end load is spread out over a greater number of years.

c. With a 12b-1 fee instead of a front-end load, the portfolio must earn a rate of return, r, that satisfies:

$$1 + r - .005 - .0075 > 1.06$$

In this case, r must exceed 7.25% regardless of the investment horizon.

17. Trading costs will reduce portfolio returns by $0.4\% \times .50 = .2\%$

18. For the bond fund, the fraction of investment earnings given up to fees is

$$\frac{.6\%}{4.0\%} = .15 = 15\%.$$

For the equity fund, the fraction of investment earnings given up to fees is

$$\frac{.6\%}{12.0\%} = .05 = 5\%.$$

Fees are a much higher fraction of expected earnings for the bond fund, and therefore may be a more important factor in selecting the bond fund.

This may help to explain why unmanaged unit investment trusts are concentrated in the fixed income market. The advantages of unit investment trusts are low turnover and low trading costs and management fees. This will be a more important concern to bond-market investors.

CHAPTER 5: HISTORY OF INTEREST RATES AND RISK PREMIUMS

1.   Your holding period return for the next year on the money market fund depends on what 30 day interest rates will be each month when it is time to roll over maturing securities. The one-year savings deposit will offer a 7.5% holding period return for the year. If you forecast the rate on money market instruments to rise significantly above the current yield of 6%, then the money market fund might result in a higher HPR for the year. While the 20-year Treasury bond is offering a yield to maturity of 9% per year, which is 150 basis points higher than the rate on the one-year savings deposit at the bank, you could wind up with a one-year HPR of much less than 7.5% on the bond if long-term interest rates rise during the year. If Treasury bond yields rise above 9% during the year, then the price of the bond will fall, and the capital loss will wipe out some or all of the 9% return you would have received if bond yields had remained unchanged over the course of the year.

2. a.   If businesses decrease their capital spending they are likely to decrease their demand for funds. This will shift the demand curve in Figure 5.1 to the left and reduce the equilibrium real rate of interest.

   b.   Increased household saving will shift the supply of funds curve to the right and cause real interest rates to fall.

   c.   An open market purchase of Treasury securities by the Fed is equivalent to an increase in the supply of funds (a shift of the supply curve to the right). The equilibrium real rate of interest will fall.

3. a.   The Inflation-Plus CD is safer because it guarantees the purchasing power of the investment. Using the approximation that the real rate equals the nominal rate minus the inflation rate, the CD provides a real rate of 3.5% regardless of the inflation rate.

   b.   The expected return depends on the expected rate of inflation over the next year. If the rate of inflation is less than 3.5% then the conventional CD will offer a higher real return than the Inflation-Plus CD; if inflation is more than 3.5%, the opposite will be true.

   c.   If you expect the rate of inflation to be 3% over the next year, then the conventional CD offers you an expected real rate of return of 4%, which is 0.5% higher than the real rate on the inflation-protected CD. But unless you know that inflation will be 3% with certainty, the conventional CD is also riskier. The question of which is the better investment then depends on your attitude towards risk versus return. You might choose to diversify and invest part of your funds in each.

   d.   No. We cannot assume that the entire difference between the nominal risk-free rate (on conventional CDs) of 7% and the real risk-free rate (on inflation-protected CDs) of 3.5% is the expected rate of inflation. Part of the difference is probably a risk premium associated with the uncertainty surrounding the real rate of return on the conventional CDs. This implies that the expected rate of inflation is less than 3.5% per year.

4. $\qquad$ $E(r) = .35 \times 44\% + .30 \times 14\% + .35 \times (-16\%) = 14\%.$

$\qquad$ Variance $= .35 \times (44-14)^2 + .30 \times (14-14)^2 + .35 \times (-16-14)^2 = 630$

$\qquad$ Standard deviation $= 25.10\%$

The mean is unchanged, but the standard deviation has increased, as the probabilities of the high and low returns have increased.

5. Probability distribution of price and 1-year holding period return on 30-year Treasuries (which will have 29 years to maturity at year's end):

State of the Economy	Probability	YTM	Price	Capital gain	Coupon	HPR
Boom	.20	11.0%	$ 74.05	−$25.95	$8.00	−17.95%
Normal Growth	.50	8.0	100.00	0.00	8.00	8.00%
Recession	.30	7.0	112.28	12.28	8.00	20.28%

6. The average risk premium on stocks for the period 1926-1996 was 8.74% per year. Adding this to a risk-free rate of 8% gives an expected return of 16.74% per year for the S&P 500 portfolio.

7. The average rate of return and standard deviation are quite different in the sub periods:

	STOCKS		BONDS	
	Mean	Std. Dev.	Mean	Std. Dev.
1926-1996	12.50%	20.39%	5.31%	7.96%
1967-1996	13.06	15.97	8.21	10.52
1926-1941	6.39	30.33	4.42	4.32

I would prefer to use the risk premiums and standard deviations estimated over the period 1967-1996, because it seems to have been a different economic regime. After 1955 the U.S. economy entered the Keynesian era, when the Federal government actively attempted to stabilize the economy and prevent extreme cycles of boom and bust. Note that the standard deviation of stocks has gone down in the later period while the standard deviation of bonds has gone up.

8. a Real holding period return $= \dfrac{1 + \text{Nominal HPR}}{1 + \text{Inflation}} - 1 = \dfrac{\text{Nominal HPR} - \text{Inflation}}{1 + \text{Inflation}}$

$\qquad\qquad\qquad\qquad\quad = \dfrac{.80 - .70}{1.70} = .0588 = 5.88\%$

b. The approximation gives a real HPR of $80\% - 70\% = 10\%$, which is clearly too high.

9. From Table 5.2, the average real rate on bills has been approximately $3.76\% - 3.22\% = .54\%$.

   a. T-bills: .54% real rate + 3% inflation = 3.54%
   b. Large stock return: 3.54% T-bill rate + 8.74% historical risk premium = 12.28%
   c. The risk premium on stocks remains unchanged. [A premium, the difference between two rates, is a real value, unaffected by inflation].

10. Real interest rates are expected to rise. The investment activity will shift the demand for funds curve to the right in Figure 5.1 and therefore increase the equilibrium real interest rate.

11. a [Expected dollar return on equity investment is $18,000 versus $5,000 return on T-bills]

12. b

13. d

14. c

15. b

16. Probability of neutral economy is .50, or 50%. *Given* a neutral economy, the stock will experience poor performance 30% of the time. The probability of both poor stock performance and a neutral economy is therefore $.30 \times .50 = .15 = 15\%$. Choice (b) is correct.

17. b.

18. a. Probability Distribution of HPR on the Stock Market and Put

State of the Economy	Probability	STOCK Ending price + $4 dividend	HPR	PUT Ending Value	HPR
Boom	.25	$144	44%	0	−100%
Normal Growth	.50	114	14%	0	−100%
Recession	.25	84	−16%	$30	150%

Remember that the cost of the stock is $100 per share, and that of the put is $12.

b. The cost of one share of stock plus a put is $112. The Probability Distribution of HPR on the Stock Market plus Put is:

State of the Economy	Probability	Stock + Put + $4 dividend Ending Value	HPR	
Boom	.25	$144	28.6%	(144 − 112)/112
Normal Growth	.50	114	1.8	(114 − 112)/112
Recession	.25	114	1.8	

c. Buying the put option guarantees you a minimum HPR of 1.8% regardless of what happens to the stock's price. Thus, it offers insurance against a price decline.

19.   The probability distribution of the dollar return on CD plus call option is:

State of the Economy	Probability	Ending Value CD	Ending Value Call	Combined Value
Boom	.25	$114	$30	$144
Normal Growth	.50	114	0	114
Recession	.25	114	0	114

CHAPTER 6 : RISK AND RISK AVERSION

1. a. The expected cash flow is: $.5 \times 70{,}000 + .5 \times 200{,}000 = \$135{,}000$. With a risk premium of 8% over the risk-free rate of 6%, the required rate of return is 14%. Therefore, the present value of the portfolio is

$$135{,}000/1.14 = \$118{,}421$$

   b. If the portfolio is purchased at \$118,421, and provides an expected payoff of \$135,000, then the expected rate of return, E(r), is derived as follows:

$$\$118{,}421 \times [1 + E(r)] = \$135{,}000$$

   so that E(r) = 14%. The portfolio price is set to equate the expected return with the required rate of return.

   c. If the risk premium over bills is now 12%, the required return is $6 + 12 = 18\%$. The present value of the portfolio is now $\$135{,}000/1.18 = \$114{,}407$.

   d. For a given expected cash flow, portfolios that command greater risk premia must sell at lower prices. The extra discount from expected value is a penalty for risk.

2. When we specify utility by $U = E(r) - .005A\sigma^2$, the utility from bills is 7%, while that from the risky portfolio is $U = 12 - .005A \times 18^2 = 12 - 1.62A$. For the portfolio to be preferred to bills, the following inequality must hold: $12 - 1.62A > 7$, or, $A < 5/1.62 = 3.09$. A must be less than 3.09 for the risky portfolio to be preferred to bills.

3. Points on the curve are derived as follows:

$$U = 5 = E(r) - .005A\sigma^2 = E(r) - .015\sigma^2$$

The necessary value of E(r), given the value of σ^2, is therefore:

σ	σ^2	E(r)
0%	0	5.0%
5	25	5.375
10	100	6.5
15	225	8.375
20	400	11.0
25	625	14.375

The indifference curve is depicted by the bold line in the graph on the next page (labeled Q3, for Question 3).

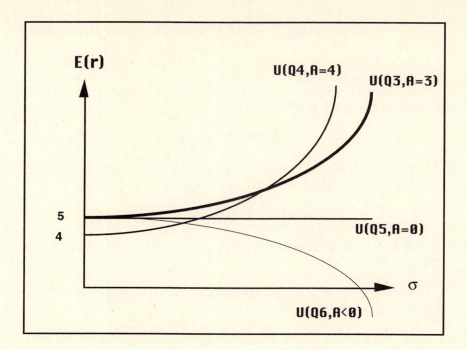

4.   Repeating the analysis in Problem 3, utility is:

$$U = E(r) - .005A\sigma^2 = E(r) - .02\sigma^2 = 4$$

leading to the equal-utility combinations of expected return and standard deviation presented in the table below. The indifference curve is the upward sloping line appearing in the graph of Problem 3 labeled Q4 (for Question 4).

σ	σ^2	$E(r)$
0%	0	4.00%
5	25	4.50
10	100	6.00
15	225	8.50
20	400	12.00
25	625	16.50

The indifference curve in Problem 4 differs from that in Problem 3 in both slope and intercept. When A increases from 3 to 4, the higher risk aversion results in a greater slope for the indifference curve since more expected return is needed to compensate for additional σ. The lower level of utility assumed for Problem 4 (4% rather than 5%), shifts the vertical intercept down by 1%.

5.   The coefficient of risk aversion of a risk neutral investor is zero. The corresponding utility is simply equal to the portfolio's expected return. The corresponding indifference curve in the expected return-standard deviation plane is a horizontal line, drawn in the graph of Problem 3, and labeled Q5.

6. A risk lover, rather than penalizing portfolio utility to account for risk, derives greater utility as variance increases. This amounts to a negative coefficient of risk aversion. The corresponding indifference curve is downward sloping, as drawn in the graph of Problem 3, and labeled Q6.

7. c [Utility for each portfolio = $E(r) - .005 \times 4 \times \sigma^2$. We choose the portfolio with the highest utility value.)

8. d [When investors are risk neutral, $A = 0$, and the portfolio with the highest utility is the one with the highest expected return.]

9. b

10. The portfolio expected return can be computed as follows:

W_{bills} ×	Return on bills	+	W_{market} ×	Exp. return on market	=	Portfolio expected return	Portfolio standard deviation (= W_{market} × 20%)
0.0	5%		1.0	13.5%		13.5%	20%
.2	5		.8	13.5		11.8	16
.4	5		.6	13.5		10.1	12
.6	5		.4	13.5		8.4	8
.8	5		.2	13.5		6.7	4
1.0	5		0.0	13.5		5.0	0

11. Computing the utility from $U = E(r) - .005 \times A\sigma^2 = E(r) - .015\sigma^2$ (because $A = 3$), we arrive at the following table.

W_{bills}	W_{market}	$E(r)$	σ	σ^2	$U(A=3)$	$U(A=5)$
0.	1.0	13.5%	20	400	7.5	3.5
.2	.8	11.8	16	256	7.96	5.4
.4	.6	10.1	12	144	7.94	6.5
.6	.4	8.4	8	64	7.43	6.8
.8	.2	6.7	4	16	6.46	6.3
1.0	0.	5.0	0	0	5.0	5.0

The utility column implies that investors with $A = 3$ will prefer a position of 80% in the market and 20% in bills over any of the other positions in the table.

12. The column labeled $U(A = 5)$ in the table above is computed from $U = E(r) - .005 A\sigma^2 = E(r) - .025\sigma^2$ (since $A = 5$). It shows that the more risk averse investors will prefer the position with 40% in the market index portfolio, rather than the 80% market weight preferred by investors with $A = 3$.

13. SugarKane is now less of a hedge, and the entire probability distribution is:

| | Normal Sugar Crop | | Sugar Crisis |
	Bullish Stock Market	Bearish Stock Market	
Probability	.5	.3	.2
Stock			
Best Candy	25%	10%	−25%
SugarKane	10	−5	20
Humanex's Portfolio	17.5	2.5	− 2.5

Using the portfolio rate of return distribution, its expected return and standard deviation can be calculated as follows:

$$E(r_p) = .5 \times 17.5 + .3 \times 2.5 + .2 \times (-2.5) = 9\%$$
$$\sigma_p = [.5(17.5 - 9)^2 + .3(2.5 - 9)^2 + .2(-2.5 - 9)^2]^{1/2} = 8.67\%$$

While the expected return has even improved slightly, the standard deviation is significantly greater and only marginally better than investing half in T-bills.

14. The expected return of Best is 10.5% and its standard deviation 18.9%. The mean and standard deviation of SugarKane are now:

$$E(r_{SK}) = .5 \times 10 + .3 \times (-5) + .2 \times 20 = 7.5\%$$

$$\sigma_{SK} = [.5(10 - 7.5)^2 - .3(-5 - 7.5)^2 + .2(20 - 7.5)^2]^{1/2} = 9.01\%$$

and its covariance with Best is

$$Cov = .5 (10 - 7.5)(25 - 10.5) + .3(-5 - 7.5)(10 - 10.5) + .2(20 - 7.5)(-25 - 10.5)$$
$$= -68.75$$

15. From the calculations in (14), the portfolio expected rate of return is

$$E(r_p) = .5 \times 10.5 + .5 \times 7.5 = 9\%$$

Using the portfolio weights $w_B = w_{SK} = .5$ and the covariance between the stocks, we can compute the portfolio standard deviation from rule 5.

$$\sigma_p = [w_B^2\sigma_B^2 + w_{SK}^2\sigma_{SK}^2 + 2w_B w_{SK}Cov(B,SK)]^{1/2}$$

$$= [.5^2 \times 18.9^2 + .5^2 \times 9.01^2 + 2 \times .5 \times .5 \times (-68.75)]^{1/2} = 8.67\%$$

CHAPTER 6: APPENDIX A

1. The current price of Klink stock is \$12. Thus, the rates of return in each scenario and their deviations from the mean are given by:

Probability	Rate of Return (%)	Deviation from the Mean (%)
.10	−100.00	−107.52
.20	−81.25	−88.77
.40	20.00	12.48
.25	71.67	64.15
.05	157.08	149.56

Mean = 7.52%
Std Dev = 70.30%

a. Mean = 7.52%
   Median = 20.00%
   Mode = 20.00%

b. Std. Dev. = 70.30%
   MAD = $\Sigma_s Pr(s) Abs[r(s) - E(r)] = 57.01\%$

c. The first moment is the mean (7.52%), the second moment around the mean is the variance (70.30^2) and the third moment is:

$$M_3 = \Sigma_s Pr(s) [r(s) - E(r)]^3 = -30,157.82$$

Therefore the probability distribution is negatively (left) skewed.

CHAPTER 6: APPENDIX B

1. Your \$50,000 investment will grow to \$50,000(1.06) = \$53,000 by year end. *Without insurance* your wealth will then be:

	Probability	Wealth
No fire:	.999	\$253,000
Fire:	.001	\$ 53,000

which gives expected utility

$$.001 \times \log_e(53,000) + .999 \times \log_e(253,000) = 12.439582$$

and a certainty equivalent wealth of

$$\exp(12.439582) = \$252,604.85$$

With fire insurance at a cost of $P, your investment in the risk-free asset will be only $(50,000 − P). Your year-end wealth will be certain (since you are fully insured) and equal to

$$(50,000 − P) \times 1.06 + 200,000.$$

Setting this expression equal to $252,604.85 (the certainty equivalent of the uninsured house) results in P = $372.79. This is the most you will be willing to pay for insurance. Note that the expected loss is "only" $200, meaning that you are willing to pay quite a risk premium over the expected value of losses. The main reason is that the value of the house is a large proportion of your wealth.

2. a. With 1/2 coverage, your premium is $100, your investment in the safe asset is $49,900 which grows by year end to $52,894. If there is a fire, your insurance proceeds are only $100,000. Your outcome will be:

	Probability	Wealth
Fire	.001	$152,894
No fire	.999	$252,894

Expected utility is

$$.001 \times \log_e(152,894) + .999 \times \log_e(252,894) = 12.440222$$

and $W_{CE} = \exp(12.440222) = \$252,767$

b. With full coverage, costing $200, end-of-year wealth is certain, and equal to

$$(50,000 − 200) \times 1.06 + 200,000 = \$252,788$$

Since wealth is certain, this is also certainty equivalent wealth of the exactly insured position.

c. With over-insurance, the insurance costs $300, and pays off $300,000 in the event of a fire. The outcomes are

Event	Probability	Wealth
fire	.001	$352,682 = (50,000 − 300) \times 1.06 + 300,000
no fire	.999	$252,682 = (50,000 − 300) \times 1.06 + 200,000

Expected utility is

$$.001 \times \log_e(352,682) + .999 \times \log_e(252,682) = 12.4402205$$

and $W_{CE} = \exp(12.4402205) = 252,766$

Therefore, full insurance dominates both over- and under-insurance. Over-insuring creates a gamble (you actually gain when the house burns down). Risk is minimized when you insure exactly the value of the house.

CHAPTER 7:
CAPITAL ALLOCATION BETWEEN
THE RISKY ASSET AND THE RISK-FREE ASSET

1. Expected return $= .3 \times 8\% + .7 \times 18\% = 15\%$ per year.

   Standard deviation $= .7 \times 28\% = 19.6\%$ per year

2. Investment proportions:

		30.0%	in T-bills
$.7 \times 25\%$	$=$	17.5%	in stock A
$.7 \times 32\%$	$=$	22.4%	in stock B
$.7 \times 43\%$	$=$	30.1%	in stock C

3. Your reward-to-variability ratio $= \dfrac{18 - 8}{28} = .3571$

   Client's reward-to-variability ratio $= \dfrac{15 - 8}{19.6} = .3571$

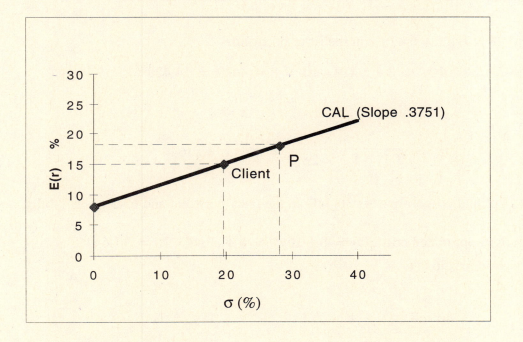

5. a. Expected return of portfolio = $r_f + (r_P - r_f)y = 8 + 10y$

If the expected return of the portfolio is equal to 16%, then solving for y we get:

$$16 = 8 + 10y, \quad \text{and} \quad y = \frac{16 - 8}{10} = .8$$

Therefore, to get an expected return of 16% the client must invest 80% of total funds in the risky portfolio and 20% in T-bills.

b. Investment proportions of the client's funds:

$$20\% \text{ in T-bills,}$$
$$.8 \times 25\% = 20.0\% \text{ in stock A}$$
$$.8 \times 32\% = 25.6\% \text{ in stock B}$$
$$.8 \times 43\% = 34.4\% \text{ in stock C}$$

c. Standard deviation $= .8 \times \sigma_P = .8 \times 28\% = 22.4\%$ per year

6. a. Portfolio standard deviation $= y \times 28\%$. If client wants a standard deviation of at most 18%, then

$$y = 18/28 = .6429 = 64.29\% \text{ in the risky portfolio.}$$

b. Expected return $= 8 + 10y = 8 + .6429 \times 10 = 8 + 6.429 = 14.429\%$

7. a.

$$y^* = \frac{E(r_P) - r_f}{.01 \times A\sigma_P^2} = \frac{18 - 8}{.01 \times 3.5 \times 28^2} = \frac{10}{27.44} = .3644$$

So the client's optimal proportions are 36.44% in the risky portfolio and 63.56% in T-bills.

b. Expected return of optimized portfolio $= 8 + 10y^* = 8 + .3644 \times 10 = 11.644\%$
Standard deviation $= .3644 \times 28 = 10.20\%$

8. a. Slope of the CML $= \frac{13 - 8}{25} = .20$

The diagram is on the following page.

b. My fund allows an investor to achieve a higher mean for any given standard deviation than would a passive strategy, i.e., a higher expected return for any given level of risk.

7-2

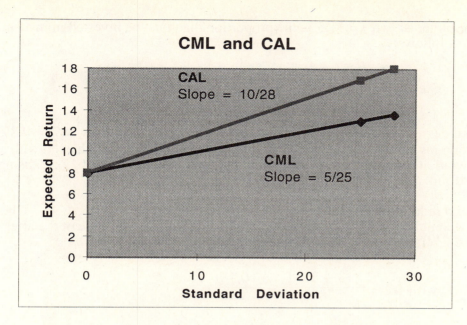

9. a. With 70% of his money in my fund's portfolio the client gets a mean return of 15% per year and a standard deviation of 19.6% per year. If he shifts that money to the passive portfolio (which has an expected return of 13% and standard deviation of 25%), his overall expected return and standard deviation would become:

$$E(r_C) = r_f + .7(r_M - r_f)$$

In this case, $r_f = 8\%$ and $r_M = 13\%$. Therefore,

$$E(r_C) = 8 + .7 \times (13 - 8) = 11.5\%$$

The standard deviation of the complete portfolio using the passive portfolio would be:

$$\sigma_C = .7 \times \sigma_M = .7 \times 25\% = 17.5\%$$

Therefore, the shift entails a decline in the mean from 14% to 11.5% and a decline in the standard deviation from 19.6% to 17.5%. Since both mean return *and* standard deviation fall, it is not yet clear whether the move is beneficial or harmful. The disadvantage of the shift is that if my client is willing to accept a mean return on his total portfolio of 11.5%, he can achieve it with a lower standard deviation using my fund portfolio, rather than the passive portfolio. To achieve a target mean of 11.5%, we first write the mean of the complete portfolio as a function of the proportions invested in my fund portfolio, y:

$$E(r_C) = 8 + y(18 - 8) = 8 + 10y$$

Because our target is: $E(r_C) = 11.5\%$, the proportion that must be invested in my fund is determined as follows:

$$11.5 = 8 + 10y, \qquad y = \frac{11.5 - 8}{10} = .35$$

The standard deviation of the portfolio would be: $\sigma_C = y \times 28\% = .35 \times 28\% = 9.8\%$. Thus, by using my portfolio, the same 11.5% expected return can be achieved with a standard deviation of only 9.8% as opposed to the standard deviation of 17.5% using the passive portfolio.

b. The fee would reduce the reward-to-variability ratio, i.e., the slope of the CAL. Clients will be indifferent between my fund and the passive portfolio if the slope of the after-fee CAL and the CML are equal. Let f denote the fee.

$$\text{Slope of CAL with fee} = \frac{18 - 8 - f}{28} = \frac{10 - f}{28}$$

Slope of CML (which requires no fee) $= \dfrac{13 - 8}{25} = .20$. Setting these slopes equal we get:

$$\frac{10 - f}{28} = .20$$

$$10 - f = 28 \times .20 = 5.6$$

$$f = 10 - 5.6 = 4.4\% \text{ per year}$$

10. a. The formula for the optimal proportion to invest in the passive portfolio is:

$$y^* = \frac{E(r_M) - r_f}{.01 \times A\sigma_M^2}$$

With $E(r_M) = 13\%$; $r_f = 8\%$; $\sigma_M = 25\%$; $A = 3.5$, we get

$$y^* = \frac{13 - 8}{.01 \times 3.5 \times 25^2} = .229$$

b. The answer here is the same as in 9b. The fee that you can charge a client is the same regardless of the asset allocation mix of your client's portfolio. You can charge a fee that will equalize the reward-to-variability *ratio* of your portfolio with that of your competition.

11. a. If 1926 - 1996 is assumed to be representative of future expected performance, A = 4, $E(r_M) - r_f = 8.7\%$, and $\sigma_M = 20.8\%$ (we use the standard deviation of the risk premium from the last column of Table 7.1), then y* is given by:

$$y^* = \frac{E(r_M) - r_f}{.01 \times A\sigma_M^2} = \frac{8.7}{.01 \times 4 \times 20.8^2} = .503$$

That is, 50.3% should be allocated to equity and 49.7% to bills.

   b. If 1979 - 1996 is assumed to be representative of future expected performance, A = 4, $E(r_M) - r_f = 6.6\%$; and $\sigma_M = 13.3\%$, then y* is given by:

$$y^* = \frac{9.6}{.01 \times 4 \times 13.5^2} = 1.317$$

Therefore, 131.7% of the complete portfolio is allocated to equity. This is accomplilshed by borrowing 31.7% of wealth and investing the entire investment portfolio (including the borrowed funds) in equity.

   c. In (b) the market risk premium and the market risk are both expected to be at a lower level than in (a). The fact that the reward-to-variability *ratio* is expected to be higher explains the greater proportion invested in equity.

12. Assuming no change in tastes, that is, an unchanged risk aversion coefficient, A, the denominator of the equation for the optimal investment in the risky portfolio will be higher. The proportion invested in the risky portfolio will depend on the relative change in the expected risk premium (the numerator) compared to the change in the perceived market risk. Investors perceiving higher risk will demand a higher risk premium to hold the same portfolio they held before. If we assume that the risk-free rate is unaffected, the increase in the risk premium would require a higher expected rate of return in the equity market.

13. a. $E(r) = 8\% = 5\% + y(11\% - 5\%)$

$$y = \frac{8 - 5}{11 - 5} = .5$$

   b. $\sigma_C = y\sigma_p = .50 \times 15\% = 7.5\%$

   c. The first client is more risk averse, allowing a smaller standard deviation.

14. Continue to assume from problem 13 that $r_f = 5\%$, $E(r_M) = 13\%$, and $\sigma_M = 25\%$. In addition, $r_f^B = 9\%$. Therefore, the CML and indifference curves are as follows:

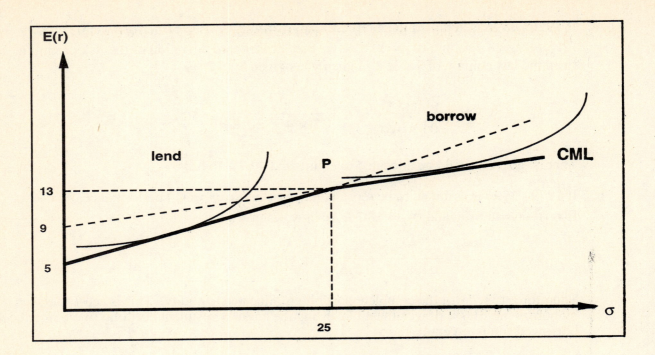

15.   For y to be less than 1.0 (so that the investor is a lender), risk aversion must be large enough that:

$$1 \geq y = \frac{E(r_M) - r_f}{.01 \times A\sigma_M^2}$$

$$A \geq \frac{13 - 5}{.01 \times 25^2} = 1.28$$

For y to be greater than 1.0 (so that the investor is a borrower), risk aversion must be small enough that:

$$1 \leq y = \frac{E(r_M) - r_f^B}{.01 \times A\sigma_M^2}$$

$$A \geq \frac{13 - 9}{.01 \times 625} = .64$$

For values of risk aversion within this range, the investor neither borrows nor lends, but instead holds a complete portfolio comprised only of the optimal risky portfolio:

$$y = 1 \text{ for } .64 \leq A \leq 1.28$$

16. a. The graph of problem 14 has to be redrawn here with $E(r) = 11\%$ and $\sigma = 15\%$

    b.   For a lending position, $A \geq \dfrac{11 - 5}{.01 \times 225} = 2.67$

            For a borrowing position, $A \leq \dfrac{11 - 9}{.01 \times 225} = .89$

            In between, $y = 1$ for $.89 \leq A \leq 2.67$

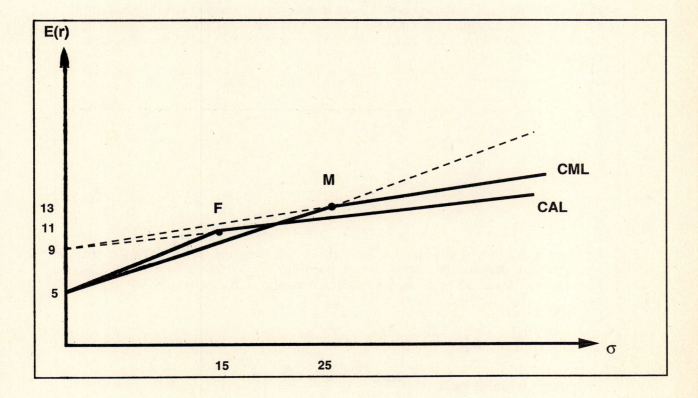

17.   The maximum feasible fee, denoted f, depends on the reward-to-variability ratio.

        For $y < 1$, the lending rate, 5%, is viewed as the relevant risk-free rate, and we solve for f from:

        $$\frac{11 - 5 - f}{15} = \frac{13 - 5}{25}$$

        $$f = 6 - \frac{15 \times 8}{25} = 1.2\%$$

For y > 1, the borrowing rate, 9%, is the relevant risk-free rate. Then we notice that even without a fee, the active fund is inferior to the passive fund because:

$$\frac{11 - 9}{15} = .13 \le \frac{13 - 9}{25} = .16$$

More risk tolerant investors (who are more inclined to borrow) therefore will not be clients of the fund even without a fee. (If you solved for the fee that would make investors who borrow indifferent between the active and passive portfolio, as we did above for lending investors, you would find that f is negative: that is, you would need to *pay* them to choose your active fund.) The reason is that these investors desire higher risk-higher return complete portfolios and thus are in the borrowing range of the relevant CAL. In this range the reward to variability ratio of the index (the passive fund) is better than that of the managed fund.

18.   b

19.   a

20.   a

21.   b

22.   (c) is the correct choice:

The expected return of your fund = T-bill rate + risk premium = 6% + 10% = 16%.
The expected return of the client's overall portfolio is .6 × 16% + .4 × 6% = 12%.
The standard deviation of the client's overall portfolio is .6 × 14% = 8.4%.

23.   (a) is the correct choice:

Reward to variability ratio $= \dfrac{\text{Risk premium}}{\text{Standard deviation}} = \dfrac{10}{14} = .71.$

CHAPTER 8 : OPTIMAL RISKY PORTFOLIOS

1. The parameters of the opportunity set are:

    $E(r_S) = 20\%$, $E(r_B) = 12\%$, $\sigma_S = 30\%$, $\sigma_B = 15\%$, $\rho = .10$

    From the standard deviations and the correlation coefficient we generate the covariance matrix [note that $Cov(r_S, r_B) = \rho\sigma_S\sigma_B$]:

	Bonds	Stocks
Bonds	225	45
Stocks	45	900

    The minimum-variance portfolio is found by applying the formula:

    $$w_{Min}(S) = \frac{\sigma_B^2 - Cov(B,S)}{\sigma_S^2 + \sigma_B^2 - 2Cov(B,S)}$$

    $$= \frac{225 - 45}{900 + 225 - 2 \times 45} = .1739$$

    $$w_{Min}(B) = .8261$$

    The minimum variance portfolio mean and standard deviation are:

    $$E(r_{Min}) = .1739 \times 20 + .8261 \times 12 = 13.39\%$$

    $$\sigma_{Min} = [W_S^2\sigma_S^2 + W_B^2\sigma_B^2 + 2W_S W_B Cov(S,B)]^{1/2}$$

    $$= [.1739^2 \times 900 + .8261^2 \times 225 + 2 \times .1739 \times .8261 \times 45]^{1/2} = 13.92\%$$

2.

% in stocks	% in bonds	Exp. return	Std. Dev	
0.00%	100.00%	12.00	15.00	
17.39%	82.61%	13.39	13.92	minimum variance
20.00%	80.00%	13.60	13.94	
40.00%	60.00%	15.20	15.70	
45.16%	54.84%	15.61	16.54	tangency portfolio
60.00%	40.00%	16.80	19.53	
80.00%	20.00%	18.40	24.48	
100.00%	0.00%	20.00	30.00	

3.

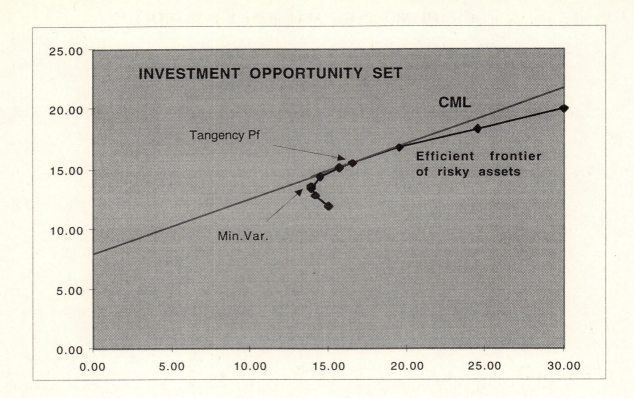

The graph approximates the points:

	E(r)	σ
Min. Variance Portf.	13.4%	13.9%
Tangency Portfolio	15.6	16.5

4. The proportion of stocks in the optimal risky portfolio is given by:

$$W_S = \frac{[E(r_S) - r_f]\sigma_B^2 - [E(r_B) - r_f]Cov(B,S)}{[E(r_S) - r_f]\sigma_B^2 + [E(r_B) - r_f]\sigma_S^2 - [E(r_S) - r_f + E(r_B) - r_f]Cov(B,S)}$$

$$= \frac{(20 - 8)225 - (12 - 8)45}{(20 - 8)225 + (12 - 8)900 - [20 - 8 + 12 - 8]45} = .4516$$

$$W_B = .5484$$

The mean and standard deviation of the optimal risky portfolio are:

$$E(r_p) = .4516 \times 20 + .5484 \times 12 = 15.61\%$$

$$\sigma_p = [.4516^2 \times 900 + .5484^2 \times 225 + 2 \times .4516 \times .5484 \times 45]^{1/2} = 16.54\%$$

5.   The reward-to-variability ratio of the optimal CAL is:

$$\frac{E(r_p) - r_f}{\sigma_p} = \frac{15.61 - 8}{16.54} = .4601$$

6. a.   If you require your portfolio to yield a mean return of 14% you can find the corresponding standard deviation from the optimal CAL. The formula for this CAL is:

$$E(r_C) = r_f + \frac{E(r_p) - r_f}{\sigma_p} \sigma_C = 8 + .4601\sigma_C$$

Setting $E(r_C)$ equal to 14% we find that the standard deviation of the optimal portfolio is 13.04%.

   b.   To find the proportion invested in T-bills we remember that the mean of the complete portfolio, 14%, is an average of the T-bill rate and the optimal combination of stocks and bonds, P. Let y be the proportion in this portfolio. The mean of any portfolio along the optimal CAL is:

$$E(r_C) = (1 - y) r_f + y \, E(r_p) = r_f + y \, [E(r_p) - r_f] = 8 + y \, (15.61 - 8)$$

Setting $E(r_C) = 14\%$ we find: $y = .7884$, and $1 - y = .2116$, the proportion in T-bills. To find the proportions invested in each of the funds we multiply .7884 by the proportions of the stocks and bonds in the optimal risky portfolio:

Proportion of stocks in complete portfolio = $.7884 \times .4516 = .3560$
Proportion of bonds in complete portfolio = $.7884 \times .5484 = .4324$

7.   Using only the stock and bond funds to achieve a portfolio mean of 14% we must find the appropriate proportion in the stock fund, w_S, and $w_B = 1 - w_S$ in the bond fund. The portfolio mean will be:

$$14 = 20w_S + 12(1 - w_S) = 12 + 8w_S \implies w_S = .25$$

So the proportions will be 25% in stocks and 75% in bonds. The standard deviation of this portfolio will be:

$$\sigma_p = (.25^2 \times 900 + .75^2 \times 225 + 2 \times .25 \times .75 \times 45)^{1/2}$$
$$= 14.13\%.$$

This is considerably larger than the standard deviation of 13.04% achieved using T-bills and the optimal portfolio.

8. With no opportunity to borrow you wish to construct a portfolio with a mean of 24%. Since this exceeds the mean on stocks of 20%, you will have to go short on bonds, which have a mean of 12%, and use the proceeds to buy additional stock. The graphical representation of your risky portfolio is point Q on the following graph:

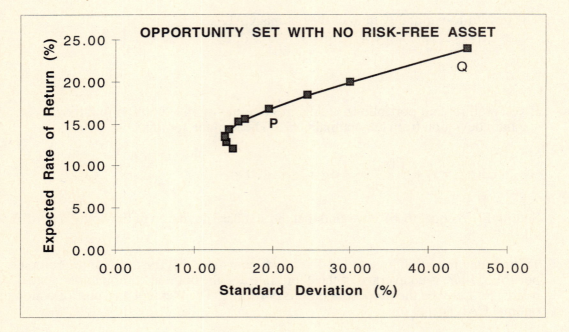

Point Q is the stock/bond combination with mean of 24%. Let w_S be the proportion of stocks and $1 - w_S$ be the proportion of bonds required to achieve the 24% mean. Then:

$$24 = 20 \times w_S + 12 \times (1 - w_S) = 12 + 8 w_S$$

$$w_S = 1.50, \quad \text{and } 1 - w_S = -.50$$

Therefore, you would have to sell short an amount of bonds equal to .50 of your total funds, and invest 1.50 times your total funds in stocks. The standard deviation of this portfolio would be:

$$\sigma_Q = [1.50^2 \times 900 + (-.50)^2 \times 225 + 2 \times (1.50) \times (-.50) \times 45]^{1/2}$$
$$= 44.87\%$$

If you were allowed to borrow at the risk-free rate of 8%, the way to achieve the target 24% would be to invest more than 100% of your funds in the optimal risky portfolio, moving out along the CAL to the right of P, up to R, on the following graph.

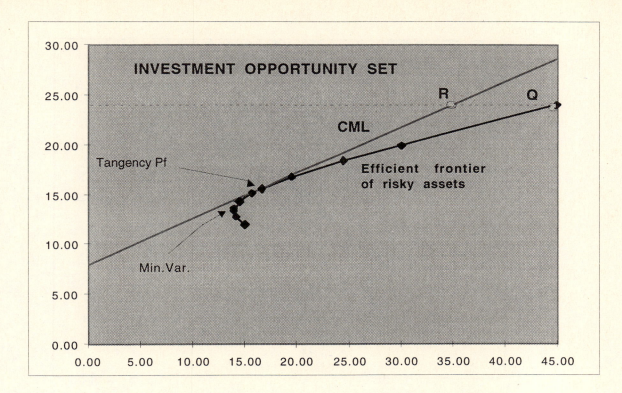

R is the point on the optimal CAL which has the mean of 24%. Using the formula for the optimal CAL we can find the corresponding standard deviation:

$$E(r_C) = 8 + .4601\sigma_C = 24$$

Setting $E(r_C) = 24$, we get: $\sigma_C = 34.78\%$, which is considerably less than the 44.87% standard deviation you would get without the possibility of borrowing at the risk-free rate of 8%.

What is the portfolio composition of point R on the optimal CAL? The mean of any portfolio along this CAL is:

$$E(r_C) = r_f + y[E(r_P) - r_f]$$

where y is the proportion invested in the optimal risky portfolio P and r_P is the mean of that portfolio, which is 15.61%.

$$24 = 8 + y(15.61 - 8)$$
$$y = 2.1025$$

This means that for every $1 of your own funds invested in portfolio P, you would borrow an additional $1.1025 and invest it also in portfolio P.

9. a.

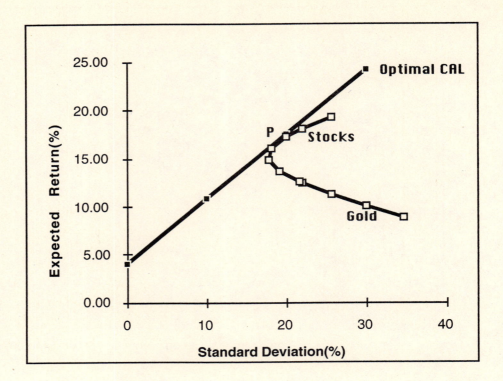

Even though gold seems dominated by stocks, it still might be an attractive asset to hold as a *part* of a portfolio. If the correlation between gold and stocks is sufficiently low, it will be held as an element in a portfolio -- the optimal tangency portfolio.

b. If gold had a correlation coefficient with stocks of +1, it would not be held. The optimal CAL would be comprised of bills and stocks only. Since the set of risk/return combinations of stocks and gold would plot as a straight line with a negative slope (see the following graph), it would be dominated by the stocks portfolio. Of course, this situation could not persist. If no one desired gold, its price would fall and its expected rate of return would increase until it became an attractive enough asset to hold.

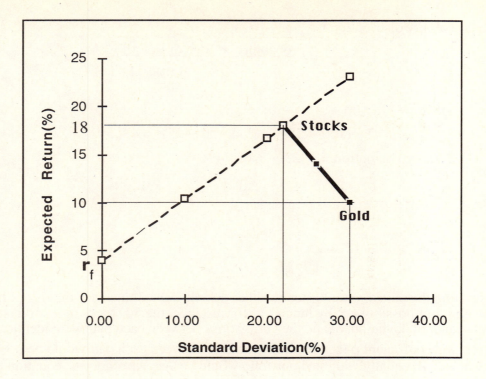

10.   Since A and B are perfectly negatively correlated, a risk-free portfolio can be created and its
        rate of return in equilibrium will be the risk-free rate. To find the proportions of this
        portfolio (with w_A invested in A and $w_B = 1 - w_A$ in B), set the standard deviation equal
        to zero. With perfect negative correlation, the portfolio standard deviation reduces to

$$\sigma_P = Abs[\ w_A\sigma_A - w_B\sigma_B]$$
$$0 = 5w_A - 10(1 - w_A)$$
$$w_A = .6667$$

The expected rate of return on this risk-free portfolio is:

$$E(r) = .6667 \times 10 + .3333 \times 15 = 11.67\%$$

Therefore, the risk-free rate must also be 11.67%.

11.   False. If the borrowing and lending rates are not identical, then depending on the tastes of
        the individuals (that is, the shape of their indifference curves), borrowers and lenders could
        have different optimal risky portfolios.

12.   False. The portfolio standard deviation equals the weighted average of the component-asset
        standard deviations *only* in the special case that all assets are perfectly positively correlated.
        Otherwise, as the formula for portfolio standard deviation shows, the portfolio standard
        deviation is *less* than the weighted average of the component-asset standard deviations. The
        portfolio *variance* will be a weighted *sum* of the elements in the covariance matrix, with the
        products of the portfolio proportions as weights.

13.   The probability distribution is:

	Probability	Rate of Return
	.7	100%
	.3	−50%

Mean = $.7 \times 100 + .3 \times (-50) = 55\%$

Variance = $.7 \times (100 - 55)^2 + .3 \times (-50 - 55)^2 = 4725$

Standard deviation = $4725^{1/2} = 68.74\%$

14. $\sigma_P = 30 = y\sigma = 40y$

$y = .75$

$E(r_p) = 12 + .75(30 - 12) = 25.5\%$

15. a. Restricting the portfolio to 20 stocks rather than 40-50 will increase the risk of the portfolio, but possibly not by much. If, for instance, the 50 stocks in a universe had the same standard deviation, σ, and the correlations between each pair were identical with correlation coefficient ρ (so that the covariance between each pair would be $\rho\sigma^2$), the variance of an equally weighted portfolio would be (see Appendix A, equation 8A.4),

$$\sigma_P^2 = \frac{1}{n} \sigma^2 + \frac{n-1}{n} \rho\sigma^2$$

The effect of the reduction in n on the second term would be relatively small (since 49/50 is close to 19/20 and $\rho\sigma^2$ is smaller than σ^2, but the denominator of the first term would be 20 instead of 50. For example, if $\sigma = 45\%$ and $\rho = .2$, then the standard deviation with 50 stocks would be 20.91%, and would rise to 22.05% when only 20 stocks are held. Such an increase might be acceptable if the expected return is sufficiently increased.

   b. Hennessy could contain the increase in risk by making sure that he maintains reasonable diversification among the 20 stocks that remain in his portfolio. This entails maintaining a low correlation among the remaining stocks. For example, in part (a), with $\rho = .2$, the increase in portfolio risk was minimal. As a practical matter, this means that Hennessy would need to spread his portfolio among many industries; concentrating on just a few would result in higher correlation among the included stocks.

16.   Risk reduction benefits from diversification are not a linear function of the number of issues in the portfolio. Rather, the incremental benefits from additional diversification are most important when you are least diversified. Restricting Hennesey to 10 instead of 20 issues would increase the risk of his portfolio by a greater amount than would reducing the size of the portfolio from 30 to 20 stocks. In our example, restricting the number of stocks to 10 will increase the standard deviation to 23.81%. The increase in standard deviation of 1.76% from giving up 10 of 20 stocks is greater than the increase of 1.14% from giving up 30 stocks when starting with 50.

17.   The point is well taken because the committee should be concerned with the volatility of the entire portfolio. Since Hennessey's portfolio is only one of six well-diversified portfolios and smaller than the average, the concentration in fewer issues could have a minimal effect on the diversification of the total fund. Hence, unleashing Hennessey to do stock picking may be advantageous.

18.   c. Intuitively, we note that since all stocks have the same expected rate of return and standard deviation, we wish to choose the stock that will result in lowest risk. This will be the one with the lowest correlation with stock A.

More formally, we note that when all stocks have the same expected rate of return, the optimal portfolio for any risk averse investor is the global minimum variance portfolio (G). When restricted to A and one more stock, the objective is to find G for any pair that includes A, and select the combination with the lowest variance. With two stocks, I and J, the formula for the weights in G is:

$$w_{Min}(I) = \frac{\sigma_J^2 - Cov(I,J)}{\sigma_I^2 + \sigma_J^2 - 2Cov(I,J)}$$

$$w_{Min}(J) = 1 - w_{Min}(I)$$

Since all standard deviations are equal to 20%,

$$Cov(I,J) = \rho\sigma_I\sigma_J = 400\rho, \text{ and}$$

$$w_{Min}(I) = w_{Min}(J) = .5$$

This intuitive result is an implication of a property of any efficient frontier, namely, that the covariance of the global minimum variance portfolio with any other asset on the frontier is identical and equal to its own variance. (Otherwise, additional diversification would further reduce the variance.) In this case, the standard deviation of G(I,J) will reduce to:

$$\sigma_{Min}(G) = [200(1 + \rho(I,J))]^{1/2}$$

This leads us directly to the intuitive result that the desired addition would be the stock with the lowest correlation with A, which is D. The optimal portfolio is equally invested in A and D, and the standard deviation will be 17.03%.

19.   No, at least as long as they are not risk lovers. Risk neutral investors will not care which portfolio they hold since all portfolios yield 8%.

20.   No change. The efficient frontier of risky assets is horizontal at 8%, so the optimal CAL runs from the risk-free rate through G. The best G is here, again, the one with the lowest variance. The optimal complete portfolio will, as usual, depend on risk aversion.

21.   d. Portfolio Y cannot be efficient because it is dominated by another portfolio. For
       example, Portfolio X has higher expected return and lower standard deviation.

22.   c.

23.   d.

24.   b.

25.   a.

26.   c.

27.   We know nothing about expected returns, so we focus exclusively on reducing variability.
       Portfolios C and A have equal standard deviations, but the correlation of Portfolio C with
       Portfolio B is lower than that of Portfolio A with Portfolio B, so a portfolio comprised of C
       and B will have lower total risk than a portfolio comprised of A and B.

28.   Rearranging the table (converting rows to columns), and computing serial correlation
       results in the following table.

Decade	Nominal	rates					
	Large Stocks	Small Stocks	L.T. Corp. Bonds	L.T. Gov't Bonds	Intermediate Gov't Bonds	T-Bills	Inflation
1920s	6.98%	-1.51%	2.05%	1.57%	1.49%	1.41%	-0.40%
1930s	-1.25%	7.28%	6.95%	4.60%	3.91%	0.30%	-2.04%
1940s	9.11%	20.63%	2.70%	3.59%	1.70%	0.37%	5.36%
1950s	19.41%	19.01%	1.02%	0.26%	1.11%	1.87%	2.22%
1960s	7.84%	13.72%	1.69%	1.14%	3.41%	3.89%	2.52%
1970s	5.90%	8.75%	6.21%	6.63%	6.11%	6.29%	7.36%
1980s	17.60%	12.46%	13.03%	11.50%	12.01%	9.00%	5.10%
1990s	7.64%	8.05%	6.58%	6.79%	5.60%	2.92%	1.99%
Serial Corr.	-0.091	0.37	0.29	0.47	0.43	0.55	0.15

For example: to compute serial correlation in decades of nominal, large-stock returns, we
set up the two columns:

	Decade	Previous
1930s	-1.25%	6.98%
1940s	9.11%	-1.25%
1950s	19.41%	9.11%
1960s	7.84%	19.41%
1970s	5.90%	7.84%
1980s	17.60%	5.90%
1990s	7.64%	17.60%

and use the "correlation" function of the spreadsheet to obtain a serial correlation of –0.091.

Note that each correlation is based on only seven observations, so we cannot really arrive at any statistically significant conclusion. Looking at the numbers, however, it appears that there is persistent serial correlation with the exception of large stocks (S&P 500). This conclusion changes when we turn to real rates in the next problem.

29. The table for real rates (using the approximation of subtracting a decade's average inflation from the decade's average nominal return) is:

Decade	**Real** Large Stocks	**Rates** Small Stocks	L.T. Corp.	L.T. Gov't	Inter. Gov't	T-Bills
1920s	7.37%	-1.11%	2.45%	1.97%	1.89%	1.81%
1930s	0.79%	9.31%	8.99%	6.64%	5.95%	2.34%
1940s	3.75%	15.27%	-2.66%	-1.77%	-3.66%	-4.99%
1950s	17.19%	16.78%	-1.20%	-1.97%	-1.11%	-0.35%
1960s	5.33%	11.21%	-0.83%	-1.38%	0.89%	1.37%
1970s	-1.46%	1.39%	-1.15%	-0.73%	-1.25%	-1.07%
1980s	12.50%	7.36%	7.94%	6.41%	6.91%	3.90%
1990s	5.65%	6.07%	4.59%	4.81%	3.62%	0.93%
Serial Corr.	-0.29	0.00	0.21	-0.08	-0.18	-0.18

The positive serial correlation in decade *nominal* returns has vanished and it appears that real rates are serially uncorrelated. The decade time series (although again too short for any decisive conclusion) suggest that real rates are independent from decade to decade.

CHAPTER 9: THE CAPITAL ASSET PRICING MODEL

1. $$E(r_P) = r_f + \beta[E(r_M) - r_f]$$
    $$18 = 6 + \beta(14 - 6)$$
    $$\beta = 12/8 = 1.5$$

2. If the covariance of the security doubles, then so will its beta and its risk premium. The current risk premium is 8% (= 14 – 6), so the new risk premium would be 16%, and the new discount rate for the security would be 16 + 6 = 22%.

    If the stock pays a level perpetual dividend, then we know from the original data that the dividend, D, must satisfy the equation for the present value of a perpetuity:

    Price = Dividend / Discount rate

    50 = D /.14

    D = 50 × .14 = $7.00

    At the new discount rate of 22%, the stock would be worth only $7/.22 = $31.82. The increase in stock risk has lowered its value by 36.36%.

3. The appropriate discount rate for the project is:

    $$r_f + \beta[E(r_M) - r_f] = 8 + 1.8(18 - 8) = 26\%$$

    Using this discount rate,

    $$NPV = -40 + \sum_{t=1}^{10} \frac{15}{1.26^t}$$
    $$= -40 + 15 \times \text{Annuity factor(26\%, 10 years)} = 11.97$$

    The internal rate of return on the project is 35.73%. The highest value that beta can take before the hurdle rate exceeds the IRR is determined by

    $$35.73 = 8 + \beta(18 - 8)$$
    $$\beta = 27.73 / 10 = 2.773$$

4. a.   False. $\beta = 0$ implies $E(r) = r_f$, not zero.

   b.   False. Investors require a risk premium only for bearing systematic (undiversifiable or market) risk. Total volatility includes diversifiable risk.

   c.   False. 75% of your portfolio should be in the market, and 25% in bills. Then,

   $$\beta_P = .75 \times 1 + .25 \times 0 = .75$$

5. a. Call the aggressive stock A and the defensive stock D. Beta is the sensitivity of the stock's return to the market return, i.e., the change in the stock return per change in the market return. Therefore, we compute each stock's beta by calculating the difference in its return across the two scenarios divided by the difference in the market return.

$$\beta_A = \frac{-2 - 38}{5 - 25} = 2.00$$

$$\beta_D = \frac{6 - 12}{5 - 25} = .30$$

b. With the two scenarios equally likely, the expected return is an average of the two possible outcomes.

$$E(r_A) = .5(-2 + 38) = 18\%$$

$$E(r_D) = .5(6 + 12) = 9\%$$

c. The SML is determined by the market expected return of $.5(25 + 5) = 15\%$, with a beta of 1, and the bill return of 6% with a beta of zero. See the following graph.

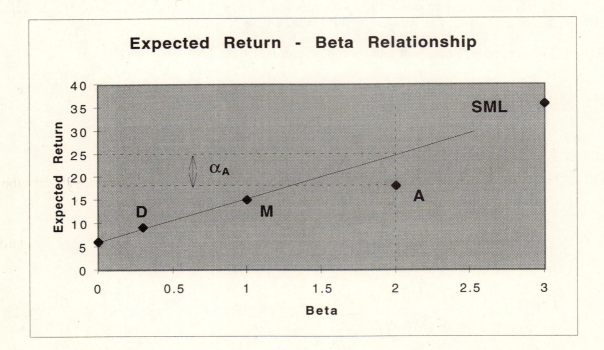

The equation for the security market line is:

$$E(r) = 6 + \beta(15 - 6).$$

d. The aggressive stock has a fair expected return of: $E(r_A) = 6 + 2.0(15 - 6) = 24\%$ but the analyst's forecast of expected return is only 18%. Thus its alpha is $18\% - 24\% = -6\%$. Similarly, the required return on the defensive stock is: $E(r_D) = 6 + .3(15 - 6) = 8.7\%$, but the analyst's forecast of expected return for D is 9%, and hence, the stock has a positive alpha:

$$\alpha_D = \text{actually expected return} - \text{required return (given risk)}$$
$$= 9 - 8.7 = +.3\%.$$

The points for each stock plot on the graph as indicated above.

e. The hurdle rate is determined by the project beta, .3, not by the firm's beta. The correct discount rate is 8.7%, the fair rate of return on stock D.

6. Not possible. Portfolio A has a higher beta than B, but its expected return is lower. Thus, thse two portfolios cannot exist in equilibrium.

7. Possible. If the CAPM is valid, the expected rate of return compensates only for systematic (market) risk represented by beta rather than for the standard deviation which includes nonsystematic risk. Thus, A's lower rate of return can be paired with a higher standard deviation, as long as A's beta is lower than B's.

8. Not possible. The reward-to-variability ratio for portfolio A is better than that of the market, which is impossible according to the CAPM, since the CAPM predicts that the market is the most efficient portfolio. Using the numbers supplied,

$$S_A = \frac{16 - 10}{12} = .5 \qquad\qquad S_M = \frac{18 - 10}{24} = .33$$

The numbers would imply that portfolio A provides a better risk-reward tradeoff than the market portfolio.

9. Not possible. Portfolio A clearly dominates the market portfolio. It has a lower standard deviation with a higher expected return.

10. Not possible. The SML for this situation is: $E(r) = 10 + \beta(18 - 10)$
Portfolios with beta of 1.5 have an expected return of $E(r) = 10 + 1.5 \times (18 - 10) = 22\%$.
A's expected return is 16%, that is, A plots below the SML (has an alpha of –6%), and hence, is an overpriced portfolio. This is inconsistent with the CAPM.

11. Not possible. Same SML as in problem 10. Here portfolio A's required expected return is: $10 + .9 \times 8 = 17.2\%$, which is still higher than 16%. A is overpriced with a negative alpha of –1.2%.

12. Possible. Same CML as shown in problem 8. Portfolio A plots below the CML, as any asset is expected to. This situation is not inconsistent with the CAPM.

13.   Since the stock's beta is equal to 1.2, its expected rate of return is $6 + 1.2(16 - 6) = 18\%$

$$E(r) = \frac{D_1 + P_1 - P_0}{P_0}$$

$$.18 = \frac{6 + P_1 - 50}{50}$$

$$P_1 = \$53$$

14.   The \$1,000 is a perpetuity. If beta is .5, the cash flow should be discounted at the rate

$$6\% + .5 \times (16\% - 6\%) = 11\%$$

$$PV = 1000/.11 = \$9,090.91$$

If, however, beta is equal to 1, the investment should yield 16%, and the price paid for the firm should be:

$$PV = 1000/.16 = \$6,250$$

The difference, \$2,840.91, is the amount you will overpay if you erroneously assumed that beta is .5 rather than 1.

15.   Using the SML: $4 = 6 + \beta(16 - 6)$

$$\beta = -2/10 = -.2$$

16. $r_1 = 19\%$; $r_2 = 16\%$; $\beta_1 = 1.5$; $\beta_2 = 1$

a.   To tell which investor was a better predictor of individual stocks we look at their abnormal return, which is the ex-post alpha, that is, the abnormal return is the difference between the actual return and that predicted by the SML. Without information about the parameters of this equation (risk-free rate and market rate of return) we cannot tell which one is more accurate.

b.   If $r_f = 6\%$ and $r_M = 14\%$, then (using the notation of alpha for the abnormal return)

$$\alpha_1 = 19 - [6 + 1.5(14 - 6)] = 19 - 18 = 1\%$$

$$\alpha_2 = 16 - [6 + 1(14 - 6)] = 16 - 14 = 2\%$$

Here, the second investor has the larger abnormal return and thus he appears to be a more accurate predictor. By making better predictions the second investor appears to have tilted his portfolio toward underpriced stocks.

c. If $r_f = 3\%$ and $r_M = 15\%$, then

$$\alpha_1 = 19 - [3 + 1.5(15 - 3)] = 19 - 21 = -2\%$$

$$\alpha_2 = 16 - [3 + 1(15 - 3)] = 16 - 15 = 1\%$$

Here, not only does the second investor appear to be a better predictor, but the first investor's predictions appear valueless (or worse).

17. a. Since the market portfolio by definition has a beta of 1, its expected rate of return is 12%.

b. $\beta = 0$ means no systematic risk. Hence, the portfolio's fair return is the risk-free rate, 5%.

c. Using the SML, the *fair* rate of return of a stock with $\beta = -0.5$ is:

$$E(r) = 5 + (-.5)(12 - 5) = 1.5\%$$

The *expected* rate of return, using the expected price and dividend for next year:

$$E(r) = 44/40 - 1 = .10 \text{ or } 10\%$$

Because the expected return exceeds the fair return, the stock must be underpriced.

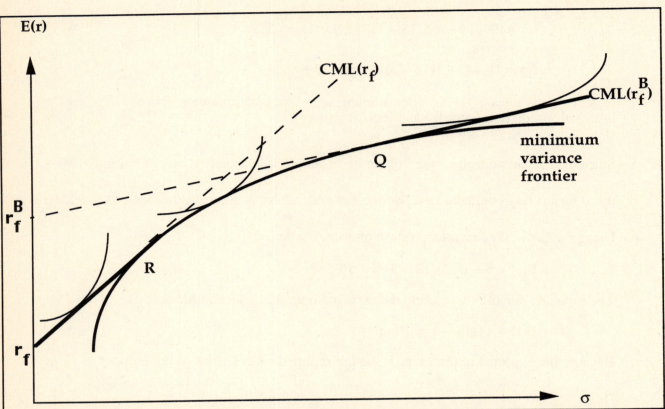

The risky portfolio selected by all defensive investors is at the tangency point between the minimum-variance frontier and the ray originating at r_f, depicted by point R on the graph. Point Q represents the risky portfolio of all aggressive investors. It is the tangency point between the minimum-variance frontier and the ray originating at r_f^B.

b. Investors who do not wish to borrow or lend will each have a unique risky portfolio at the tangency of their own individual indifference curves with the minimum-variance frontier in the section between R and Q.

c. The market portfolio is clearly defined (in all circumstances) as the portfolio of all risky securities, with weights in proportion to their market value. Thus, by design, the average investor holds the market portfolio. The average investor in turn, neither borrows nor lends. Hence, the market portfolio is on the efficient frontier between R and Q.

d. Yes, the zero-beta CAPM is valid in this scenario as shown in the following graph:

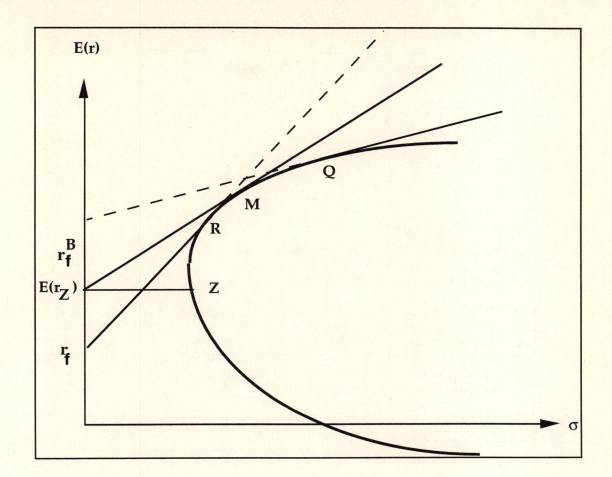

19. Assume that stocks pay no dividends and hence the rate of return on stocks is essentially tax-free. Thus, both taxed and untaxed investors compute identical efficient frontiers. The situation is analogous to that with different lending and borrowing rates as depicted in the graph of Problem 18. Taxed investors are analogous to lenders with a lending rate of $r_f(1 - t)$. Their relevant CML is drawn from $r_f(1 - t)$ to the efficient frontier with tangency at point R on the graph. Untaxed investors are analogous to borrowers who must use the (now higher) rate of r_f to get a tangency at Q. Between them, both classes of investors hold the market portfolio which is a weighted average of R and Q, with weights proportional to the aggregate wealth of the investors in each class.

Since any combination of two efficient frontier portfolios is also efficient, the average (market) portfolio will also be efficient here, as depicted by point M. Moreover, the Zero Beta model must now apply, because the market portfolio is efficient and all investors choose risky portfolios that lie on the efficient frontier. As a result, the ray from the expected return on the efficient portfolio with zero correlation with M (and hence zero beta), to the efficient frontier, will be tangent at M. This can only happen if $r_f(1 - t) < E(r_Z) < r_f$.

More generally, consider the case of any number of classes of investors with individual risk-free borrowing and lending rates. As long as the same efficient frontier of risky assets applies to all of them, the Zero-Beta model will apply, and the equilibrium zero-beta rate will be a weighted average of each individual's risk-free borrowing and lending rates.

20.   In the Zero-Beta CAPM the zero-beta portfolio replaces the risk-free rate, thus,

$$E(r) = 8 + .6(17 - 8) = 13.4\%$$

21.   a.

22.   d.

23.   d.

24.   c.

25.   d.

26.   d. [You need to know the risk-free rate]

27.   d. [You need to know the risk-free rate]

28.   Under the CAPM, the only risk that investors are compensated for bearing is the risk that cannot be diversified away (systematic risk). Because systematic risk (measured by beta) is equal to 1.0 for both portfolios, an investor would expect the same rate of return form both portfolios A and B. Moreover, since both portfolios are well diversified, it doesn't matter if the specific risk of the individual securities is high or low. The firm-specific risk has been diversified away for both portfolios.

CHAPTER 10: SINGLE-INDEX AND MULTIFACTOR MODELS

1. a.   To optimize this portfolio one would need:

$$n \quad = \quad 60 \quad \text{estimates of means}$$
$$n \quad = \quad 60 \quad \text{estimates of variances}$$
$$\frac{n^2 - n}{2} \quad = \quad 1770 \quad \text{estimates of covariances}$$

$$\frac{n^2 + 3n}{2} \quad = \quad 1890 \quad \text{estimates}$$

b.   In a single index model: $r_i - r_f = \alpha_i + \beta_i(r_M - r_f) + e_i$

The variance of the rate of return on each stock can be decomposed into the components:

(1) $\beta_i^2 \sigma_M^2$ The variance due to the common market factor

(2) $\sigma^2(e_i)$ The variance due to firm specific unanticipated events

In this model $Cov(r_i,r_j) = \beta_i\beta_j\sigma_M^2$. The number of parameter estimates required will be:

$n = 60$ estimates of the mean $E(r_i)$,

$n = 60$ estimates of the sensitivity coefficient β_i,

$n = 60$ estimates of the firm-specific variance $\sigma^2(e_i)$, and

1 estimate of the market mean $E(r_M)$

1 estimate for the market variance σ_M^2

182 estimates

Thus, the single index model reduces the total number of required parameter estimates from 1,890 to 182, and in general from $(n^2 + 3n)/2$ to $3n + 2$.

2. a.   The standard deviation of each individual stock is given by:

$$\sigma_i = [\beta_i^2 \sigma_M^2 + \sigma^2(e_i)]^{1/2}$$

Since $\beta_A = .8$, $\beta_B = 1.2$, $\sigma(e_A) = 30\%$, $\sigma(e_B) = 40\%$, and $\sigma_M = 22\%$ we get:

$$\sigma_A = (.8^2 \times 22^2 + 30^2)^{1/2} = 34.78\%$$

$$\sigma_B = (1.2^2 \times 22^2 + 40^2)^{1/2} = 47.93\%$$

b. The expected rate of return on a portfolio is the weighted average of the expected returns of the individual securities:

$$E(r_p) = w_A E(r_A) + w_B E(r_B) + w_f r_f$$

where w_A, w_B, and w_f are the portfolio weights of stock A, stock B, and T-bills, respectively.

Substituting in the formula we get:

$$E(r_p) = .30 \times 13 + .45 \times 18 + .25 \times 8 = 14\%$$

The beta of a portfolio is similarly a weighted average of the betas of the individual securities:

$$\beta_P = w_A \beta_A + w_B \beta_B + w_f \beta_f$$

The beta of T-bills (β_f) is zero. The beta of the portfolio is therefore:

$$\beta_P = .30 \times .8 + .45 \times 1.2 + 0 = .78$$

The variance of this portfolio is :

$$\sigma_P^2 = \beta_P^2 \sigma_M^2 + \sigma^2(e_P)$$

where $\beta_P^2 \sigma_M^2$ is the systematic component and $\sigma^2(e_P)$ is the nonsystematic component. Since the residuals, e_i are uncorrelated, the non-systematic variance is:

$$\sigma^2(e_P) = w_A^2 \sigma^2 (e_A) + w_B^2 \sigma^2(e_B) + w_f^2 \sigma^2(e_f)$$
$$= .30^2 \times 30^2 + .45^2 \times 40^2 + .25^2 \times 0$$
$$= 405$$

where $\sigma^2(e_A)$ and $\sigma^2(e_B)$ are the firm-specific (nonsystematic) variances of stocks A and B, and $\sigma^2(e_f)$, the nonsystematic variance of T-bills, is zero. The residual standard deviation of the portfolio is thus:

$$\sigma(e_P) = (405)^{1/2} = 20.12\%$$

The total variance of the portfolio is then:

$$\sigma_P^2 = .78^2 \times 22^2 + 405 = 699.47$$

and the standard deviation is 26.45%.

3. a.   The two figures depict the stocks' security characteristic lines (SCL). Stock A has a higher firm-specific risk because the deviations of the observations from the SCL are larger for A than for B. Deviations are measured by the vertical distance of each observation from the SCL.

   b.   Beta is the slope of the SCL, which is the measure of systematic risk . Stock B's SCL is steeper, hence stock B's systematic risk is greater.

   c.   The R^2 (or squared correlation coefficient) of the SCL is the ratio of the explained variance of the stock's return to total variance, and the total variance is the sum of the explained variance plus the unexplained variance (the stock's residual variance).

$$R^2 = \frac{\beta_i^2 \sigma_M^2}{\beta_i^2 \sigma_M^2 + \sigma^2(e_i)}$$

   Since stock B's explained variance is higher (its explained variance is $\beta_B^2 \sigma_M^2$, which is greater since its beta is higher), *and* its residual variance $\sigma^2(e_B)$ is smaller, its R^2 is higher than stock A's.

   d.   Alpha is the intercept of the SCL with the expected return axis. Stock A has a small positive alpha whereas stock B has a negative alpha, hence stock A's alpha is larger.

   e.   The correlation coefficient is simply the square root of R^2, so stock B's correlation with the market is higher.

4. a.   Firm-specific risk is measured by the residual standard deviation. Thus, stock A has more firm-specific risk: $10.3 > 9.1$.

   b.   Market risk is measured by beta, the slope coefficient of the regression. A has a larger beta coefficient: $1.2 > .8$.

   c. R^2 measures the fraction of total variance of return explained by the market return. A's R^2 is larger than B's: $.576 > .436$.

   d.   The average rate of return in *excess* of that predicted by the CAPM is measured by alpha, the intercept of the SCL. Alpha(A) = 1% is larger than alpha(B) = –2%.

   e.   Rewriting the SCL equation in terms of total return (r) rather than excess return (R):

$$r_A - r_f = \alpha + \beta(r_M - r_f)$$
$$r_A = \alpha + r_f(1 - \beta) + \beta r_M$$

   The intercept is now equal to:

$$\alpha + r_f(1 - \beta) = 1 + r_f(1 - 1.2)$$

   Since $r_f = 6\%$, the intercept would be: $1 - 1.2 = -.2\%$.

5. The standard deviation of each stock can be derived from the following equation for R^2:

$$R_i^2 = \frac{\beta_i^2 \sigma_M^2}{\sigma_i^2} = \frac{\text{Explained variance}}{\text{Total variance}}$$

Therefore,

$$\sigma_A^2 = \frac{\beta_A^2 \sigma_M^2}{R_A^2} = \frac{.7^2 \times 20^2}{.20} = 980$$

$$\sigma_A = 31.30\%$$

For stock B

$$\sigma_B^2 = \frac{1.2^2 \times 20^2}{.12} = 4800$$

$$\sigma_B = 69.28\%$$

6. The systematic risk for A is

$$\beta_A^2 \sigma_M^2 = .70^2 \times 20^2 = 196$$

and the firm-specific risk of A (the residual variance) is the difference between A's total risk and its systematic risk,

$$980 - 196 = 784$$

B's systematic risk is:

$$\beta_B^2 \sigma_M^2 = 1.2^2 \times 20^2 = 576$$

and B's firm-specific risk (residual variance) is:

$$4800 - 576 = 4224$$

7. The covariance between the returns of A and B is (since the residuals are assumed to be uncorrelated):

$$\text{Cov}(r_A, r_B) = \beta_A \beta_B \sigma_M^2 = .70 \times 1.2 \times 400 = 336$$

The correlation coefficient between the returns of A and B is:

$$\rho(A,B) = \frac{Cov(r_A,r_B)}{\sigma_A\sigma_B} = \frac{336}{31.30 \times 69.28} = .155$$

8.   Note that the correlation is the square root of R^2: $\rho = \sqrt{R^2}$

$$Cov(r_A,r_M) = \rho\sigma_A\sigma_M = .20^{1/2} \times 31.30 \times 20 = 280$$

$$Cov(r_B,r_M) = \rho\sigma_B\sigma_M = .12^{1/2} \times 69.28 \times 20 = 480$$

9.   The non-zero alphas from the regressions are inconsistent with the CAPM. The question is whether the alpha estimates reflect sampling errors or real mispricing. To test the hypothesis of whether the intercepts (3% for A, and –2% for B), are significantly different from zero, we would need to compute t-values for each intercept.

10.   For portfolio P we can compute:

$$\sigma_P = [.6^2 \times 980 + .4^2 \times 4800 + 2 \times .4 \times .6 \times 336]^{1/2}$$

$$= [1282.08]^{1/2} = 35.81\%$$

$$\beta_P = .6 \times .70 + .4 \times 1.2 = .90$$

$$\sigma^2(e_P) = \sigma_P^2 - \beta_P^2\sigma_M^2 = 1282.08 - .90^2 \times 400 = 958.08$$

$$Cov(r_P, r_M) = \beta_P\sigma_M^2 = .90 \times 400 = 360$$

This same result can be also attained using the covariances of the individual stocks with the market:

$$Cov(r_P, r_M) = Cov(.6r_A+.4r_B, r_M) = .6\ Cov(r_A, r_M) + .4\ Cov(r_B, r_M)$$

$$= .6 \times 280 + .4 \times 480 = 360$$

11.   Note that the variance of T-bills and their covariance with any asset are zero. Therefore, for portfolio Q

$$\sigma_Q = w_P^2\sigma_P^2 + w_M^2\sigma_M^2 + 2 \times w_P \times w_M \times Cov(r_P, r_M)$$

$$\sigma_Q = [.5^2 \times 1282.08 + .3^2 \times 400 + 2 \times .5 \times .3 \times 360]^{1/2}$$

$$= [464.52]^{1/2} = 21.55\%$$

$$\beta_Q = .5 \times .90 + .3 \times 1 + 0 = .75$$

$$\sigma^2(e_Q) = \sigma_Q^2 - \beta_Q^2 \sigma_M^2 = 464.52 - .75^2 \times 400 = 239.52$$

$$\text{Cov}(r_Q, r_M) = \beta_Q \sigma_M^2 = .75 \times 400 = 300$$

12. In a two-stock capital market, the capitalization of A being twice that of B implies that

$$w_A = 2/3 \text{ and } w_B = 1/3. \quad \sigma_A = 30\%, \ \sigma_B = 50\%, \ \rho(A,B) = .7$$

a. The variance of the market index portfolio is:

$$\sigma_M^2 = w_A^2 \sigma_A^2 + w_B^2 \sigma_B^2 + 2 w_A w_B \rho \ \sigma_A \sigma_B$$

$$= (2/3)^2 30^2 + (1/3)^2 50^2 + 2(2/3)(1/3).7 \times 30 \times 50 = 1144.4$$

$$\sigma_M = 33.83\%$$

b. The beta of stock A is:

$$\beta_A = \text{Cov}(r_A, r_M) / \sigma_M^2$$

where

$$\text{Cov}(r_A, r_M) = \text{Cov}[r_A, (2/3 \ r_A + 1/3 \ r_B)] = 2/3 \times \sigma_A^2 + 1/3 \times \text{Cov}(r_A, r_B)$$

$$= (2/3) \times 30^2 + (1/3) \times .7 \times 30 \times 50 = 950$$

so that

$$\beta_A = \frac{950}{1144.4} = .83$$

For stock B,

$$\text{Cov}(r_B, r_M) = \text{Cov}[r_B, (2/3 \ r_A + 1/3 \ r_B)] = 2/3 \times \text{Cov}(r_A, r_B) + 1/3 \times \sigma_B^2$$

$$= 2/3 \times .7 \times 30 \times 50 + 1/3 \times 50^2 = 1533.3$$

so that,

$$\beta_B = \frac{1533.3}{1144.4} = 1.34$$

c. The residual variance of each stock is:

$$\sigma^2(e_A) = \sigma_A^2 - \beta_A^2 \sigma_M^2 = 30^2 - .83^2 \times 1144.4 = 111.6$$

and

$$\sigma^2(e_B) = \sigma_B^2 - \beta_B^2 \sigma_M^2 = 50^2 - 1.34^2 \times 1144.4 = 445.1$$

d.   If the index model holds, then the following holds too:

$$(r_A - r_f) = \beta_A(r_M - r_f)$$

$$11\% = .83(r_M - r_f)$$

Thus the market risk premium must be

$$r_M - r_f = 11\%/.83 = 13.25\%$$

Since A's beta is smaller than 1.0, its risk premium is smaller than the market's risk premium.

13. a.   Merrill Lynch adjusts beta by taking the sample estimate of beta and averaging it with 1.0, using the weights of 2/3 and 1/3, as follows:

$$\text{adjusted beta} = (2/3) \times 1.24 + (1/3) \times 1 = 1.16$$

   b.   If you use your current estimate of beta to be $\beta_{t-1} = 1.24$, then

$$\beta_t = .3 + .7 \times (1.24) = 1.168$$

which is the prediction of beta for next year.

14.   The regression results provide quantitative measures of return and risk based on monthly returns over the 1989-1998 period.

ABC: β for ABC is .60, considerably below the average stock's β of 1.0, indicating that when the S&P 500 rises or falls one percentage point, ABC's return on averages rises or falls only 0.60 percentage point. As such it indicates ABC's systematic risk or market risk is low relative to the typical value for stocks. ABC's α or unique return was –3.2%, indicating that when the market return was zero percent, the average return on ABC was –3.2%. ABC's unsystematic or residual risk, as measured by $\sigma(e)$, was 13.02%. Its R^2 was .35, indicating closeness of fit to the linear regression above the value for a typical stock.

XYZ: β for XYZ was somewhat higher at .97, indicating XYZ's return pattern was very similar to the market index's β of 1.0 and the stock therefore had average systematic risk over the period examined. α for XYZ was positive and quite large, indicating an almost 7.3% return, on average, for XYZ independent of market return. Residual risk was 21.45%, half again as much as ABC, indicating a wider scatter of observations around the regression line for XYZ. Correspondingly the fit of the regression model was considerably less, consistent with an R^2 of only .17.

10-7

The effects of including one stock or the other in a diversified portfolio may be quite different, if it can be assumed that both stocks' betas will remain stable over time, since there is such a large difference in their systematic risk level. The betas obtained from the two brokerage houses may help the analyst draw inferences for the future. ABC's β estimates are similar regardless of the sample period of the underlying data. They range from .60 to .71, all well below the market average β of 1.0. XYZ's β varies significantly among the three sources of calculations, ranging as high as 1.45 for the weekly price change observations over the most recent two years. One could infer that XYZ's beta for the future might be well above 1.0, meaning it may have somewhat more systematic risk than was implied by the quarterly regression for the 1989 - 1998 period.

The upshot is that these stocks appear to have significantly different systematic risk characteristics. If these stocks are added to a diversified portfolio, XYZ will add more to total volatility.

15. a. The α of stock A is:

$$\alpha_A = r_A - [r_f + \beta_A(r_M - r_f)]$$

$$= 11 - [6 + .8(12 - 6)] \ = \ .2\%$$

For stock B:

$$\alpha_B = 14 - [6 + 1.5(12 - 6)] = -1\%$$

Stock A would be a good addition. A short position in B may be desirable.

   b. The reward to variability ratio of the stocks is :

$$S_A = \frac{11 - 6}{10} = .5$$

$$S_B = \frac{14 - 6}{11} = .73$$

Stock B is superior when only one can be held.

16.   c. The R^2 of the regression is $.7^2 = .49$, leaving 51% of total variance unexplained by the market, and therefore, interpreted as firm-specific.

17.   b.

18.   d.

19.   b.

CHAPTER 11: ARBITRAGE PRICING THEORY

1. The revised estimate of the expected rate of return of the stock would be the old estimate plus the sum of the unexpected changes in the factors times the sensitivity coefficients, i.e.,

    $$\text{revised estimate} = 12\% + [1 \times 2\% + .5 \times 3\%] = 15.5\%$$

2. Equation 11.6 applies here:

    $$E(r_p) = r_f + \beta_{p1}[E(r_1) - r_f] + \beta_{p2}[E(r_2) - r_f]$$

    We need to find the risk premium, RP, of the two factors; $RP_1 = [E(r_1) - r_f]$ and $RP_2 = [E(r_2) - r_f]$. To do so, the following two equations with two unknowns must be solved:

    $$31 = 6 + 1.5 \times RP_1 + 2.0 \times RP_2$$

    $$27 = 6 + 2.2 \times RP_1 + (-.2) \times RP_2$$

    The solution to this set of equations is

    $$RP_1 = 10\% \text{ and } RP_2 = 5\%$$

    Thus, the expected return-beta relationship is:

    $$E(r_p) = 6\% + \beta_{p1} \times 10\% + \beta_{p2} \times 5\%$$

3. The expected return of portfolio F equals the risk-free rate since its beta equals 0. Portfolio A's ratio of risk premium to beta is: $(12 - 6)/1.2 = 5$, whereas, portfolio E's ratio is lower at $(8 - 6)/.6 = 3.33$. This implies that an arbitrage opportunity exists. For instance, you can create a portfolio G with beta equal to .6 (the same as E's) by mixing portfolios A and F in equal weights. The expected return and beta of G is then:

    $$E(r_G) = .5 \times 12\% + .5 \times 6\% = 9\%$$

    $$\beta_G = .5 \times 1.2 + .5 \times 0 = 0.6$$

    Comparing G to E, G has the same beta and higher return. Therefore, an arbitrage opportunity exists by buying portfolio G and selling and equal amount of portfolio E. If you do so, your profit will be

    $$r_G - r_E = (9\% + .6 \times .F) - (8\% + .6 \times F) = 1\%$$

    of the funds (long or short) in each portfolio.

4. a. As a first step, convert the scenario rates of return to dollar payoffs per share, as shown in the following table:

	Price	Scenarios 1	2	3
A	$10	10(1 − .15) = $ 8.5	10(1 + .20) = $12	10(1 + .30) = $13
B	$15	15(1 + .25) = $18.75	15(1 + .10) = $16.5	15(1 − .10) = $13.5
C	$50	50(1 + .12) = $56	50(1 + .15) = $57.5	50(1 + .12) = $56

Identifying an arbitrage opportunity always involves constructing a zero investment portfolio. This portfolio must show non-negative payoffs in all scenarios.

For example, the proceeds from selling short two shares of A *and* two shares of B will be sufficient to buy one share of C.

$$(-2)10 + (-2)15 + 50 = 0$$

The payoff table for this zero investment portfolio in each scenario is:

	Price	# of shares	Investment	Scenarios 1	2	3
A	$10	−2	−20	−17	−24	−26
B	$15	−2	−30	−37.5	−33	−27
C	$50	+1	50	56	57.5	56
			$0	+1.5	+.5	+3

This portfolio qualifies as an arbitrage portfolio because it is both a zero investment portfolio and has positive returns in all scenarios.

b. Should prices of A and B go down due to excess short selling and price of C go up because of buying pressures, then the rate of return on (A + B) will go up and the rate of return on C will fall.

We now find a price change that will eliminate the arbitrage opportunity shown above. First note that as the price of C changes, so will the number of shares of stock that can be purchased for the investment portfolio. Second, the weakest scenario for a portfolio long on C and short on (A + B) appears to be scenario 2. Focusing on scenario 2, we call X the number of shares of A and B that will drive profits in that scenario down to zero. Next we we find the price of C that will enable us to buy only that number of shares. Denote by X the number of shares of A and B sold short and let the proceeds be sufficient to long one share of C. First we set the payoff in scenario 2 to zero.

$$12X + 16.5X + 57.5 = 0 \quad ; \quad X = -2.0175$$

meaning that we short 2.0175 shares of A and shares of B for each share of C held long. (Note that in the previous arbitrage portfolio X = −2).

11-2

Next, with this number of shares of A and B short, we ask: what is the price of one share of C that would make the portfolio investment zero? In other words, how high a price for will enable us to buy only one share of C with the proceeds of the short sale?

$$10X + 15X + P_C = 0$$

where P_C is the new price of C. Substituting $X = -2.0175$ we find that:

$$10\ (-2.0175)\ +\ 15\ (-2.0175) + P_C = 0$$

$$P_C = 50.4375$$

This means that the minimum price change that is needed to eliminate the arbitrage opportunity is 43.75 cents. To check our result, let's look at the following payoff table for a price change of 50 cents, that is, $P_C = \$50.50$.

	Price	# of shares	Investment	1	Scenarios 2	3
A	$10	−2.02	−20.2	−17.17	−24.24	−26.26
B	$15	−2.02	−30.3	−37.875	−33.33	−27.27
C	$50.50	+1	50.50	56	57.5	56
			$0	+.955	−.07	+2.47

Note that the zero investment portfolio must be recalculated ($X = -2.02$) and indeed the payoffs are no longer positive across the board but negative for scenario 2. Thus the arbitrage opportunity has been eliminated. This exercise proves that the price increase of C will eliminate the arbitrage opportunity we found in 4a, the one that uses an equal number of shares of A and B to go short. However, it does not eliminate *all* arbitrage opportunities. For example, with $P_C = \$50.50$ an arbitrage portfolio can be formed with $X_A = -1.95$, and $X_B = -2.07$ for the number of shares sold short of A and B respectively.

5.   Substituting the portfolio return and the betas in the expected return-beta relationship, we obtain two equations in the unknowns, the risk-free rate and the factor risk premium, RP.

$$12\ =\ r_f + 1.2 \times RP$$

$$9\ =\ r_f + 0.8 \times RP$$

Solving these equations, we obtain

$$r_f = 3\% \text{ and } RP = 7.5\%$$

6. a. Shorting equally the 10 negative-alpha stocks and investing the proceeds equally in the 10 positive-alpha stocks eliminates the market exposure and creates a zero-investment portfolio. The expected dollar return is:

$$1,000,000 \times .02 + (-1,000,000)(-.02) = \$40,000.$$

The beta of this portfolio is zero because it is equally weighted, with half of the weights negative, and all betas equal to one. Thus, the systematic component of the total risk is also zero. The variance of the analyst's profit is not zero, however, since this portfolio is not well diversified. Total variance amounts to the non-systematic risk.

$$\sigma^2 = \sigma^2(e_p) = \frac{\sigma^2(e_i)}{n} = \frac{30^2}{20} = 45 \quad \text{so} \quad \sigma = 6.71\%$$

b. The only change from increasing the number of stocks is that the portfolio risk falls to:

$$\sigma^2(50) = \frac{30^2}{50} = 18 \text{ and } \sigma = 4.24\%$$

$$\sigma^2(100) = \frac{30^2}{100} = 9 \text{ and } \sigma = 3\%$$

7 a.

$$\sigma^2 = \beta^2 \sigma_M^2 + \sigma^2(e)$$

The standard deviations are:

	$\sigma(e)$
A	25
B	10
C	20

and $\sigma_M = 20$. Thus,

$$\sigma_A^2 = .8^2 \times 20^2 + 25^2 = 881$$

$$\sigma_B^2 = 1.0^2 \times 20^2 + 10^2 = 500$$

$$\sigma_C^2 = 1.2^2 \times 20^2 + 20^2 = 976$$

b. If there is an infinite number of assets with identical characteristics, a well-diversified portfolio of each type will have only systematic risk since the non-systematic risk will approach zero with large n. The mean will equal that of the individual (identical) stocks.

c. There is no arbitrage opportunity because the well-diversified portfolios all plot on the security market line (SML). Because they are fairly priced, there is no arbitrage.

8. a.   A long position in an equally-weighted portfolio, P, of stocks A and B will have $\beta_P = \beta_C$ but return higher than that of portfolio C.   Hence, combining P with a short position in C will create an arbitrage portfolio with zero investment, zero beta, and positive rate of return.

   b.   The argument in (a) leads to the proposition that the coefficient of β^2 must be zero to preclude arbitrage opportunities.

9.   Any pattern of returns can be "explained" if we are free to choose an indefinitely large number of explanatory factors. If a theory of asset pricing is to have value, it must explain returns using a reasonably limited number of explanatory variables (systematic factors).

10.   The APT factors must correlate with major sources of uncertainty, i.e., sources of uncertainty that are of concern to many investors. Researchers should investigate factors that correlate with uncertainty in consumption and investment opportunities. GDP, the inflation rate, and interest rates are among the factors that can be expected to determine risk premiums. In particular, industrial production (IP) is a good indicator of changes in the business cycle. Thus, IP is a candidate for a factor that is highly correlated with uncertainties that have to do with investment and consumption opportunities in the economy.

11. a. $E(r) = 6 + 1.2 \times 6 + .5 \times 8 + .3 \times 3 = 18.1\%$

   b. Surprises in the macroeconomic factors will result in surprises in the return of the stock:

   Unexpected return from macro factors $= 1.2 (4 - 5) + .5(6 - 3) + .3 (0 - 2) = -.3\%$

12.   The APT *required* return on the stock based on r_f and the factor betas is:

        required $E(r) = 6 + 1 \times 6 + .5 \times 2 + .75 \times 4 = 16\%$

   According to the equation for the return on the stock, the actually expected return on the stock is 15% (because the *expected* surprises on all factors by definition are zero). Because the required return based on risk exceeds the actually expected return, we conclude that the stock is overpriced.

13.   b.

14.   c.

15.   d.

16.   d.

17.   (c) Investors will take on as large a position as possible only if the mispricing opportunity is an arbitrage. Otherwise, considerations of risk and diversification will limit the position they attempt to take in the mispriced security.

18.   d.

19.   d.

CHAPTER 12: MARKET EFFICIENCY

1. Zero. If not, one could use returns from one period to predict returns in later periods and make abnormal profits.

2. c. This is a predictable pattern in returns which should not occur if the weak-form EMH is valid.

3. c. This is a classic filter rule which should not work in an efficient market.

4. b. This is the definition of an efficient market.

5. c. The P/E ratio is public information and should not predict abnormal security returns.

6. b. Semi-strong efficiency implies that market prices reflect all *publicly available* information concerning past trading history as well as fundamental aspects of the firm.

7. a. The full price adjustment should occur just as the news about the dividend becomes publicly available.

8. d. If low P/E stocks consistently provide positive abnormal returns, this would represent an unexploited profit opportunity that would provide evidence that investors are not using all available information to make profitable investments.

9. c. In an efficient market, no securities are consistently overpriced or underpriced. While some securities will turn out after any investment period to have provided positive alphas (i.e., risk-adjusted abnormal returns) and some negative alphas, these past returns are not predictive of future returns.

10. c. A random walk implies that stock price changes are unpredictable, using past price changes or any other data.

11. d. A gradual adjustment to fundamental values would allow for strategies based on past price movements to generate abnormal profits.

12. a.

13. b. The contrarian strategist would notice that other investors have become deeply pessimistic about prices, and therefore would take this as a *bullish* indicator, reasoning that market sentiment swings too widely and that the stock prices reflect a too-pessimistic view of the economy.

14. No. Microsoft's continuing high return on assets does not imply that stock market investors who purchased Microsoft shares after its success already was evident would have earned a high return on their investments.

15. The question for market efficiency is whether investors can earn abnormal risk-adjusted profits. If the stock price run-up occurs when only insiders are aware of the coming dividend increase, then it is a violation of strong-form, but not semi-strong form efficiency. If the public already knows of the increase, then it is a violation of semi-strong form efficiency.

16. While positive beta stocks will respond well to favorable new information about the economy's progress through the business cycle, they should not show abnormal returns around already anticipated events. If a recovery, for example, already is anticipated, the actual recovery is not news. The stock price already should reflect the coming recovery.

17. a. Consistent. Based on pure luck, half of all managers should beat the market in any year.

    b. Inconsistent. This would be the basis of an "easy money" rule: simply invest with last year's best managers.

    c. Consistent. In contrast to predictable returns, predictable *volatility* does not convey a means to earn abnormal returns.

    d. Inconsistent. The abnormal performance ought to occur in January when earnings are announced.

    e. Inconsistent. Reversals offer a means to earn easy money: just buy last week's losers.

18. Expected rates of return will differ because of differential risk premiums.

19. The return on the market was 8%. Therefore, the forecast return on GM given the market's return is $.10\% + 1.1 \times 8\% = 8.9\%$. GM's actual return was 7%, meaning that the abnormal return was −1.9%.

20. a. Based on broad market trends, the CAPM suggests that AmbChaser stock should have increased by $1\% + 2.0(1.5\% - 1\%) = 2\%$. Its firm-specific (nonsystematic) return due to the lawsuit is $1 million per $100 million initial equity, or 1%. Therefore, the total return should be 3%. (It is assumed here that the outcome of the lawsuit had a zero expected value).

    b. If the settlement was expected to be $2 million, then the actual settlement was a "$1 million disappointment," and so the firm-specific return would be −1%, for a total return of $2\% - 1\% = 1\%$.

21. Given market performance, predicted returns on the two stocks would be:

Apex: $.2\% + 1.4 \times 3\% = 4.4\%$
Bpex: $-.1\% + .6 \times 3\% = 1.7\%$

Apex underperformed this prediction; Bpex overperformed. We conclude that Bpex won the suit.

22. a. $E(r_M) = 12\%$, $r_f = 4\%$, and $\beta = .5$. Therefore, the expected rate of return is

$$4\% + .5(12\% - 4\%) = 8\%.$$

If the stock is fairly priced, then $E(r) = 8\%$.

b. If r_M falls short of your expectation by 2% (that is, 10% – 12%) then you would expect the return on Changing Fortunes to fall short of your original expectation by $\beta \times 2\% = 1\%$. So you would forecast a "revised" expectation for Changing Fortunes of 8% – 1% = 7%.

c. Given a market return of 10%, you would forecast a return for Changing Fortunes of 7%. The actual return is 10%. Therefore, the surprise due to firm-specific factors is 10% – 7% = 3% which we attribute to the settlement. Because the firm initially is worth $100 million, the surprise amount of the settlement must be 3% of $100 million, or $3 million, implying that the prior expectation for the settlement was only $2 million.

23. Implicit in the dollar-cost averaging strategy is the notion that stock prices fluctuate around a "normal" level. Otherwise, there is no meaning to statements like, "when the price is high." How do we know, for example, that a price of $25 today will turn out to be viewed as high or low compared to the stock price in 6 months?

24. No. The value of dividend predictability will already be reflected in the stock price.

25. The market responds positively to *new* news. If the eventual recovery is anticipated, then the recovery already is reflected in stock prices. Only a better-than-expected recovery should affect stock prices.

26. Over the long haul, there is an expected upward drift in stock prices based on their fair expected rates of return. The fair expected return over any single day is very small (e.g., 12% per year is only about .03% per day), so that on any day the price is virtually equally likely to rise or fall. However, over longer periods, the small expected daily returns accumulate, and upward moves are indeed more likely than downward ones.

27. Buy. In your view, the firm is not as bad as everyone else believes it to be. Therefore, you view the firm as undervalued by the market. You are less pessimistic about the firm's prospects than the beliefs built into the stock price.

28. The negative abnormal returns (downward drift in CAR) just prior to stock purchases suggest that insiders deferred their purchases until *after* bad news was released to the public. This is evidence of valuable inside information. The positive abnormal returns after purchase suggest insider purchases in anticipation of good news. The analysis is symmetric for insider sales.

29. Here we need a two-factor model relating Ford's return to those of both the broad market and the auto industry. If we call r_I the industry return, then we first would estimate parameters a,b,c in the regression

$$r_{Ford} = a + br_M + cr_I + e$$

Given these estimates we would calculate Ford's firm-specific return as

$$r_{Ford} - [\ a + br_M + cr_I\ ].$$

This estimate of firm-specific news would measure the market's assessment of the potential profitability of Ford's new model.

30. The market may have anticipated even greater earnings. *Compared to prior expectations,* the announcement was a disappointment.

31. a. Some empirical evidence that supports the EMH is that (i) professional money managers do not typically earn higher returns than comparable risk, passive index strategies; (ii) event studies typically show that stocks respond immediately to the public release of relevant news; (iii) most tests of technical analysis find that it is difficult to identify price trends that can be exploited to earn superior risk-adjusted investment returns.

   b. Some evidence that is difficult to reconcile with the EMH concerns simple portfolio strategies that apparently would have provided high risk-adjusted returns in the past. Some examples of portfolios with attractive historical returns: (i) low P/E stocks; (ii) high book-to-market ratio stocks; (iii) small firms in January; (iv) firms with very poor stock price performance in the last few months. Other evidence concerns post-earnings-announcement stock price drift and intermediate-term price momentum.

   c. An investor may choose not to index even if markets are efficient because he or she may want to tailor a portfolio to specific tax considerations or to specific risk management issues, for example, the need to hedge (or at least not add to) exposure to a particular source of risk (e.g., industry exposure).

32. a. The efficient market hypothesis (EMH) states that a market is efficient if security prices immediately and fully reflect all available relevant information. If the market fully reflects information, the knowledge of that information would not allow anyone to profit from it because stock prices already incorporate the information.

   i. The *weak form* asserts that stock prices already reflect all the information that can be derived by examining market trading data such as the history of past prices and trading volume.

   A strong body of evidence supports weak-form efficiency in the major U.S. securities markets. For example, test results suggest that technical trading rules do not produce superior returns after adjusting for transactions costs and taxes.

   ii. The *semistrong form* says that a firm's stock price already reflects all publicly available information about a firm's prospects. Examples of publicly available information are annual reports of companies and investment advisory data.

Evidence strongly supports the notion of semistrong efficiency, but occasional studies (e.g., those identifying market anomalies such as the small-firm-in-January or book-to-market effects) and events such as the stock market crash of October 19,1987) are inconsistent with this form of market efficiency. However, there is a question concerning the extent to which these "anomalies" result from data mining.

iii. The *strong form* of the EMH holds that current market prices reflect *all* information (whether publicly available or privately held) that can be relevant to the valuation of the firm.

Empirical evidence suggests that strong-form efficiency does not hold. If this form were correct, prices would fully reflect all information. Therefore even insiders could not earn excess returns. But the evidence is that corporate officers do have access to pertinent information long enough before public release to enable them to profit from trading on this information.

b. *Technical analysis* involves the search for recurrent and predictable patterns in stock prices to enhance returns. The EMH implies that technical analysis is without value. If past prices contain no useful information for predicting future prices, there is no point in following any technical trading rule.

Fundamental analysis uses earnings and dividend prospects of the firm, expectations of future interest rates, and risk evaluation of the firm to determine proper stock prices. The EMH predicts that most fundamental analysis is doomed to failure. According to semistrong-form efficiency, no investor can earn excess returns from trading rules based on publicly available information. Only analysts with unique insight receive superior returns.

In summary, the EMH holds that the market appears to adjust so quickly to information about individual stocks and the economy as a whole that no technique of selecting a portfolio using either technical or fundamental analysis can consistently outperform a strategy of simply buying and holding a diversified group of securities, such as those making up the popular market indexes.

c. Portfolio managers have several roles and responsibilities even in perfectly efficient markets. The most important responsibility is to identify the risk/return objectives for the portfolio given the investor's constraints. In an efficient market, portfolio managers are responsible for tailoring the portfolio to meet the investor's needs rather than to beat the market, which requires identifying the client's return requirements and risk tolerance. Rational portfolio management also requires examining the investor's constraints, such as liquidity, time horizon, laws and regulations, taxes, and unique preferences and circumstances such as age and employment.

33. a. The earnings (and dividend) growth rate of growth stocks may be consistently overestimated by investors. Investors may extrapolate recent earnings (and dividend) growth too far into the future and downplay the inevitable slowdown. At any given time, growth stocks are likely to revert to (lower) mean returns and value stocks are likely to revert to (higher) mean returns, often over an extended future time horizon.

b. In efficient markets, the current prices of stocks already reflect all known relevant information. In this situation, growth stocks and value stocks will provide the same risk-adjusted expected return.

CHAPTER 13: EMPIRICAL EVIDENCE ON SECURITY RETURNS

Note: In Chapter 13's end-of-chapter-problems the focus is on the estimation *procedure*. To keep the exercise feasible the sample was limited to returns on 9 stocks plus a market index and a second factor over 12 years. The data were generated to conform to a two-factor CAPM so that actual rates of return equal CAPM expectations plus random noise and the true intercept of the SCL is zero for all stocks. The exercise will give you a feel for the pitfalls of verifying social-science models. However, due to the small size of the sample, results are not always consistent with the findings of the studies reported in the chapter itself.

1. Using the regression feature of Excel with the data presented in the text, the first-pass (SCL) estimation results are:

Stock:	A	B	C	D	E	F	G	H	I
R Square	0.06	0.06	0.06	0.37	0.41	0.59	0.24	0.67	0.70
Intercept	9.00	-0.63	-0.64	-5.05	0.73	-4.52	5.94	-2.41	5.92
Beta	-0.47	0.59	0.42	1.38	0.90	1.78	0.66	1.91	1.983
t-Intercept	0.73	-0.04	-0.06	-0.41	0.05	-0.45	0.33	-0.26	-0.13
t-Beta	-0.81	0.78	0.78	2.42	1.42	3.83	0.78	4.51	2.08

2. The hypotheses for the second-pass regression for the SML are that the intercept is zero and the slope is equal to the average excess return on the index portfolio.

3. The second-pass data from the first-pass (SCL) estimates are:

	Average Excess Return	Beta
A	5.18	-0.47
B	4.19	0.59
C	2.75	0.42
D	6.15	1.38
E	8.05	0.90
F	9.90	1.78
G	11.32	0.66
H	13.11	1.91
I	22.83	2.08
M	8.12	

The second-pass regression yields:

Regression Statistics	
Multiple R	0.707426
R Square	0.500452
Adjusted R Square	0.429087
Standard Error	4.623741
Observations	9

	Coefficients	Standard Error	t-statistic
Intercept	3.923452	2.541849	1.543543
Slope	5.205081	1.96556	2.648142

The results are reflected in the regression equation above, with intercept, slope coefficients, standard errors, and t-statistics as shown.

4. As regression theory predicts, and as we have seen in the chapter, the intercept is too high (3.92%/year instead of zero), and the slope too flat (5.21% instead of 8.12%). The fact that the intercept is not significantly greater than zero (the t-statistic is less than 2) and the slope's deviation from the theoretical value (5.21 – 8.12 = –2.91) is not statistically significant (its magnitude is less than twice the standard error of 1.97) is probably due to the small size of the sample.

5. Arranging the securities in three portfolios based on betas from the SCL estimates, the first pass input data is:

Year	ABC	DEG	FHI
1	15.05	25.86	56.70
2	-16.76	-29.74	-50.85
3	19.67	-5.68	8.98
4	-15.83	-2.58	35.41
5	47.18	37.70	-3.24
6	-2.26	53.86	75.44
7	-18.67	15.32	12.50
8	-6.35	36.33	32.12
9	7.85	14.08	50.42
10	21.41	12.66	52.14
11	-2.53	-50.71	-66.12
12	-0.30	-4.99	-20.10

which result in first-pass (SCL) estimates:

	ABC	DEG	FHI
Multiple R	0.19	0.69	0.91
R Square	0.04	0.48	0.82
Adjusted R Square	-0.06	0.42	0.81
Standard Error	19.86	22.36	19.38
Observations	12	12	12
Alpha	2.58	0.54	-0.34
Beta	0.18	0.98	1.92
t-alpha	0.41	0.08	-0.06
t-beta	0.62	3.02	6.83

Grouping into portfolios has improved the SCL estimates, as is evident from the higher R-square. This means that the beta (slope) is measured with greater precision, reducing the error-in-measurement problem at the expense of leaving fewer observations for the second pass.

Estimating the second pass regression we have

	Avg. excess return	Beta
ABC	4.04	0.18
DEG	8.51	0.98
FHI	15.28	1.92
Multiple R	0.9975	
R Square	0.9949	
Adjusted R Square	0.9899	
Standard Error	0.5696	
Observations	3	

	Coefficients	Standard Error	t-statistic
Intercept	2.62	0.58	4.54
Slope	6.47	0.46	14.02

Despite the drop in the intercept and increase in slope, the intercept is now significantly positive and the slope is below the hypothesized value by more than twice the standard error, that is, significantly so.

6. Roll's critique suggests that the problem begins with the market index which isn't the theoretical portfolio against which the second pass regression is supposed to hold. Hence, even if the relationship is true with respect to the true (unknown) index, we may not find it. As a result, the second pass relationship may be meaningless.

7.

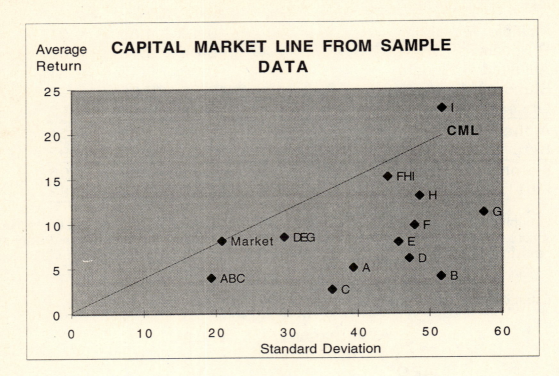

CAPITAL MARKET LINE FROM SAMPLE DATA

Except for Stock I, which realized an extremely positive surprise, the CML shows that the index dominates all other securities, and the three portfolios dominate most of the individual stocks. The power of diversification is evident even using the very short sample period.

8. The first-pass (SCL) regression results are summarized below.

	A	B	C	D	E	F	G	H	I
R-Sqr	0.07	0.36	0.11	0.44	0.24	0.84	0.12	0.68	0.71
St. Err.	41.62	45.50	37.91	38.79	43.86	21.22	59.63	30.17	30.72
Obs.	12	12	12	12	12	12	12	12	12
Intercept	9.19	-1.89	-1.00	-4.48	0.17	-3.47	5.32	-2.64	5.66
Beta M	-0.47	0.58	0.41	1.39	0.89	1.79	0.65	1.91	2.08
Beta F	-0.35	2.33	0.67	-1.05	1.03	-1.95	1.15	0.43	0.48
t-(a)	0.71	-0.13	-0.08	-0.37	0.01	-0.52	0.29	-0.28	0.59
t-(bM)	-0.77	0.87	0.75	2.46	1.40	5.81	0.75	4.35	4.65
t-(bF)	-0.34	2.06	0.71	-1.08	0.94	-3.69	0.77	0.57	0.63

9. The hypotheses for the two-factor model are: (1) the intercept is zero, (2) the market-index slope coefficient equals the market-index average excess return (note that hypotheses 1 and 2 are the same as with a single-factor model), and (3) the factor slope coefficient equals the average excess return on the factor.

10.   The input into the second pass is:

Average excess return	Beta M	Beta F
5.18	-0.47	-0.35
4.19	0.58	2.33
2.75	0.41	0.67
6.15	1.39	-1.05
8.05	0.89	1.03
9.90	1.79	-1.95
11.32	0.65	1.15
13.11	1.91	0.43
22.83	2.08	0.48

which results in second-pass estimates:

R Square	0.52		
St. Error	4.88		
Obs.	9		

Intercept	3.36	2.88	1.16
Beta M	5.53	2.16	2.56
Beta F	0.80	1.42	0.56

This result is slightly better than the single factor test; that is, the intercept is smaller and the slope on M is slightly greater. We cannot expect a great improvement in the first place since the factor we added does not appear to carry much of a risk premium (its average return is less than 1%); its effect on mean returns is therefore small. The data do not reject the second factor because the slope is close to the average and the difference is less than one standard error. However, with this sample size, the power of this test is extremely low.

11.   A candidate for any factor portfolio should maximize the correlation with the factor itself. Thus, by taking the factor, we implicitly assumed that there a perfectly correlated

12.   (i) Betas as empirically estimated are computed with respect to market indexes that are at best proxies for the true market portfolio, which is inherently not observable.

(ii) Empirical tests of the CAPM show that average returns are not related to beta in the manner predicted by the theory. The empirical SML is flatter than the theoretical one.

(iii) Multi-factor models of security returns show that beta, which is a one-dimensional view of risk, may not capture the true risk of the stock or portfolio.

13.   [From the CFA Study Guide]

a.   The basic procedure in portfolio evaluation is to compare the returns on a managed portfolio to the return expected on an unmanaged portfolio having the same risk, via use of the SML. That is, expected return is calculate from:

$$E(r_p) = r_f + \beta_P[E(r_M) - r_f]$$

where r_f is the risk-free rate, $E(r_M)$ is the *unmanaged* portfolio (or the market) expected return and β_P is the beta coefficient (or systematic risk) of the managed portfolio. The benchmark of performance then is the unmanaged portfolio. The typical proxy for this unmanaged portfolio is some aggregate stock market index such as the S&P 500.

b.   The benchmark error may occur when the unmanaged portfolio used in the evaluation process is not "optimized." That is, market indices, such as the S&P 500, chosen as benchmarks are not on the manager's *ex ante* mean/variance efficient frontier.

c.   Your graph should show an efficient frontier obtained from actual returns, and a different one which represents (unobserved) ex-ante expectations. The CML and SML generated from actual returns do not conform to the CAPM predictions, while the hypothesized lines do.

d.   The answer to this question depends on one's prior beliefs. Given a consistent track record, an agnostic observer might conclude that the data support the claim of superiority. Other observers might start with a strong prior that, since so many managers are attempting to beat a passive portfolio, a small number are bound to come up with seemingly convincing track records.

e.   The question is really whether the CAPM is at all testable. The problem is that even a slight inefficiency in the benchmark portfolio may completely invalidate any test of the expected return-beta relationship. It appears from Roll's argument that the best guide to the question of the validity of the CAPM is the difficulty of beating a passive strategy.

CHAPTER 14

BOND PRICES AND YIELDS

1. a.   Effective annual rate on 3-month T-bill:

$$(\frac{100,000}{97,645})^4 - 1 = 1.02412^4 - 1 = .10 \text{ or } 10\%$$

   b.   Effective annual interest rate on coupon bond paying 5% semiannually:

$$(1.05)^2 - 1 = .1025 \text{ or } 10.25\%$$

2.   The effective annual yield on the semiannual coupon bonds is 8.16%. If the annual coupon bonds are to sell at par they must offer the same yield, which will require an annual coupon of 8.16%.

3.   The bond callable at 105 should sell at a lower price because the call provision is more valuable to the firm. Therefore, its YTM should be higher.

4.   Lower. As time passes, the bond price, which now must be above par value, will approach par.

5.   We find the yield to maturity from our financial calculator using the following inputs: n = 3, FV = 1000, PV = 953.10, PMT = 80. This results in

   YTM = 9.88%

   <u>Realized compound yield</u>: First find the future value, FV, of reinvested coupons and principal:

   FV = $(80 \times 1.10 \times 1.12) + (80 \times 1.12) + 1080 = \$1268.16$

   Then find the rate, y, that makes the FV of the purchase price equal to $1268.16.

$$953.10(1 + y)^3 = 1268.16$$
$$y = 10\%$$

6. a.   A sinking fund is a provision that calls for the mandatory early redemption of a bond issue. The provision may be for a specific number of bonds or a percentage of bonds over a specified time horizon. The sinking fund can retire all or a portion of an issue over its life.

   b.   (i) Compared to a bond without a sinking fund, the sinking fund will reduce the average life of the overall issue because some of the bonds are retired before stated maturity.

(ii) The company will make the same total principal payments over the life of the issue, although the timing of the payments will be affected. The total interest payments associated with the issue will be reduced given the early redemption of principal.

c. From the investor's point of view, the key reason for demanding a sinking fund is to reduce credit risk. Default risk is reduced by the orderly retirement of the issue.

7. a. (i) Current yield = Coupon/Price = 70/960 = .073 = 7.3%

(ii) YTM = 4% semiannually or 8% annual bond equivalent yield.

On your calculator, set   n = 10 (semiannual payments)
                                        PV = (–)960
                                          FV = 1,000
                                          PMT = 35
Compute the interest rate.

(iii) Realized compound yield is 4.166% (semiannually), or 8.33% annual bond equivalent yield. To obtain this value, first calculate the future value of reinvested coupons. There will be 6 payments of $35 each, reinvested semiannually at a per period rate of 3%: PV = 0; PMT = $35; n = 6; i = 3%. Compute FV = $226.39.

The bond will be selling at par value of $1,000 in 3 years, since coupon is forecast to equal yield to maturity.

Therefore, total proceeds in 3 years will be $1,226.39. To find realized compound yield on a semiannual basis (i.e., for 6 half-year periods), we solve:

$$\$960 \times (1 + y)^6 = \$1,226.39$$

Which implies that y = 4.166% (semiannual)

b. Shortcomings of each measure:

(i) Current yield does not account for capital gains or losses on bonds bought at prices other than par value. It also does not account for reinvestment income on coupon payments.

(ii) Yield to maturity assumes the bond is held until maturity and that all coupon income can be reinvested at a rate equal to the yield to maturity.

(iii) Realized compound return is affected by the forecast of reinvestment rates, holding period, and yield of the bond at the end of the investor's holding period.

8.

	Zero	8% coupon	10% coupon
a. Current prices	$463.19	$1000	$1134.20
b. Price 1 year from now	$500.25	$1000	$1124.94
Price increase	$ 37.06	$ 0.00	− 9.26
Coupon income	$ 0.00	$ 80.00	$ 100.00
Pre-tax income	$ 37.06	$ 80.00	$ 90.74
Pre-tax rate of return	8.00%	8.00%	$ 8.00%
Taxes*	$11.12	$24	$ 28.15
After-tax income	$25.94	$56	$ 62.59
After-tax return	5.60%	5.60%	5.52%
c. Price 1 year from now	$543.93	$1065.15	$1195.46
Price increase	$80.74	$65.15	$61.26
Coupon income	$0	$80	$100.00
Pre-tax income	$80.74	$145.15	$161.26
Pre-tax return	17.4%	14.5%	14.2%
Taxes	$24.22	$37.03	$42.25
After-tax income	$56.52	$108.12	$119.01
After-tax return	12.20%	10.81%	10.49%

* In computing taxes, we assume that the 10% coupon bond was issued at par and that the drop in price when the bond is sold at year end is treated as a capital loss and not as an offset to ordinary income.

9.   a.   Use the following inputs: n = 40, FV = 1000, PV = (−)950, PMT = 40. You will find that the yield to maturity on a semi-annual basis is 4.26%. This implies a bond equivalent yield to maturity of 4.26% × 2 = 8.52%.

Effective annual yield to maturity $= (1.0426)^2 - 1 = .0870 = 8.70\%$

b.   Since the bond is selling at par, the yield to maturity on a semi-annual basis is the same as the semi-annual coupon, 4%. The bond equivalent yield to maturity is 8%.

Effective annual yield to maturity $= (1.04)^2 - 1 = .0816 = 8.16\%$

c.   Keeping other inputs unchanged but setting PV = (−)1050, we find a bond equivalent yield to maturity of 7.52%, or 3.76% on a semi-annual basis.

Effective annual yield to maturity $= (1.0376)^2 - 1 = .0766 = 7.66\%$

10.   Since the bond now makes annual payments instead of semi-annual payments, the bond equivalent yield to maturity will be the same as the effective annual yield to maturity. The inputs are: n = 20, FV = 1000, PV = (−)price, PMT = 80. The resulting yields for the three bonds are:

Bond Price	Bond equivalent yield = Effective annual yield
$950	8.53%
$1000	8.00%
$1050	7.51%

The yields computed in this case are lower than the yields calculated when the coupon payments were semi-annual. All else equal, annual payments make the bonds less attractive to the investor, since more time elapses before payments are received. If the bond price is no lower when the payments are made annually, the bond's yield to maturity must be lower.

11. Remember that the convention is to use semi-annual periods:

Price	Maturity (years)	Maturity (half-years)	Semi annual YTM	Bond equivalent yield to maturity
$400	20	40	2.317%	4.634%
$500	20	40	1.748%	3.496%
$500	10	20	3.526%	7.052%
$376.89	10	20	5.000%	10.000%
$456.39	10	20	4.000%	8.000%
$400	11.68	23.36	4.000%	8.000%

12. a. The bond pays $50 every 6 months

Current price $50 × Annuity factor(4%, 6) + $1000 × PV factor(4%, 6) = $1052.42

Assuming the market interest rate remains 4% per half year:

Price 6 months from now =

$50 × Annuity factor(4%, 5) + $1000 × PV factor(4%, 5) = $1044.52

b. Rate of return $= \dfrac{\$50 + (\$1044.52 - \$1052.42)}{\$1052.42}$

$= \dfrac{\$50 - \$7.90}{\$1052.42} = \dfrac{\$42.10}{\$1052.42} = .04$ or 4% per six months

13. a. Initial price, $P_0 = 705.46$ [n = 20; PMT = 50; FV = 1000; i = 8]

Next year's price, $P_1 = 793.29$ [n = 19; PMT = 50; FV = 1000; i = 7]

$\text{HPR} = \dfrac{50 + (793.29 - 705.46)}{705.46} = .1954 = 19.54\%$

b. Using OID tax rules, the price path of the bond under the constant yield method is obtained by discounting at an 8% yield, and simply reducing maturity by one year at a time:

Constant yield prices

$P_0 = 705.46$
$P_1 = 711.89$ implies implicit interest over first year = $6.43
$P_2 = 718.84$ implies implicit interest over second year = $6.95

Tax on explicit plus implicit interest in first year = $.40 \times (\$50 + \$6.43) = \$22.57$

Capital gain in first year   = Actual price – constant yield price
                         = 793.29 – 711.89 = $81.40

Tax on capital gain = $.30 \times \$81.40 = \$24.42$

Total taxes = $22.57 + $24.42 = $46.99

c. After tax HPR $= \dfrac{50 + (793.29 - 705.46) - 46.99}{705.46} = .1288 = 12.88\%$

d. Value of bond after 2 years equals $798.82 [using n = 18; i = 7%]

Reinvested coupon income from the two coupons equals $50 \times 1.03 + \$50 = \$101.50$

Total funds after two years equals $798.82 + $101.50 = $900.32.

Therefore, the $705.46 investment grows to $900.32 after 2 years.

$705.46 (1 + r)^2 = 900.32$ which implies that r = .1297 = 12.97%

e.

Coupon received in first year:	$50
Tax on coupon @ 40%	– 20
Tax on imputed interest (.40 × $6.43)	– 2.57
Net cash flow in first year	$27.43

If you invest the year-1 CF at an after-tax rate of $3\% \times (1 - .40) = 1.8\%$ it will grow by year 2 to $27.43 \times (1.018) = \$27.92$.

You sell the bond in the second year for	$798.82	[n = 18; i = 7%]
Tax on *imputed* interest in second year	– 2.78	[.40 × $6.95]
Coupon received in second year net of tax	+ 30.00	[$50 × (1 – .40)]
Capital gains tax on	– 23.99	[.30 × (798.82 – 718.84)]
sales price – constant yield value		
CF from first year's coupon (reinvested)	+ 27.92	[from above]
TOTAL	$829.97	

$705.46 (1 + r)^2 = 829.97$

r = .0847 = 8.47%

14. The *reported* bond price is 100 2/32 percent of par, which equals $1,000.625. However, 15 days have passed since the last semiannual coupon was paid, so accrued interest equals $35 \times (15/182) = $2.885. The invoice price is the reported price plus accrued interest, or $1003.51.

15. If the yield to maturity is greater than current yield, the bond must offer the prospect of price appreciation as it approaches its maturity date. Therefore, the bond must be selling below par value.

16. The coupon rate must be below 9%. If coupon divided by price equals 9%, and price is less than par, then price divided by par must be less than 9%.

17. The price schedule is as follows:

Year	Remaining Maturity, T	Constant yield value $1000/(1.08)^T$	Imputed interest (Increase in constant yield value)
0 (now)	20 years	214.55	
1	19	231.71	17.16
2	18	250.25	18.54
19	1	925.93	
20	0	1000.00	74.07

18. The bond is issued at a price of $800. Therefore, its yield to maturity is 6.824%. Using the constant yield method, we can compute that its price in one year (when maturity falls to 9 years) will be (at an unchanged yield) $814.60, representing an increase of $14.60. Total taxable income is $40 + $14.60 = $54.60.

19. a. The bond sells for $1,124.72 based on the 3.5% yield to *maturity*. [n = 60; i = 3.5%; FV = 1,000; PMT = 40]

   Therefore, yield to call is 3.368% semiannually. [n = 10 semiannual periods; PV = (–)1,124.72 ; FV = 1,100; PMT = 40]

   b. If the call price were $1,050, we would set FV = 1,050 and redo part (a) to find that yield to call is 2.976%. With a lower call price, the yield to call is lower.

   c. Yield to call is 3.031% semiannually. [n = 4; (–)PV = 1,124.72 ; FV = 1,100; PMT = 40]

20. The yield to maturity based on promised payments equals 16.07%. [n = 10; PV = (–)900; FV = 1,000; PMT = 140]

   Based on *expected* coupon payments of $70 annually, the expected yield to maturity would be only 8.526%.

21. The bond is selling at par value. Its yield to maturity equals the coupon rate, 10%. If the first-year coupon is reinvested at an interest rate of r percent, then total proceeds at the end of the second year will be $100 \times (1+r) + 1100$. Therefore, realized compound yield to maturity will be a function of r as given in the following table:

r	Total proceeds	Realized YTM = $\sqrt{\text{Proceeds}/1000} - 1$
8%	$1208	$\sqrt{1208/1000} - 1 = .0991 = 9.91\%$
10%	$1210	$\sqrt{1210/1000} - 1 = .1000 = 10.00\%$
12%	$1212	$\sqrt{1212/1000} - 1 = .1009 = 10.09\%$

22. Zero coupon bonds provide no coupons to be reinvested. Therefore, the final value of the investor's proceeds from the bond are independent of the rate at which coupons could be reinvested (if they were paid). There is no reinvestment rate uncertainty with zeros.

23. April 15 is midway through the semiannual coupon period. Therefore, the invoice price will be higher than the stated ask price by an amount equal to one-half of the semiannual coupon. The ask price is 101.125 percent of par, so the invoice price is

$1011.25 + 1/2 \times \$50 = \$1036.25$

24. Factors which might make the ABC debt more attractive to investors, therefore justifying a lower coupon rate and yield to maturity, are:

a. The ABC debt is a larger issue and therefore may sell with more liquidity.

b. An option to extend the term from 10 years to 20 years is favorable if interest rates in 10 years are lower than today's. In contrast, if interest rates are rising, the investor can present the bond for payment and reinvest the money for better returns.

c. In the event of trouble, the ABC debt is a more senior claim. It has more underlying security in the form of a first claim against real property.

d. The call feature on the XYZ bonds makes the ABC bonds relatively more attractive since ABC bonds cannot be called from the investor.

e. The XYZ bond has a sinking fund requiring XYZ to retire part of the issue each year. Since most sinking funds give the firm the option to retire this amount at the lower of par or market value, the sinking fund can work to the detriment of bondholders.

25. a. The floating rate note pays a coupon that adjusts to market levels. Therefore, it will not experience dramatic price changes as market yields fluctuate. The fixed rate note therefore will have a greater price range.

b. Floating rate notes may not sell at par for any of the several reasons:

The yield spread between 1-year Treasury bills and other money market instruments of comparable maturity could be wider than when the bond was issued.

The credit standing of the firm may have eroded relative to Treasury securities which have no credit risk. Therefore, the 2% premium would become insufficient to sustain the issue at par.

The coupon increases are implemented with a lag, i.e., once every year. During a period of rising interest rates, even this brief lag will be reflected in the price of the security.

c. The risk of call is low. Because the bond will almost surely not sell for much above par value (given its adjustable coupon rate), it is unlikely that the bond will ever be called.

d. The fixed-rate note currently sells at only 88% of the call price. Call risk is currently low, since yields would need to fall substantially for the firm to use its option to call the bond.

e. The 9% coupon notes currently have a remaining maturity of 15 years and sell at a yield to maturity of 9.9%. This is the coupon rate that would be needed for a newly-issued 15-year maturity bond to sell at par.

f. Because the floating rate note consists of a *variable stream* of interest payments to maturity, the effective maturity for comparative purposes with other debt securities is closer to next coupon reset date than the final maturity date. Therefore, yield-to-maturity is an indeterminable calculation for a floating rate note, with "yield-to-recoupon date" a more meaningful measure of return.

26. a. The yield on the par bond equals its coupon rate, 8.75%. All else equal, the 4% coupon bond would be more attractive because its coupon rate is far below current market yields, and its price is far below the call price. Therefore, if yields do fall, capital gains on the bond will not be limited by the call price. In contrast, the 8 3/4% coupon bond can increase in value to at most $1050, offering a maximum possible gain of only 0.5%. The disadvantage of the 8 3/4% coupon bond in terms of vulnerability to being called shows up in its higher *promised* yield to maturity.

b. If an investor expects yields to fall substantially, the 4% bond will offer a greater expected return.

c. Implicit call protection is offered in the sense that any likely fall in yields would not be nearly enough to make the firm consider calling the bond. In this sense, the call feature is almost irrelevant.

27. Market conversion price = value if converted into stock

= 20.83 × $28 = $583.24

Conversion premium = Bond price – value if converted into stock

= $775 – $583.24 = 191.76

28. a. The call provision requires the firm to offer a higher coupon (or higher promised yield to maturity) on the bond to compensate the investor for the firm's option to call back the bond at a specified price if interest rate falls sufficiently. Investors are willing to grant this valuable option to the issuer, but only for a price that reflects the possibility that the bond will be called. That price is the higher promised yield at which they are willing to buy the bond.

   b. The call option will reduce the expected life of the bond. If interest rates fall substantially and the likelihood of call increases, investors will begin to treat the bond as if it will "mature" and be paid off at the call date, not at the stated maturity date. On the other hand if rates rise, the bond must be paid off at the maturity date, not later. This asymmetry means that the expected life of the bond will be less than the stated maturity.

   c. The advantage of a callable bond is the higher coupon (and a higher promised yield to maturity) when the bond is issued. If the bond turns out not to be called, then one will earn a higher realized compound yield on a callable bond issued at par than a non-callable bond issued at par on the same date. The disadvantage of the callable bond is the risk of call. If rates fall and the bond is called, the investor will receive the call price and will have to reinvest the proceeds at now-lower interest rates than the yield to maturity at which the bond originally was issued. In this event, the firm's savings in interest payments is the investor's loss.

29. a. (iv) The Euless, Texas, General Obligation Bond, which has been refunded and secured by U.S. Government bonds held in escrow, has as good a credit quality as the U.S. bonds backing it. Euless, Texas has issued new bond to refund this issue, and with the proceeds purchased U.S. Government bonds. They did this rather than simply retire the old bonds because the old bonds are not callable yet and because Euless gets to earn the rate on T-bonds while paying a lower rate on its own bonds.

   The University of Kansas Medical Center Bonds are insured by a body which is not backed by the taxing power of the U.S. Treasury and therefore do not have as high a credit quality as the Euless bonds.

   The other two bonds have indeterminate quality. Since both are bonds of small local governments they may be subject to significant risk. The Sumter, South Carolina, Water and Sewer Revenue Bond probably is less likely to default because the revenues from such essential services are more reliable than the general taxing power of Riley County, Kansas.

   b. (ii) Economic uncertainty increases the chances of default and therefore widens the spread between Treasury and BAA corporate bond yields.

   c. (iii)

   d. (iii) The yield on the callable bond must compensate the investor for the risk of call.

   Choice (i) is wrong because, although the owner of a callable bond receives a premium plus the principal in the event of a call, the interest rate at which he can reinvest will be low. The low interest rate which makes it profitable for the issuer to call the bond makes it a bad deal for the bond's holder.

Choice (ii) is wrong because a bond is more apt to be called when interest rates are low. Only if rates are low will there be an interest saving for the issuer.

e. (ii) is the only correct choice.

   (i) is wrong because the YTM exceeds the coupon rate when a bond sells at a discount and is less than the coupon rate when the bond sells at a premium.

   (iii) is wrong because adding the *average* annual capital gain rate to the current yield does not give the yield to maturity. For example, assume a 10-year bond with a 6% coupon rate paying interest annually and a YTM of 8% per year. Its price is $865.80. The average annual capital gain is equal to ($1000 – 865.80)/10 years = $13.42 per year. Using this number results in an average capital gains rate per year of $13.42/$865.80 = 1.55%. The current coupon yield is $60/$865.80 = .0693 per year or 6.93%. Therefore, the "total yield" is 8.48% (=1.55% + 6.93%) which is greater than the YTM.

   (iv) is wrong because YTM is based on the assumption that any payments received are reinvested at the YTM and not at the coupon rate.

f. $(1+.12/4)^4 = 1.1255$. The effective annual YTM is 12.55%. Choice (iii) is correct.

g. (iii)

h. (ii)

i. (iii)

j. (iv)

k. (iii)

l. (iii)

m. (iv)

n. (iii)

o. (i)

p. (iii)

q. (ii)

CHAPTER 15: THE TERM STRUCTURE OF INTEREST RATES

1. Expectations hypothesis.
   The yields on long-term bonds are geometric averages of present and expected future short rates. An upward sloping curve is explained by expected future short rates being higher than the current short rate. A downward-sloping yield curve implies expected future short rates are lower than the current short rate. Thus bonds of different maturities have different yields if expectations of future short rates are different from the current short rate.

   Liquidity preference hypothesis.
   Yields on long-term bonds are greater than the expected return from rolling-over short-term bonds in order to compensate investors in long-term bonds for bearing interest rate risk. Thus bonds of different maturities can have different yields even if expected future short rates are all equal to the current short rate. An upward sloping yield curve can be consistent even with expectations of falling short rates if liquidity premiums are high enough. If, however, the yield curve is downward sloping and liquidity premiums are assumed to be positive, then we can conclude that future short rates are expected to be lower than the current short rate.

   Segmentation hypothesis.
   This hypothesis would explain a sloping yield curve by an imbalance between supply and demand for bonds of different maturities. An upward sloping yield curve is evidence of supply pressure in the long-term market and demand pressure in the short-term market. According to the segmentation hypothesis expectations of future rates have little to do with the shape of the yield curve.

2. d.

3. b.

4. True. Under the expectations hypothesis, there are no risk premia built into bond prices. The only reason for long-term yields to exceed short-term yields is an expectation of higher short-term rates in the future.

5. Uncertain. Lower inflation will usually lead to lower nominal interest rates. Nevertheless, if the liquidity premium is sufficiently great, long-term yields may exceed short-term yields *despite* expectations of falling short rates.

6.

Maturity	Price	YTM	Forward Rates
1	$943.40	6.00%	
2	$898.47	5.50%	5.00% $(1.055^2/1.06 - 1)$
3	$847.62	5.67%	6.00% $(1.0567^3/1.055^2 - 1)$
4	$792.16	6.00%	7.00% $(1.06^4/1.0567^3 - 1)$

7. The expected price path of the 4-year zero coupon bond is as follows. (We discount the face value by the appropriate sequence of forward rates implied by this year's yield curve.)

Beginning of Year	Expected Price	Expected Rate of Return
1	$792.16	6.00% (839.69/792.16 – 1)
2	$\dfrac{1000}{1.05 \times 1.06 \times 1.07}$ = 839.69	5.00% (881.68/839.69 – 1)
3	$\dfrac{1000}{1.06 \times 1.07}$ = 881.68	6.00% (934.58/881.68 – 1)
4	$\dfrac{1000}{1.07}$ = 934.58	7.00% (1000/934.58 – 1)

8. a. $(1+y_4)^4 = (1+ y_3)^3 (1 + f_4)$

   $(1.055)^4 = (1.05)^3 (1 + f_4)$

   $1.2388 = 1.1576 (1 + f_4)$

   $f_4 = .0701$, or 7.01%

   b. The conditions would be those that underlie the pure expectations theory of the term structure: risk neutral market participants who are willing to substitute among maturities solely on the basis of yield differentials. This behavior would rule out liquidity or term premia relating to risk as well as market segmentation based on maturity preferences.

   c. Under the expectations hypothesis, lower implied forward rates would indicate lower expected future spot rates for the corresponding period. Since the lower expected future rates embodied in the term structure are nominal rates, either lower expected future real rates or lower expected future inflation rates would be consistent with the specified change in the observed (implied) forward rate.

9. You should expect it to lie above the curve since the bond must offer a premium to investors to compensate them for the option granted to the issuer.

10. The interest rates are annual, but each period is a half-year. Therefore, the per period spot rates are 2.5% on one-year bonds and 2% on six-month bonds. The semiannual forward rate is

$$1 + f = \frac{1.025^2}{1.02} = 1.03$$

which means that the forward rate is 3% semiannually, or 6% annually. Therefore, choice d is correct.

11. The present value of each bond's payments can be derived by discounting each cash flow by rates from the spot interest rate (i.e., the pure yield) curve.

Bond A: $PV = \dfrac{10}{1.05} + \dfrac{10}{1.08^2} + \dfrac{110}{1.11^3} = \$98.53$

Bond A: $PV = \dfrac{6}{1.05} + \dfrac{6}{1.08^2} + \dfrac{106}{1.11^3} = \$88.36$

Bond A sells for $.13 (i.e., .13% of par value) less than the present value of its stripped payments. Bond B sells for $.02 less than the present value of its stripped payments. Bond A seems to be more attractively priced.

12. a. We obtain forward rates from the following table:

Maturity	YTM	Price	Forward rate	
1 year	10%	909.09		
2	11	811.62	12.01%	$(1.11^2/1.10 - 1)$
3	12	711.78	14.03%	$(1.12^3/1.11^2 - 1)$

b. We obtain next year's prices and yields by discounting each zero's face value at the forward rates for next year that we derived in part (a):

Maturity	Price	YTM
1 year	892.78 [= 1000/1.1201]	12.01%
2 years	782.93 [= 1000/(1.1201 × 1.1403)]	13.02%

Note that this year's upward sloping yield curve implies, according to the expectations hypothesis, a shift upward in next year's curve.

c. Next year, the 2-year zero will be a 1-year zero, and will therefore sell at $1000/1.1201 = $892.78. Similarly, the current 3-year zero will be a 2-year zero and will sell for $782.93.

Expected total rate of return:

2-year bond: $\dfrac{892.78}{811.62} - 1 = 1.1000$ or 10%

3-year bond: $\dfrac{782.93}{711.78} - 1 = 1.1000$ or 10%

d. The current price of the bond should equal the value of each payment times the present value of $1 to be received at the "maturity" of that payment. The present value schedule can be taken directly fom the prices of zero-coupon bonds calculated above.

Current price $= 120 \times (.90909) + 120 \times (.81162) + 1{,}120 \times (.71178)$
$$= 109.09 + 97.39 + 797.19$$
$$= \$1{,}003.67$$

Similarly, the expected prices of zeros in 1 year can be used to calculate the expected bond value at that time:

Expected price 1 year from now
$$= 120 \times .89278 + 1120 \times .78293$$
$$= 107.1336 + 876.8816$$
$$= \$984.02$$

Total expected rate of return $= \dfrac{120 + (984.02 - 1003.67)}{1003.68}$

$$= \dfrac{120 - 19.65}{1003.68} = .1000 \text{ or } 10\%$$

13. a. A 3-year zero with face value \$100 will sell today at a yield of 6% and a price of $\$100/1.06^3 = \$83.96$. Next year, the bond will have a two-year maturity, and therefore a yield of 6% (reading from next year's forecasted yield curve). The price will be \$89.00, resulting in a holding period return of 6%.

b. The forward rates based on today's yield curve are as follows:

Year	Forward Rate	
2	6.01%	$(1.05^2/1.04 - 1)$
3	8.03%	$(1.06^3/1.05^2 - 1)$

Using the forward rates, the yield curve *next* year is forecast as:

Maturity	YTM	
1	6.01%	
2	7.02%	$[(1.0601 \times 1.0803)^{1/2} - 1]$

The market forecast is for a higher YTM on 2–year bonds than your forecast. Thus, the market predicts a lower price and higher rate of return.

14. a. $P = \dfrac{9}{1.07} + \dfrac{109}{(1.08)^2} = 101.86$

b. YTM = 7.958%, which is the solution to:

$$\dfrac{9}{1+y} + \dfrac{109}{(1+y)^2} = 101.86$$

[On your calculator, input n = 2; FV = 100; PMT = 9; PV = (−)101.86; compute i]

c. The forward rate for next year derived from the zero-coupon yield curve is approximately 9%:

$$1 + f_2 = \frac{(1.08)^2}{1.07} = 1.0901 \quad \text{which implies} \quad f_2 = 9.01\%.$$

Therefore, using an expected rate for next year of $r_2 = 9.01\%$, we find that the forecast bond price is

$$P = \frac{109}{1.0901} = 99.99$$

d. If the liquidity premium is 1% then the forecast interest rate is :
$E(r_2) = f_2 - \text{liquidity premium} = 9.01\% - 1\% = 8.01\%$

and you forecast the bond to sell at $\frac{109}{1.0801} = 100.92$.

15. The coupon bonds may be viewed as portfolios of stripped zeros: each coupon can stand alone as an independent zero-coupon bond. Therefore, yields on coupon bonds will reflect yields on payments with dates corresponding to each coupon. When the yield curve is upward sloping, coupon bonds will have lower yields than zeros with the same maturity, because the yields to maturity on coupon bonds will reflect the yields on the earlier, interim coupon payments.

16. a. The current bond price is $85 \times .9434 + 85 \times .87352 + 1085 \times .81637 = 1040.20$ which implies a yield to maturity of 6.97% [since $85 \times$ Annuity factor(6.97%, 3) + $1000 \times$ PV factor(6.97%, 3) = 1040.20].

b. If next year, y = 8%, then the bond price will be

$85 \times$ Annuity factor(8%,2) + $1000 \times$ PV factor(8%,2) = 1008.92

for a rate of return equal to [85 + (1008.92 – 1040.20)]/1040.20 = .0516 or 5.16%.

17.

Year	Forward rate	PV of $1 received at period end	
1	5%	1/1.05	= $.9524
2	7%	1/(1.05)(1.07)	= .8901
3	8%	1/(1.05)(1.07)(1.08)	= .8241

a. Price = (60 × .9524) + (60 × .8901) + (1060 × .8241) = 984.10

b. 984.10 = 60 × Annuity factor(y, 3) + 1000 × PV factor(y, 3)

which can be solved to show that y = 6.60%

c.

Period	Payment Received at end of period	Will grow by a factor of	To a future value of
1	$ 60	(1.07) (1.08)	69.34
2	$ 60	(1.08)	64.80
3	$1060	1	1060.00
			1194.14

$$984.10 \, (1 + RCY)^3 = 1194.14$$

$$1 + RCY = \left(\frac{1194.14}{984.10}\right)^{1/3} = 1.0666$$

$$RCY = 6.66\%$$

d. Next year, the bond will sell for

$$60 \times \text{Annuity factor}(7\%, 2) + 1000 \times \text{PV factor}(7\%,2) = 981.92$$

which implies a capital loss of $984.10 - 981.92 = \$2.18$.

The holding period return is $\dfrac{60 + (-2.18)}{984.10} = .0588$ or 5.88%.

18. a. The return on the one-year bond will be 6.1%. The price of the 4-year zero today is $\$1000/1.064^4 = \$780.25$. Next year, if the yield curve is unchanged, the bond will have a 3-year maturity, a YTM of 6.3%, and therefore sell for $\$1000/1.063^3 = \$832.53$, resulting in a one-year return of 6.7%. The longer-term bond gave the higher return in this case because its YTM fell during the holding period.

b. If you believe in the expectations theory, you could not believe that the yield curve next year will be the same as today's curve. The upward slope in today's curve would be evidence that expected short rates are rising and that the yield curve will shift upward, reducing the holding period return on the four-year bond. Under the expectations hypothesis, all bonds have equal expected holding period returns. Therefore, you would predict that the HPR for the 4-year bond would be 6.1%, the same as for the 1-year bond.

19 a. <u>Five-year Spot Rate</u>:

$$1000 = \frac{70}{(1 + y_1)^1} + \frac{70}{(1 + y_2)^2} + \frac{70}{(1 + y_3)^3} + \frac{70}{(1 + y_4)^4} + \frac{1070}{(1 + y_5)^5}$$

$$1000 = \frac{70}{1.05} + \frac{70}{(1.0521)^2} + \frac{70}{(1.0605)^3} + \frac{70}{(1.0716)^4} + \frac{1070}{(1 + y_5)^5}$$

$$1000 = 66.67 + 63.24 + 58.69 + 53.08 + \frac{1070}{(1 + y_5)^5}$$

$$758.32 = \frac{1070}{(1 + y_5)^5}$$

$$(1 + y_5)^5 = \frac{1070}{758.32} \quad \Rightarrow \quad y_5 = \sqrt[5]{1.411} - 1 = \underline{7.13\%}$$

Five-year Forward Rate:

$$\frac{(1.0713)^5}{(1.0716)^4} - 1 = 1.0701 - 1 = \underline{7.01\%}$$

b. Yield to maturity is the single discount rate that equates the present value of a series of cash flows to a current price. It is the internal rate of return.

The spot rate for a given period is the yield to maturity on a zero-coupon bond which matures at the end of the period. A spot rate is the discount rate for each period. Spot rates are used to discount each cash flow of a coupon bond to calculate a current price. Spot rates are the rates appropriate for discounting future cash flows of different maturities.

A forward rate is the implicit rate that links any two spot rates. Forward rates are directly related to spot rates, and therefore yield to maturity. Some would argue (as in the expectations theory) that forward rates are the market expectations of future interest rates. Regardless, a forward rate represents a break-even rate that links two spot rates. It is important to note that forward rates link spot rates, not yields to maturity.

Yield to maturity is not unique for any particular maturity. In other words, two bonds with the same maturity but different coupon rates may have different yields to maturity.   In contrast, spot rates and forward rates for each date are unique.

c. The 4-year spot rate is 7.16%. Therefore, 7.16% is the theoretical yield to maturity for the zero coupon U.S. Treasury note. The price of the zero coupon discounted at 7.16% is the present value of $1000 to be received in 4 years.

Using annual compounding, $PV = \dfrac{1000}{(1.0716)^4} = 758.35$

20. The price of the coupon bond, based on its yield to maturity, is

120 × Annuity factor(5.8%, 2) + 1000 × PV factor(5.8%, 2) = \$1113.99.

If the coupons were stripped and sold separately as zeros, then based on the yield to maturity of zeros with maturities of one and two years, the coupon payments could be sold separately for

$$\frac{120}{1.05} + \frac{1120}{1.06^2} = \$1111.08.$$

The arbitrage strategy is to buy zeros with face values of $120 and $1120 and respective maturities of one and two years, and simultaneously sell the coupon bond. The profit equals $2.91 on each bond.

21. a.   The one-year bond has a yield to maturity of 6%:

$$94.34 = \frac{100}{1+y_1} \quad \Rightarrow \quad y_1 = .06$$

The yield on the two-year zero is 8.472%:

$$84.99 = \frac{100}{(1+y_2)^2} \quad \Rightarrow \quad y_2 = .08472$$

The price of the coupon bond is $\dfrac{12}{1.06} + \dfrac{112}{(1.08472)^2} = 106.51$

Therefore its yield to maturity is 8.333% [on your calculator: n = 2; PV = (−)106.51; FV = 100; PMT = 12]

b. $f_2 = \dfrac{(1 + y_2)^2}{1 + y_1} - 1 = \dfrac{(1.08472)^2}{1.06} - 1 = .11 = 11\%$

c.   Expected price $= \dfrac{112}{1.11} = 100.90$. (Note that next year, the coupon bond will have one payment left.)

Expected rate of return $= \dfrac{12 + (100.90 - 106.51)}{106.51} = .06 = 6\%$

which is the same as the return on the one-year zero.

d.   If there is a liquidity premium, then

$E(r_2) < f_2$

$E(\text{Price}) = \dfrac{112}{1 + E(r)} > 100.90$

$E(\text{HPR}) > 6\%$

CHAPTER 16: FIXED INCOME PORTFOLIO MANAGEMENT

1. The percentage bond price change will be

$$- \text{Duration} \times \frac{\Delta y}{1+y} = -7.194 \times \frac{.005}{1.10} = -.0327 \text{ or a 3.27\% decline.}$$

2. Computation of duration:
   a. <u>YTM = 6%</u>

(1) Time Until Payment (in years)	(2) Payment	(3) Payment Discounted at 6%	(4) Weight of each Payment	(5) Column (1) × Column (4)
1	60	56.60	.0566	.0566
2	60	53.40	.0534	.1068
3	1060	890.00	.8900	2.6700
Column Sum		1000.00	1.0000	2.8334

Duration = 2.833 years

   b. <u>YTM = 10%</u>

(1) Time Until Payment (in years)	(2) Payment	(3) Payment Discounted at 10%	(4) Weight of each Payment	(5) Column (1) × Column (4)
1	60	54.55	.0606	.0606
2	60	49.59	.0551	.1102
3	1060	796.39	.8844	2.6532
Column Sum		900.53	1.0000	2.8240

Duration = 2.824 years, which is less than the duration at the YTM of 6%.

3. For a semiannual 6% coupon bond selling at par, we use parameters c = 3% per half-year period, y = 3%, T = 6 semiannual periods. Using Rule 8, we find that

$$D = (1.03/.03) \left[1 - (1/1.03)^6 \right]$$

$$= 5.58 \text{ half year periods}$$

$$= 2.79 \text{ years}$$

If the bond's yield is 10%, use Rule 7, setting the semiannual yield to 5%, and semiannual coupon to 3%:

$$D = \frac{1.05}{.05} - \frac{1.05 + 6(.03 - .05)}{.03[(1.05)^6 - 1] + .05}$$

$$= 21 - 15.448 = 5.552 \text{ half-year periods} = 2.776 \text{ years}$$

4. a. Bond B has a higher yield to maturity than bond A since its coupon payments and maturity are equal to those of A, while its price is lower. (Perhaps the yield is higher because of differences in credit risk.) Therefore, its duration must be shorter.

   b. Bond A has a lower yield and a lower coupon, both of which cause it to have a longer duration than B. Moreover, A cannot be called, which makes its maturity at least as long as that of B, which generally increases duration.

5.

t	CF	PV(CF)	Weight	w × t
1	10	9.09	.786	.786
5	4	2.48	.214	1.070
		11.57	1.0	1.856

   a. D = 1.856 years = required maturity of zero coupon bond

   b. The market value of the zero must be $11.57 million, the same as the market value of the obligations. Therefore, the face value must be $11.57 × $(1.10)^{1.856}$ = $13.81 million.

6. a. The call feature provides a valuable option to the issuer, since it can buy back the bond at a given call price even if the present value of the scheduled remaining payments are worth more than the call price. The investor will demand, and the issuer will be willing to pay, a higher yield on the issue as compensation for this feature.

   b. The call feature will reduce both the duration (interest rate sensitivity) and the convexity of the bond. The bond will not experience as large a price increase if interest rates fall. Moreover the usual curvature that would characterize a straight bond will be reduced by a call feature. The price-yield curve (see Figure 16.7) flattens out as the interest rate falls and the option to call the bond becomes more attractive. In fact, at very low interest rates, the bond exhibits "negative convexity."

7. Choose the longer-duration bond to benefit from a rate decrease.

   a. The Aaa-rated bond will have the lower yield to maturity and the longer duration.

   b. The lower-coupon bond will have the longer duration *and* more de facto call protection.

   c. Choose the lower coupon bond for its longer duration.

8.   a.   (iv)
     b.   (ii)
     c.   (i)
     d.   (i)
     e.   (iii)
     f.   (i)
     g.   (i)
     h.   (iii)

9.   You should buy the 3-year bond because it will offer a 9% holding-period return over the next year, which is greater than the return on either of the other bonds.

Maturity:	1 year	2 years	3 years
YTM at beginning of year	7%	8%	9%
Beginning of year prices	$1009.35	$1000.00	$974.69
Prices at year end (at 9% YTM)	$1000.00	$ 990.83	$982.41
Capital gain	–$ 9.35	–$ 9.17	$ 7.72
Coupon	$ 80.00	$ 80.00	$ 80.00
1-year total $ return	$ 70.65	$ 70.83	$ 87.72
1-year total rate of return	7%	7.08%	9%

The 3-year bond provides the greatest holding period return.

10. a.   Modified duration = $\dfrac{\text{Macaulay duration}}{1 + \text{YTM}}$

If the Macaulay duration is 10 years and the yield to maturity is 8%, then the modified duration equals 10/1.08 = 9.26 years.

   b. For option-free coupon bonds, modified duration is better than maturity as a measure of the bond's sensitivity to changes in interest rates. Maturity considers only the final cash flow, while modified duration includes other factors such as the size and timing of coupon payments and the level of interest rates (yield to maturity). Modified duration, unlike maturity, tells us the approximate proportional change in the bond price for a given change in yield to maturity.

   c. i.   Modified duration increases as the coupon decreases.
       ii.   Modified duration decreases as maturity decreases.

   d. Convexity measures the curvature of the bond's price-yield curve. Such curvature means that the duration rule for bond price change (which is based only on the slope of the curve at the original yield) is only an approximation. Adding a term to account for the convexity of the bond will increase the accuracy of the approximation. That convexity adjustment is the last term in the following equation:

$$\frac{\Delta P}{P} = -D^* \Delta y \ + \ \frac{1}{2} \times \text{Convexity} \times (\Delta y)^2$$

11. a. PV of the obligation = $10,000 × Annuity factor (8%, 2) = $17,832.65
    Duration = 1.4808 years, which can be verified from rule 6 or a table like Table 15.3.

    b. To immunize my obligation I need a zero-coupon bond maturing in 1.4808 years. Since the present value must be $17,832.65, the face value (i.e., the future redemption value) must be $17,832.65 × $1.08^{1.4808}$ or $19,985.26.

    c. If the interest rate increases to 9%, the zero-coupon bond would fall in value to

$$\frac{\$19,985.26}{1.09^{1.4808}} = \$17,590.92$$

and the present value of the tuition obligation would fall to $17,591.11. The net position decreases by $.19.

If the interest rate falls to 7%, the zero-coupon bond would rise in value to

$$\frac{\$19,985.26}{1.07^{1.4808}} = \$18,079.99$$

and the present value of the tuition obligation would rise to $18,080.18. The net position decreases by $.19.

The reason the net position changes at all is that as the interest rate changes so does the duration of the stream of tuition payments.

12.   a. In an interest rate swap, one firm exchanges or "swaps" a fixed payment for another payment that is tied to the level of interest rates. One party in the swap agreement must pay a fixed interest rate on the notional principal of the swap. The other party pays the floating interest rate (typically LIBOR) on the same notional principal. For example, in a swap with a fixed rate of 8% and notional principal of $100 million, the *net* cash payment for the firm that pays the fixed and receives the floating rate would be (LIBOR − .08) × $100 million. Therefore, if LIBOR exceeds 8%, the firm receives money; if it is less than 8%, the firm pays money.

    b. There are several applications of interest rate swaps. For example, a portfolio manager who is holding a portfolio of long-term bonds, but is worried that interest rates might increase, causing a capital loss on the portfolio, can enter a swap to pay a fixed rate and receive a floating rate, thereby converting the holdings into a synthetic floating rate portfolio. Or, a pension fund manager might identify some money market securities that are paying excellent yields compared to other comparable-risk short-term securities. However, the manager might believe that such short-term assets are inappropriate for the portfolio. The fund can hold these securities and enter a swap in which it receives a fixed rate and pays a floating rate. It thus captures the benefit of the advantageous *relative* yields on these securities, but still establishes a portfolio with interest-rate risk characteristics more like those of long-term bonds.

13. The answer depends on the nature of the long-term assets which the corporation is holding. If those assets produce a return which varies with short-term interest rates then an interest-rate swap would not be appropriate. If, however, the long-term assets are fixed-rate financial assets like fixed-rate mortgages then a swap might be risk-reducing. In such a case the corporation would swap its floating-rate bond liability for a fixed-rate long-term liability.

14. The firm should enter a swap in which it pays a 7% fixed rate and receives LIBOR on $10 million of notional principal. Its total payments will be as follows:

Interest payments on bond	$(LIBOR + .01) \times \$10$ million par value
Net cash flow from swap	$(.07 - LIBOR) \times \$10$ million notional principle
TOTAL	$.08 \times \$10$ million

The interest rate on the synthetic fixed-rate loan is 8%.

15. a. PV of obligation = $2 million/.16 = $12.5 million.
   Duration of obligation = 1.16/.16 = 7.25 years

   Call w the weight on the 5-year maturity bond (which has duration of 4 years). Then
   $$w \times 4 + (1 - w) \times 11 = 7.25$$

   which implies that w = .5357.

   Therefore, .5357 × $12.5 = $6.7 million in the 5-year bond and
   .4643 × $12.5 = $5.8 million in the 20-year bond.

   b. The price of the 20-year bond is

   60 × Annuity factor(16%,20) + 1000 × PV factor(16%, 20) = $407.12.

   Therefore, the bond sells for .4071 times its par value, and

   Market value = Par value × .4071
   $5.8 million = Par value × .4071
   Par value = $14.25 million

   Another way to see this is to note that each bond with par value $1000 sells for $407.11. If total market value is $5.8 million, then you need to buy 14,250 bonds, resulting in total par value of $14,250,000.

16. a. The duration of the perpetuity is 1.05/.05 = 21 years. Let w be the weight of the zero-coupon bond. Then we find w by solving:

   $$w \times 5 + (1 - w) \times 21 = 10$$
   $$21 - 16w = 10 \qquad \Rightarrow \qquad w = 11/16 = .6875$$

Therefore, your portfolio would be 11/16 invested in the zero and 5/16 in the perpetuity.

b. The zero-coupon bond now will have a duration of 4 years while the perpetuity will still have a 21-year duration. To get a portfolio duration of 9 years, which is now the duration of the obligation, we again solve for w:

$$w \times 4 \ + \ (1 - w) \times 21 = 9$$

$$21 - 17w = 9$$

$$w = 12/17 \text{ or } .7059$$

So the proportion invested in the zero has to increase to 12/17 and the proportion in the perpetuity has to fall to 5/17.

17. a. From Rule 6, the duration of the annuity *if* it were to start in 1 year would be

$$\frac{1.10}{.10} - \frac{10}{(1.10)^{10} - 1} = 4.7255 \text{ years}$$

Because the payment stream starts in 5 years, instead of one year, we must add 4 years to the duration, resulting in duration of 8.7255 years.

b. The present value of the deferred annuity is

$$\frac{10,000 \times \text{Annuity factor}(10\%, 10)}{1.10^4} = \$41,968.$$

Call w the weight of the portfolio in the 5-year zero. Then

$$5w + 20(1 - w) = 8.7255$$

which implies that w = .7516 so that the investment in the 5-year zero equals

$$.7516 \times \$41,968 = \$31,543.$$

The investment in 20-year zeros is .2484 × $41,968 = $10,425.

These are the present or *market* values of each investment. The face values of each are the future values of the investments.

The face value of the 5-year zeros is

$$\$31,543 \times (1.10)^5 = \$50,800$$

meaning that between 50 and 51 zero coupon bonds, each of par value $1,000, would need to be purchased. Similarly, the face value of the 20-year zeros would be:

$$\$10,425 \times (1.10)^{20} = \$70,134.$$

18. Using a financial calculator, the price of the bond for a yield to maturity of 7% is $1620.45; for YTM of 8%, the price is $1450.31; and for YTM of 9% the price is $1308.21.

Using the Duration Rule, assuming yield to maturity falls to 7%

$$\text{Predicted price change} = -\text{Duration} \times \frac{\Delta y}{1+y} \times P_0$$

$$= -11.54 \times \frac{-.01}{1.08} \times 1450.31 = 154.97$$

Therefore, predicted new price = 154.97 + 1450.31 = $1605.28

The true price at a 7% yield to maturity is $1620.45. Therefore,

$$\% \text{ error} = \frac{1620.45 - 1605.28}{1620.45} = .0094 = .94 \% \text{ (too low)}$$

Using the Duration Rule, assuming yield to maturity increases to 9%

$$\text{Predicted price change} = -\text{Duration} \times \frac{\Delta y}{1+y} \times P_0$$

$$= -11.54 \times \frac{+.01}{1.08} \times 1450.31 = -154.97$$

Therefore, predicted new price = -154.97 + 1450.31 = $1295.34

The true price at a 9% yield to maturity is $1308.21. Therefore,

$$\% \text{ error} = \frac{1308.21 - 1295.34}{1308.21} = .0098 = .98 \% \text{ (too low)}$$

Using Duration-with-Convexity Rule, assuming yield to maturity falls to 7%

$$\text{Predicted price change} = [(-\text{Duration} \times \frac{\Delta y}{1+y}) + (0.5 \times \text{convexity} \times \Delta y^2)] \times P_0$$

$$= [-11.54 \times \frac{-.01}{1.08} + 0.5 \times 192.4 \times (-0.01)^2] \times 1450.31 = 168.92$$

Therefore, predicted price = 168.92 + 1450.31 = $1619.23

The true price at a 7% yield to maturity is $1620.45. Therefore,

$$\% \text{ error} = \frac{1620.45 - 1619.23}{1620.45} = .00075 = .075\% \text{ (too low)}$$

<u>Using Duration-with-Convexity Rule, assuming yield to maturity rises to 9%</u>

Predicted price change $= [(-\text{Duration} \times \frac{\Delta y}{1+y}) + (0.5 \times \text{convexity} \times \Delta y^2)] \times P_0$

$= [-11.54 \times \frac{.01}{1.08} + 0.5 \times 192.4 \times (0.01)^2] \times 1450.31 = -141.02$

Therefore, predicted price $= -141.02 + 1450.31 = \$1309.29$

The true price at a 9% yield to maturity is \$1308.21. Therefore,

$\% \text{ error} = \frac{1309.29 - 1308.21}{1308.21} = .00083 = .083\% \text{ (too high)}$

Conclusion: the duration-with-convexity rule provides more accurate approximations to the true change in price. In this example, the percentage error using convexity with duration is less than one-tenth the error using only duration to estimate the price change.

19. a. The price of the zero coupon bond (\$1000 face value) selling at a yield to maturity of 8% is \$374.84 and that of the coupon bond is \$774.84.

   At a YTM of 9% the price of the zero coupon bond is \$333.28 and that of the coupon bond is \$691.79.

   <u>Zero coupon bond</u>

   Actual % loss $= \frac{333.28 - 374.84}{374.84} = -.1109$, an 11.09% loss

   The percentage loss predicted by the duration-with-convexity rule is:

   Predicted % loss $= [(-11.81) \times .01 + 0.5 \times 150.3 \times (0.01)^2]$

   $= -.1106$, an 11.06% loss

   <u>Coupon bond</u>

   Actual % loss $= \frac{691.79 - 774.84}{774.84} = -.1072$, a 10.72% loss

   The percentage loss predicted by the duration-with-convexity rule is:

   Predicted % loss $= [(-11.79) \times .01 + 0.5 \times 231.2 \times (0.01)^2]$
   $= -.1063$, a 10.63% loss

b. Now assume yield to maturity falls to 7%. The price of the zero increases to $422.04, and the price of the coupon bond increases to $875.91.

<u>Zero coupon bond</u>

Actual % gain $= \dfrac{422.04 - 374.84}{374.84} = .1259$, a 12.59% gain

The percentage gain predicted by the duration-with-convexity rule is:

Predicted % gain $= [(-11.81) \times (-.01) + 0.5 \times 150.3 \times (0.01)^2]$

$= .1256$, an 12.56% gain

<u>Coupon bond</u>

Actual % gain $= \dfrac{875.91 - 774.84}{774.84} = .1304$, a 13.04% gain

The percentage gain predicted by the duration-with-convexity rule is:

Predicted % gain $= [(-11.79) \times (-.01) + 0.5 \times 231.2 \times (0.01)^2]$
$= .1295$, a 12.95% gain

c. The 6% coupon bond -- which has higher convexity -- outperforms the zero regardless of whether rates rise or fall. This can be seen to be a general property by noting from the duration-with-convexity formula that the duration effect on the two bonds due to any change in rates will be equal (since their durations are virtually equal), but the convexity effect, which is always positive, will always favor the higher convexity bond. Thus, if the yields on the bonds always change by equal amounts, as we have assumed in this example, the higher convexity bond will always outperform a lower convexity bond with equal duration and initial yield to maturity.

d. This situation cannot persist. No one will be willing to buy the lower convexity bond if it always underperforms the other bond. Its price will fall and its yield to maturity will rise. Thus, the lower convexity bond will sell at a higher initial yield to maturity. That higher yield is compensation for lower convexity. If rates change by only a little, the higher yield-lower convexity bond will do better; if rates change by a lot, the lower yield-higher convexity bond will do better.

20. a. The following spreadsheet shows that the convexity of the bond is 64.933. The present value of each cash flow is obtained by discounting at 7%. (since the bond has a 7% coupon and sells at par, its YTM must be 7%.) Convexity equals the sum of the last column, 7434.175, divided by $[P \times (1 + y)^2] = 100 \times (1.07)^2$.

Time (t)	Cash flow, CF	PV(CF)	$t + t^2$	$(t + t^2) \times$ PV(CF)
1	7	6.542	2	13.084
2	7	6.114	6	36.684
3	7	5.714	12	68.569
4	7	5.340	20	106.805
5	7	4.991	30	149.727
6	7	4.664	42	195.905
7	7	4.359	56	244.118
8	7	4.074	72	293.333
9	7	3.808	90	342.678
10	107	54.393	110	5983.271
Sum:		100		7434.175
Convexity:				64.933

The duration of the bond is (from rule 8)

$$D = \frac{1.07}{.07} [1 - \frac{1}{1.07^{10}}] = 7.515 \text{ years}$$

b. If the yield to maturity increases to 8%, the bond price will fall to 93.29% of par value, a percentage decline of 6.71%.

c. The duration rule would predict a percentage price change of

$$-\frac{D}{1.07} \times .01 = -\frac{7.515}{1.07} \times .01 = -.0702 = -7.02\%$$

This overstates the actual percentage decline in price by .31%.

d. The duration with convexity rule would predict a percentage price change of

$$-\frac{7.515}{1.07} \times .01 + .5 \times 64.933 \times (.01)^2 = .0670 = -6.70\%$$

which results in an approximation error of only .01%, far smaller than the error using the duration rule.

21. The economic climate is one of impending interest rate increases. Hence, we will want to shorten portfolio duration.

a. Choose the short maturity (2001) bond.

b. The Arizona bond likely has lower duration. The Arizona coupons are slightly lower, but the Arizona yield is substantially higher.

c. Choose the 15 3/8 coupon bond. Maturities are about equal, but its coupon is much higher, resulting in lower duration.

d. The duration of the Shell bond will be lower if the effect of the higher yield to maturity and earlier start of sinking fund redemption dominates its slightly lower coupon rate.

e. The floating rate bond has a duration that approximates the adjustment period, which is only 6 months.

22. a. A manager who believes that the level of interest rates will change should engage in a rate anticipation swap, lengthening duration if rates are expected to fall, and shortening if rates are expected to rise.

b. A change in yield spreads across sectors would call for an intermarket spread swap, in which the manager buys bonds in the sector for which yields are expected to fall and sells bonds in the sector for which yields are expected to rise.

c. A belief that the yield spread on a particular instrument will change calls for a substitution swap in which that security is sold if its relative yield is expected to rise or is bought if its yield is expected to fall compared to other similar bonds.

23. While it is true that short-term rates are more volatile than long-term rates, the longer duration of the longer-term bonds makes their rates of return and prices more volatile. The higher duration magnifies the sensitivity to interest-rate savings.

24. The minimum terminal value that the manager is willing to accept is determined by the requirement for a 3% annual return on the initial investment. Therefore, the floor equals $1 million $\times (1.03)^5 = \$1.16$ million. Three years after the initial investment, only two years remain until the horizon date, and the interest rate has risen to 8%. Therefore, at this time, the manager needs a portfolio worth $1.16 million$/(1.08)^2 = \$.9945$ million to be assured that the target value can be attained. This is the trigger point.

25. The maturity of the 30-year bond will fall to 25 years, and its yield is forecast to be 8%. Therefore, the price forecast for the bond is $893.25 [n = 25; i = 8; FV = 1000; PMT = 70]. At a 6% interest rate, the five coupon payments will accumulate to $394.60 after 5 years. Therefore, total proceeds will be $394.60 + $893.25 = $1,287.85. The 5-year return is therefore 1,287.85/867.42 = 1.485. This is a 48.5% 5-year return, or 8.22% annually.

The maturity of the 20-year bond will fall to 15 years, and its yield is forecast to be 7.5%. Therefore, the price forecast for the bond is $911.73 [n = 15; i = 7.5; FV = 1000; PMT = 65]. At a 6% interest rate, the five coupon payments will accumulate to $366.41 after 5 years. Therefore, total proceeds will be $366.41 + $911.73 = $1,278.14. The 5-year return is therefore 1,278.14/879.50 = 1.453. This is a 45.3% 5-year return, or 7.76% annually. The 30-year bond offers the higher expected return.

26. a. <u>First Scenario</u>. The first scenario envisions a period of decreasing rates and increasing volatility. An interest rate decline implies that longer-duration portfolios will have larger price increases than shorter duration portfolios. Lower rates and/or increasing volatility will cause portfolios with call or prepayment features to underperform because the holders of the callable bonds have, in effect, sold a call option to the bond issuer, and the value of the embedded call option will increase to the detriment of the bondholder. The right to call the bond (that is, to buy it back at a fixed call price) or to prepay a mortgage is more valuable when future bond and mortgage prices are less predictable. For example, the potential profit from the right to call is higher when bond prices are more volatile.

Under the first scenario, the best performing index will Index #3, followed by Index #2 and then Index #1. The reasons for the rankings are as follows:

- Index #1 has the shortest duration. This results in a drag on relative performance as rates decline.

- Index #1 has a high proportion of corporates and mortgages and, therefore, has more callable bonds. As a result, Index #1 has a significant exposure to call risk. The value of the call and prepayment options has gone up because of an increase in volatility. Yield to maturity (YTM) and duration may be significantly less than initially expected. This will hurt relative performance.

- Index #2 has a long duration. This will aid relative performance in a falling rate environment.

- Index #2 has a high proportion of corporates and mortgages and, therefore has more callable bonds. As noted, this will hurt relative performance in a high-volatility environment.

- Index #3 has a long duration. This will aid relative performance.

- Index #3 has a low proportion of corporates and mortgages and, therefore, has few callable bonds. Hence, it is relatively immune to changes in volatility. This will aid relative performance at a time when volatility increases.

<u>Second Scenario</u>. The second scenario also envisions a period of high volatility of interest rates, but in this scenario the rates forecast for the end of the period are similar to rates at the beginning of the period. The significant factors affecting returns will be the high volatility and the index's YTM. Because there is no trend in rates, duration is not as significant a factor as in the first scenario. However, the apparently positively sloped yield curve means that the longer durations pick up additional return from their higher YTM. (We infer an upward sloping yield curve by noting that the low duration index has the lowest yield to maturity.) As in scenario 1, high volatility will cause portfolios with call or prepayment features to underperform because, as noted above, the right to call or prepay is more valuable when security values are more volatile.

Under the second scenario, the rankings are unchanged from the first scenario. The best performing index will be Index #3, followed by Index #2 and then Index #1. The reasons for the rankings are as follows:

- Index #1's low YTM will hurt relative performance.

- Index #1 has a high proportion of corporates and mortgages and, therefore, has more callable bonds. In an environment of high volatility, there will be an increased likelihood that issuers will exercise their call/prepayment option (i.e., call/prepay and refinance at lower rates), thereby reducing the expected rate of return. This will hurt relative performance.

- Index #2 has the highest YTM. This will help its relative performance.

- Index #2 has a high proportion of corporates and mortgages that are callable. As a result, Index #2 has a short call option position. This will hurt relative performance.

- Index #3 has a relatively high YTM, in fact nearly as high as that of Index #2.

- Index #3 has a low proportion of corporates and mortgages and hence fewer callable bonds. Therefore, it is relatively immune to changes in volatility. This will significantly aid relative performance.

- Index #3 will have the best or second-best performance depending on the trade-off between the YTM and the effect of high volatility on the callable bonds. Because the beginning YTM differential between Index #2 and Index #3 is only 5 basis points, the volatility impact will exceed the importance of the YTM differential, making Index #3 the best performing index.

b. The trustees have indicated that the endowment is an aggressive investor with a long-term investment horizon and a high risk tolerance. Therefore, the longer duration Indices (#2 and #3) are more appropriate. These indices have a 55/50 basis point YTM pick-up versus the shorter duration index. A YTM pick-up of 55/50 basis points would have a very significant impact on the assets of the endowment over long time periods, all other things remaining equal. Given the forecast for lower rates and higher volatility, Index #3 appears to be the best choice.

c. Unlike equity funds, bond index funds cannot purchase all securities contained in the selected index. Most fixed income indices contain thousands of securities; investing in all of those in the appropriate proportion would result in holdings that are too small for rebalancing and trading. Furthermore, a significant portion of the securities contained in the index are typically illiquid or do not trade frequently. The more practical approach to setting up a fixed income index is to select a basket of securities whose profile characteristics (such as yield, duration, sector weights and convexity) and expected total returns match those of the index. We consider two methodologies to constructing such an index.

Full Replication: This method involves purchasing each security in the index at the appropriate market weighting. Although this method will track the index exactly (excluding transaction costs and management fees), in the real world it is impossible due to considerations such as transaction costs, illiquidity of many issues, and large numbers of issues in the indices (thousands).

Advantages: This method will have a tracking error of zero (excluding transaction costs) and is easy to explain and interpret.

Disadvantages: This method is impossible due to the large number of issues involved and the lack of availability of many of those issues. Investing in the appropriate proportion of each bond will result in holdings too small to actually implement transactions. Many bond issues trade infrequently and/or are illiquid.

Cellular or Stratified Sampling: Stratified sampling is simple and flexible. In stratified sampling, an index is divided into subsectors or cells. The division is made on the basis of such parameters as sector, coupon, duration and quality. This stratification is followed by the selection of securities to represent each cell.

Advantages: The key advantage to this method is its simplicity. It relies on the portfolio manager's expertise to appropriately select the significant cells and select a basket of securities that will closely match the index. Another advantage is that it is very flexible and is equally effective with all types of indexes. Finally, stratified sampling lends itself to the use of securities that are not in the index. Securities with complex structures such as derivative mortgage-backed securities can be substituted for more generic mortgage-backed securities.

Disadvantages: Stratified sampling is labor intensive. The manager must determine the cellular structure based on the size of the portfolio and type of benchmark. In addition, this method also makes it very difficult to determine whether the portfolio has been optimally constructed (e.g., whether it achieves the highest yield for a given structure).

27. a. *Scenario 1*: strong economic recovery with rising inflationary expectations. Interest rates and bond yields will most likely rise, and the prices of both bonds will fall. The probability that the callable bond will be called declines, and it will behave more like the non-callable bond -- notice that they have similar durations when priced to maturity. The slightly lower duration of the callable bond will result in somewhat better performance in the high interest rate scenario.

Scenario 2: economic recession with reduced inflation expectations. Interest rates and bond yields will most likely fall. The callable bond is likely to be called. The relevant duration calculation for the callable bond is now modified duration to call. Price appreciation is limited as indicated by the lower duration. The non-callable bond, on the other hand, continues to have the same modified duration and hence has greater price appreciation.

b. If yield to maturity (YTM) on Bond B falls 75 basis points:

Projected price change = (modified duration) × (change in YTM)

$$= (-6.80) \times (-.75\%) = 5.1\%$$

So the price will rise to $105.10 from its current level of $100.

c. For Bond A (the callable bond) bond life and therefore bond cash flows are uncertain. If one ignores the call feature and analyzes the bond on a "to maturity" basis, all calculations for yield and duration are distorted. Durations are too long and yields are too high.

On the other hand, if one treats the premium bond selling above the call price on a "to call" basis, the duration is unrealistically short and yields too low.

The most effective approach is to use an option evaluation approach. The callable bond can be decomposed into two separate securities: a non-callable bond and an option.

Price of callable bond = Price of non-callable bond − price of option

Since the option to call the bond will always have some positive value, the callable bond will always have a price which is less than the price of the non-callable security.

CHAPTER 17: MACROECONOMIC AND INDUSTRY ANALYSIS

1. Expansionary (looser) monetary policy to lower interest rates would help stimulate investment and expenditures on consumer durables. Expansionary fiscal policy – lower taxes, higher government spending, increased welfare transfers – would stimulate aggregate demand directly.

2. a. <u>Gold Mining</u>. Gold traditionally is viewed as a hedge against inflation. Expansionary monetary policy may lead to increased inflation, and thus could enhance the value of gold mining stocks.

   b. <u>Construction</u>. Expansionary monetary policy will lead to lower interest rates which ought to stimulate housing demand. The construction industry should benefit.

3. a. Lowering reserve requirements would allow banks to lend out a higher fraction of deposits and thus increase the money supply.

   b. The Fed would buy T-bonds, thereby increasing the money supply.

   c. The discount rate would be reduced, allowing banks to borrow additional funds at a lower rate.

4. a. Expansionary monetary policy will be likely to increase the inflation rate, either because it may overstimulate the economy, or ultimately because the end result of more money in the economy is higher prices.

   b. Real output and employment should increase in response to the expansionary policy, at least in the short run.

   c. The real interest rate should fall, at least in the short-run, as the supply of funds to the economy has increased.

   d. The nominal interest rate may rise or fall. On the one hand, the real rate may fall, [see part (c)] but the the inflation premium may rise [see part (a)]. The nominal rate is the sum of these two components.

5. A depreciating dollar makes imported cars more expensive and American cars cheaper to foreign consumers. This should benefit the U.S. auto industry.

6. Supply side economists believe that a reduction in income tax rates will make workers more willing to work at current or even slightly lower (gross-of-tax) wages. Such an effect ought to mitigate cost pressures on the inflation rate.

7. a. The robotics process entails higher fixed costs and lower variable (labor) costs. This firm therefore will perform better in a boom and worse in a recession. For example, costs will rise less rapidly than revenue when sales volume expands during a boom.

    b. Because its profits are more sensitive to the business cycle, the robotics firm will have the higher beta.

8. Deep recession: Health care (a non-cyclical industry)
    Superheated economy: Steel production (cyclical industry)
    Healthy expansion: Housing construction (cyclical but interest-rate sensitive)
    Stagflation: Gold mining (counter-cyclical)

9. a. Oil well equipment: Decline (Environmental pressures, decline in easily-developed new oil fields)

    b. Computer hardware: consolidation

    c. Computer software: consolidation

    d. Genetic engineering: Start-up

    e. Railroads: Relative decline

10. a. General Autos. Pharmaceuticals are less of a discretionary purchase than automobiles.

    b. Friendly Airlines. Travel expenditure is more sensitive to the business cycle than movie consumption.

11. This exercise is left to the student

12. The index of consumer expectations is a useful leading economic indicator because if consumers are optimistic about the future they will be more willing to spend money, especially on consumer durables, which will increase aggregate demand and stimulate the economy.

13. Labor cost per unit is a lagging indicator because wages typically start rising only well into an economic expansion. At the beginning of an expansion, there is considerable slack in the economy and output can expand without employers bidding up the price of inputs or the wages of employees. By the time wages start increasing due to high demand for labor, the boom period has already progressed considerably.

14. a. The concept of an industrial life cycle refers to the tendency of most industries to go through various stages of growth. The rate of growth, the competitive environment, profit margins and pricing strategies tend to shift as an industry

moves from one stage to the next although it is usually difficult to pinpoint exactly when one stage has ended and the next begun.

The initial start-up stage is characterized by perceptions of a large potential market and by a high optimism for potential profits. In this stage, however, there is usually a high rate of failure. In the second stage, often called rapid growth or consolidation, growth is high and accelerating, the markets are broadening, unit costs are declining and quality is improving. In this stage, industry leaders begin to emerge. The third stage, usually called mature growth, is characterized by decelerating growth caused by such things as maturing markets and/or competitive inroads by other products. Finally, an industry reaches a stage of full maturity in which sales slow or even decline.

Product pricing, profitability and industry competitive structure often vary by phase. Thus, for example, the first phase usually encompasses high product prices, high costs (R&D, marketing, etc.) and a (temporary) monopolistic industry structure. In phase two (rapid expansion), new entrants begin to appear and costs fall rapidly due to the learning curve. Prices generally don't fall as rapidly, however, allowing profit margins to increase. In phase three (mature growth), growth begins to slow as the product or service begins to saturate the market, and margins are eroded by significant price reductions. In the final stage, industry cumulative production is so high that production costs have stopped declining, profit margins are thin (assuming competition exists), and the fate of the industry depends on the extent of replacement demand and the existence of substitute products/services.

b. The passenger car business in the United States has probably entered the final stage in the industrial life cycle because normalized growth is quite low. The information processing business, on the other hand, is undoubtedly earlier in the cycle. Depending on whether or not growth is still accelerating, it is either in the second or third stage.

c. Cars: in the final phases of the life cycle, demand tends to be price sensitive. Thus, Universal can't raise prices without losing volume. Moreover, given the industry's maturity, cost structures are likely to be similar across all competitors, and any price cuts can be matched immediately. Thus, Universal's car business is boxed in: Product pricing is determined by the market, and the company is a "price-taker."

Idata: Idata should have much more pricing flexibility given its earlier phase in the industrial life cycle. Demand is growing faster than supply, and, depending on the presence and/or actions of an industry leader, Idata may price high to maximize current profits and generate cash for product development or price low in an effort to gain market share.

15. a. A basic premise of the business cycle approach to investing is that stock prices anticipate fluctuations in the business cycle. For example, there is evidence that stock prices tend to move about six months ahead of the economy. In fact, stock prices are a leading indicator for the economy.

Over the course of a business cycle this approach to investing would work roughly as follows. As the top of a business cycle is perceived to be approaching, stocks purchased should not be vulnerable to a recession. When a downturn is perceived to be at hand, stock holdings should be lightened with proceeds invested in fixed-income securities. Once the recession has matured to some extent, and interest rates fall, bond prices will rise. As it's perceived the recession is about to end, profits should be taken in the bonds and reinvested in stocks, particularly those in cyclical industries with a high beta.

Abnormal returns generally will only be earned if these asset allocation switches are timed better than those of other investors. Switches made after the turning points may not lead to excess returns.

b.   Based on the business cycle approach to investment timing, the ideal time to invest in a cyclical stock like a passenger car company would be just before the end of a recession. If the recovery is aleady underway, Adam's recommendation would be too late. The equities market generally anticipates the changes in the economic cycle. Therefore, since the "recovery is underway," the price of Universal Auto should already reflect the anticipated improvements in the economy.

16. The expiration of its patent means that General Weedkiller will soon face considerably greater competition from its competitors. We would expect prices and profit margins to fall, and total industry sales to increase somewhat as prices decline. The industry will probably enter the consolidation stage in which producers are forced to compete more extensively on the basis of price.

17. a.   Expected profit = Sales – fixed costs – variable costs
$$= \$120,000 - \$30,000 - (1/3) \times \$120,000 = \$50,000$$

b. $\text{DOL} = 1 + \dfrac{\text{fixed costs}}{\text{profits}} = 1 + \dfrac{\$30,000}{\$50,000} = 1.6$

c.   If sales are only $108,000, profits will fall to

$$\$108,000 - \$30,000 - (1/3) \times \$108,000 = \$42,000$$

which is a decline of 16% from the forecasted value.

d.   The decrease in profits is 16%, which equals DOL times the 10% drop in sales.

e.   Profits must drop more than 100% for earnings to turn negative. For profits to fall 100%, sales must fall by

$$\frac{100\%}{\text{DOL}} = \frac{100\%}{1.6} = 62.5\%.$$

Therefore, revenues would be only 37.5% of the original forecast. At this level, sales will be .375 × $120,000 = $45,000.

f.   If sales are $45,000, profits will be:

$$\$45,000 - \$30,000 - (1/3) \times \$45,000 = \$0$$

18. a. Relevant data items from the table that support the conclusion that the retail auto parts industry as a whole is in the maturity phase of the industry life cycle are:

1. The population of 18-29 year olds, a major customer base for the industry, is gradually declining.

2. The number of households with the income less than $35,000, another important consumer base, is not expanding.

3. The number of cars 5-15 years old, an important end market, has experienced low annual growth (or actual declines in some years), so the number of units that potentially need parts is not growing.

4. Automotive aftermarket industry retail sales have been growing slowly for several years.

5. Consumer expenditures on automotive parts and accessories have grown slowly for several years.

6. Average operating margins of all retail autoparts companies have steadily declined.

b. Relevant items of data from the table that support the conclusion that Wigwam Autoparts Heaven, Inc. (WAH) and its major competitors are in the consolidation stage of their life cycle are:

1. Sales growth of retail autoparts companies with 100 or more stores have been growing rapidly and at an increasing rate.

2. Market share of retail autoparts stores with 100 or more stores has been increasing but is still less than 20 percent, leaving room for much more growth.

3. Average operating margins for retail autoparts companies with 100 or more stores are high and rising.

Because of industry fragmentation (i.e., most of the market share is distributed among many companies with only a few stores), the retail autoparts industry apparently is undergoing marketing innovation and consolidation. The industry is moving toward the "category killer" format, in which a few major companies control large market shares through proliferation of outlets. The evidence suggests that a new "industry within an industry" is emerging in the form of "category killer" large chain-store company. This industry subgroup is in its consolidation stage (i.e., rapid growth with its high operating profit margins and emerging market leaders) despite the fact that the industry is in the maturity stage of its life cycle.

19. a. (iv)

b. (iii)

c. (iv)

d. (iii)

e. (iii)

f. (iv)

g. (iii)

h. (i)

CHAPTER 18: EQUITY VALUATION MODELS

1. a. $k = D_1/P_0 + g$

    $.16 = 2/50 + g$

    $g = .12$

    b. $P_0 = D_1/(k - g) = 2/(.16 - .05) = 18.18$

    The price falls in response to the more pessimistic dividend forecast. The forecast for *current* earnings, however, is unchanged. Therefore, the P/E ratio must fall. The lower P/E ratio is evidence of the diminished optimism concerning the firm's growth prospects.

2. a. $g = ROE \times b = 16\% \times .5 = 8\%$

    $D_1 = \$2(1 - b) = \$2(1 - .5) = \$1$

    $P_0 = D_1/(k - g) = \$1/(.12 - .08) = \$25$

    b. $P_3 = P_0(1 + g)^3 = \$25(1.08)^3 = \$31.49$

3. a.   This director is confused. In the context of the constant growth model that $P_0 = D_1/(k - g)$, it is true that price is higher when dividends are higher *holding everything else, including dividend growth, constant.* But everything else will not be constant. If the firm raises the dividend payout rate, the growth rate g will fall, and stock price will not necessarily rise. In fact if ROE > k, price will fall.

    b.   An increase in dividend payout will reduce the sustainable growth rate as less funds are reinvested in the firm. The sustainable growth rate is ROE × plowback, which will fall as plowback ratio falls. The increased dividend payout rate will reduce the growth rate of book value for the same reason -- less funds are reinvested in the firm.

4. a. $k = 6\% + 1.25(14\% - 6\%) = 16\%$; $g = 2/3 \times 9\% = 6\%$

    $D_1 = E_0 (1 + g) (1 - b) = 3(1.06) (1/3) = 1.06$

    $P_0 = \dfrac{D_1}{k - g} = \dfrac{1.06}{.16 - .06} = 10.60$

    b.   Leading $P_0/E_1 = 10.60/3.18 = 3.33$

    Trailing $P_0/E_0 = 10.60/3 = 3.53$

c. $PVGO = P_0 - \dfrac{E_1}{k} = 10.60 - \dfrac{3}{.16} = -8.15$

The low P/E ratios and negative PVGO are due to a poor ROE, 9%, that is less than the market capitalization rate, 16%.

d. Now, you revise b to 1/3, g to $1/3 \times .09 = .03$, and D_1 to $E_0 (1.03) \times (2/3) =$ 2.06. Thus, $V_0 = 2.06/(.16 - .03) = \$15.85$. V_0 increases because the firm pays out more earnings instead of reinvesting them at a poor ROE. This information is not yet known to the rest of the market, and therefore, V_0 diverges from P_0.

5. Because beta = 1.0, k = market return, 15%. Therefore $15\% = D_1/P_0 + g = 4\% + g$. Therefore g = 11%.

6. <u>FI Corporation.</u>

a. $g = 5\%$; $D_1 = \$8$; $k = 10\%$

$$P_0 = \dfrac{D_1}{k - g} = \dfrac{\$8}{.10 - .05} = \$160$$

b. The dividend payout ratio is 8/12 = 2/3, so the payout ratio is b = 1/3. The implied value of ROE on future investments is found by solving: $g = b \times ROE$ with $g = 5\%$ and b = 1/3. ROE = 15%.

c. Assuming ROE = k, the price is EPS/k. $P_0 = \$12/.10 = \$120$. Therefore, the market is paying $40 per share ($160 - $120) for growth opportunities.

7. a. $k = 4\% + 1.15 \times (10\% - 4\%) = 10.9\%$

b. Using Emmas's short term growth projections of 25%, we obtain a two-stage DDM value as follows:

$$P_0 = \dfrac{D_1}{1 + k} + \dfrac{D_2}{(1 + k)^2} + \dfrac{D_3}{(1 + k)^3} + \dfrac{D_4 + D_5/(k - g)}{(1 + k)^4}$$

$$= \dfrac{.287}{1.109} + \dfrac{.359}{1.109^2} + \dfrac{.448}{1.109^3} + \dfrac{.561 + .701/(.109 - .093)}{1.109^4}$$

$$= .259 + .292 + .329 + 29.336$$

$$= 30.216$$

c. With these new assumptions, Disney stock has an intrinsic value below its market price of $37.75. This analysis indicates a sell recommendation. Even though Disney's 5-year growth rate increases so does its beta and risk premium. The intrinsic value falls.

8. <u>High-Flyer stock.</u>

$k = r_f + \beta (k_M - r_f) = 10\% + 1.5(15\% - 10\%) = 10\% + 7.5\% = 17.5\%,$

and $g = 5\%$.

Therefore, $P_0 = \dfrac{D_1}{k - g} = \dfrac{\$2.50}{.175 - .05} = \dfrac{\$2.50}{.125} = \$20.$

9.

	Stock	
	A	B
Market capitalization rate, k	10%	10%
Expected return on equity, ROE	14%	12%
Estimated earnings per share, E_1	$2.00	$1.65
Estimated dividends per share, D_1	$1.00	$1.00
Current market price per share, P_0	$27	$25
a. Dividend payout ratio, $1 - b$	.5	.606
b. Growth rate, $g = ROE \times b$	7%	4.728%
c. Intrinsic value, V_0	$33.33	$18.97

   d. Stock A is the one you would invest in since its intrinsic value exceeds its price. You might want to sell short stock B.

10. a. It is true that NewSoft sells at higher multiples of earnings and book value than Capital Corp. But this difference may be justified by NewSoft's higher expected growth rate of earnings and dividends. NewSoft is in a growing market with abundant profit and growth opportunities. Capital Corp is in a mature industry with fewer growth prospects. Both the price-to-earnings and price-to-book ratios will reflect the prospect of growth opportunities, implying that the ratios for these firms ratios do not necessarily indicate mispricing.

    b. The most important weakness of the constant-growth dividend discount model in this application is that it assumes perpetual constant growth rate of dividends. While dividends may be on a steady growth path for Capital Corp, which is a more mature firm, that is far less likely to be a realistic assumption for NewSoft.

    c. NewSoft should be valued using a multi-stage DDM, which allows for rapid growth in the early years, but that recognizes that growth ultimately must slow to a more sustainable rate.

$$\frac{\left[1.5 + (X - 26)\right]}{X} = 15\%$$

$.15X = 1.5 - 26 + X$

$.15X = 24.5 + X$

$-.85X = 24.5$

11. Nogro Corporation.

   a. $P_0 = \$10$, $E_1 = \$2$, $b = .5$, ROE $= .2$

      $k = D_1/P_0 + g$

      $D_1 = .5 \times \$2 = \$1$

      $g = b \times$ ROE $= .5 \times .2 = .1$

      Therefore, $k = \$1/\$10 + .1 = .1 + .1 = .2$ or 20%

   b. Since $k =$ ROE, the NPV of future investment opportunities is zero:

$$PVGO = P_0 - \frac{E_1}{k} = 10 - 10 = 0$$

   c. Since $k =$ ROE, the stock price would be unaffected by cutting the dividend and investing the additional earnings.

      Even if the dividend were eliminated altogether, this should have no impact on the stock's price since the NPV of the firm's investments is zero.

12. a. $E_0 = 1$; $D_0 = .50$; ROE $= 20\%$; $k = 15\%$; $b = .5$.

      Therefore, $g =$ ROE $\times b = 20\% \times .5 = 10\%$

$$P_0 = \frac{D_1}{k - g} = \frac{D_0(1 + g)}{k - g} = \frac{.50 \times 1.10}{.15 - .10} = \$11$$

   b.

time	EPS	Dividend	Comment
0	1	.50	This figure is given in the question.
1	1.10	.55	$g = 10\%$, plowback $= .50$
2	1.21	.726	EPS has grown by 10% based on last year's earnings plowback and ROE; this year's earnings plowback ratio now falls to .40 and payout ratio $= .60$
3	1.283	.7696	EPS grows by $.4 \times 15\% = 6\%$ and payout ratio $= .60$

$$\text{At time 2, } P_2 = \frac{D_3}{k - g} = \frac{.7696}{.15 - .06} = \$8.551$$

$$\text{At time 0, } V_0 = \frac{.55}{1.15} + \frac{.726 + 8.551}{(1.15)^2} = \$7.493$$

   c. $P_0 = \$11$ and $P_1 = P_0(1 + g) = \$12.10$. (Because the market is unaware of the changed competitive situation, it believes the stock price should grow at 10% per year.

$P_2 = \$8.551$ *after* the market becomes aware of the changed competitive situation.

$P_3 = \$8.551 \times 1.06 = \$9.064$. The new growth rate is 6%.

Year	Return	
1	$\dfrac{(12.10 - 11) + .55}{11}$	$= .15$
2	$\dfrac{(8.551 - 12.10) + .726}{12.10}$	$= -.233$
3	$\dfrac{(9.064 - 8.551) + .7696}{8.551}$	$= .15$

Moral: In "normal periods" when there is no special information, the stock return equals $k = 15\%$. When special information arrives, all the abnormal return accrues *in that period*, as one would expect in an efficient market.

13. <u>Xyrong Corporation</u>

a. $k = r_f + \beta[E(r_M) - r_f] = 8\% + 1.2(15\% - 8\%) = 16.4\%$

$g = b \times ROE = .6 \times 20\% = 12\%$

$$V_0 = \frac{D_0(1 + g)}{k - g} = \frac{\$4 \times 1.12}{.164 - .12} = \$101.82$$

b. $P_1 = V_1 = V_0(1 + g) = 101.82 \times 1.12 = \$114.04$

$$E(r) = \frac{D_1 + P_1 - P_0}{P_0} = \frac{\$4.48 + \$114.04 - \$100}{\$100} = .1852 = 18.52\%$$

14. <u>DEQS Corporation.</u>

	0	1	5	6	. . .
E_t	10	12	24.883	\$29.860	
D_t	0	0	0	\$11.944	
b	1	1	1	.6	
g	.2	.2	.2	.09	

a. $P_5 = \dfrac{D_6}{k - g} = \dfrac{\$11.944}{.15 - .09} = \$199.07$

$$P_0 = \frac{P_5}{(1 + k)^5} = \$98.97$$

b. The price should rise by 15% per year until year 6: because there is no dividend, the entire return must be in capital gains.

c. It would have no effect since ROE = k.

15. a. The formula for a multistage DDM model with *two* distinct growth stages consisting of a first stage with five years of above-normal constant growth followed by a second stage of normal constant growth is:

$$P_0 = \frac{D_1}{(1 + k)^1} + \frac{D_2}{(1 + k)^2} + \frac{D_3}{(1 + k)^3} + \frac{D_4}{(1 + k)^4} + \frac{D_5}{(1 + k)^5} + \frac{\frac{D_6}{(k - g)}}{(1 + k)^5}$$

$$= \frac{\$2.29}{1.10^1} + \frac{\$2.75}{1.10^2} + \frac{\$3.30}{1.10^3} + \frac{\$3.96}{1.10^4} + \frac{\$4.75}{1.10^5} + \frac{\frac{\$5.09}{(0.10 - 0.07)}}{1.10^5}$$

$$= \underline{\$117.84}$$

where:

D_1	=	$D_0 (1 + 0.20) = 2.29$
D_2	=	$D_1 (1 + 0.20) = 2.75$
D_3	=	$D_2 (1 + 0.20) = 3.30$
D_4	=	$D_3 (1 + 0.20) = 3.96$
D_5	=	$D_4 (1 + 0.20) = 4.75$
D_6	=	$D_5 (1 + 0.07) = 5.09$
k	=	Equity required return = 0.10
g	=	Growth in second stage = 0.07

b.

Philip Morris P/E (12/31/91)	=	$80.25/$4.24	=	18.9
S&P 500 P/E (12/31/91)	=	$417.09/$16.29	=	25.6
Philip Morris relative P/E	=	18.9/25.6	=	0.74

c.

Philip Morris book value (12/31/91)	=	$12,512/920	= $13.60 per share
Philip Morris P/B (12/31/91)	=	$80.25/$13.60	
	=	5.90	
S&P 500 P/B (12/31/91)	=	$417.09/$161.08	
	=	2.59	
Philip Morris relative P/B	=	5.90/2.59	
	=	2.28	

16.   a.   **Multistage Dividend Discount Model**

Advantages	**Disadvantages**
1. Excellent for comparing greatly different companies	1. Need to forecast well into the future.
2. Solid theoretical framework.	2. Problem with non-dividend paying companies.
3. Ease in adjusting for risk levels.	3. Problem with high growth companies (g>k).
4. Dividends relatively easy to project.	4. Problems projecting "forever after" ROE and payout ratio.
5. Dividends not subject to distortions from arbitrary accounting rules.	5. Small changes in assumptions can have big impact.
6. Flexibility in use and more realistic than constant growth model.	6. Need technology for more advanced models.

Absolute and Relative Price/Earnings Ratio

Advantages	**Disadvantages**
1. Widely used by investors.	1. Difficult with volatile earnings.
2. Easy to compare with market and other companies in specific industries.	2. Need to determine what is a "normal" P/E ratio.
	3. Difficult to project earnings.
	4. Effect of accounting differences.
	5. Many factors influence multiples.
	6. Can be used only for relative rather than absolute measurement.
	7. Doesn't address quality of earnings.
	8. Problem with companies with no income.

Absolute and Relative Price/Book Ratio

Advantages	**Disadvantages**
1. Incorporates some concept of asset values.	1. Subject to differing accounting rules.
2. Easy to compute even for companies with volatile or negative earnings.	2. Affected by non-recurring items.
3. Easy to compare with market and specific industries.	3. Subject to historical costs.
	4. Book may be poor guide to actual asset values.
	5. Ignores future earnings prospects and growth potential.

b. Support can be given to either position.

Philip Morris is undervalued because:
1. DDM indicates intrinsic value above current market price.
2. Given forecasts of dividends over two stages, DDM is best to use for this situation and should be given more weight.
3. P/E below market despite past growth and forecast of superior future growth.
4. P/E relative below 10-year average.

Philip Morris is overvalued because:
1. P/B considerably higher than market.
2. P/B relative higher than 10-year average.
3. DDM discount rate used should be higher than market's 10% due to large potential risks in cigarette manufacturing business (although whether this risk is systematic is far from clear).
4. P/E on Philip Morris should be low relative to market and past growth due to risks inherent in its business.

17. Duo Growth Co.

	0	1	2	3	4	5	. . .
D_t	1	1.25	1.5625	1.953			
g	.25	.25	.25	.05	. . . .		

a. The dividend to be paid at the end of year 3 is the first installment of a dividend stream that will increase indefinitely at the constant growth rate of 5%. Therefore, we may use the constant growth model as of the end of year 2, and can calculate intrinsic value by adding the present value of the first two dividends plus the present value of the sales price of the stock at the end of year 2.

The expected price 2 years from now is:

$P_2 = D_3 / (k - g) = 1.953 / (.20 - .05) = \$13.02$

The PV of this expected price is $13.02 / 1.20^2 = \$9.04$

The PV of expected dividends in years 1 and 2 is:

$$\frac{D_1}{1.20} + \frac{D_2}{1.20^2} = \$2.13$$

Thus the current price should be $\$9.04 + \$2.13 = \$11.17$.

b. Expected dividend yield $= D_1 / P_0 = 1.25/11.17 = .112$ or 11.2%

c. The expected price one year from now is the PV of P_2 and D_2:

$P_1 = (D_2 + P_2) / 1.20 = (1.5625 + 13.02) / 1.20 = \$12.15.$

The implied capital gain is $(P_1 - P_0) / P_0$

$= (12.15 - 11.17) / 11.17 = .088 \text{ or } 8.8\%$

The implied capital gains rate and the expected dividend yield sum to the market capitalization rate. This is consistent with the DDM.

18. Generic Genetics (GG) Corporation.

	0	1	. . .	4	5
E_t	5	6		10.368	12.4416
D_t	0	0		0	12.4416

$k = 15\%$, and we are told that dividends $= 0$, so that $b = 1.0$ (100% plowback ratio).

a. $P_4 = \dfrac{D_5}{k} = \dfrac{12.4416}{.15} = \$82.944$

$V_0 = \dfrac{P_4}{(1 + k)^4} = \$47.42$

b. Its price should increase at a rate of 15% over the next year, so that the HPR will equal k. ✓

19. MoMi Corporation.

	Projected Free Cash Flow in Year 1
Before-tax cash flow from operations	$2,100,000
Depreciation	210,000
Taxable Income	1,890,000
Taxes (@ 34%)	642,600
After-tax unlevered income	1,247,400
After-tax cash flow from operations (After-tax unlevered income + depreciation)	1,457,400
New investment (20% of cash flow from operations)	420,000
Free cash flow (After-tax cash flow from operations – new investment)	1,037,400

$k = 12\%$ Debt = $4 million

The value of the whole firm, debt plus equity, is

$$V_0 = \frac{C_1}{k - g} = \frac{\$1037400}{.12 - .05} = \$14,820,000$$

Since the value of the debt is $4 million, the value of the equity is $10,820,000.

20. <u>CPI Corporation.</u>

    a. $k^* = D_1^* / P_0 + g^*$

          $= 1/20 + .04 = .05 + .04 = .09$ or 9% per year.

    b. Nominal capitalization rate:

          $k = (1 + k^*)\,(1 + i) - 1$

              $= 1.09 \times 1.06 - 1 = .1554$ or 15.54%

    Nominal dividend yield:

    $D_1/P_0 = 1 \times 1.06/20 = .053$ or 5.3%

    Growth rate of nominal dividends:

    $g = (1 + g^*)\,(1 + i) - 1$

      $= 1.04 \times 1.06 - 1 = .1024$ or 10.24%

    c. If expected real EPS are $1.80, then the estimate of intrinsic value using the simple capitalized earnings model is:

        $V_0 = \$1.80 / .09 = \$20$

21. a. (ii)

    b. (iv)

    c. (ii)

    d. (ii)

    e. (iii)

    f. (i)

    g. (i)

    h. (iii)

    i. (iii)

    j. (iv)

    k. (iii)

    l. (iii)

CHAPTER 19: FINANCIAL STATEMENT ANALYSIS

1. ROA = ROS × ATO. The only way that Crusty Pie can have an ROS higher than the industry average and an ROA equal to the industry average is for its ATO to be lower than the industry average.

2. ABC's ATO must be above the industry average.

3. ROE = (1 − tax rate)[ROA + (ROA − Interest rate)Debt/Equity]

   $ROE_A > ROE_B$

   Firms A and B have the same ROA. Assuming the same tax rate, they must have different interest rates and/or debt ratios.

4. a.

Palomba Pizza Stores
Statement of Cash Flows
For Year Ended December 31,1991

Cash Flows from Operating Activities

Cash Collections from Customer	$250,000	
Cash Payments to Suppliers	(85,000)	
Cash Payments for Salaries	(45,000)	
Cash Payments for Interest	(10,000)	
Net Cash Provided by Operating Activities		$110,000

Cash Flows from Investing Activities

Sale of Equipment	38,000	
Purchase of Equipment	(30,000)	
Purchase of Land	(14,000)	
Net Cash Used by Investing Activities		(6,000)

Cash Flows from Financing Activities

Retirement of Common Stock	(25,000)	
Payment of Dividends	(35,000)	
Net Cash Used by Financing Activities		(60,000)
Net Increase in Cash		44,000
Cash at Beginning of Year		50,000
Cash at End of Year		$94,000

b. The cash flow from operations (CFO) focuses on measuring the cash flow generated by operations and not on measuring profitability. If used as a measure of performance, CFO is less subject to distortion than the net income figure. Analysts use the CFO as a check on the quality of earnings. The CFO then becomes a check on the reported net earnings figure but not as a substitute for net earnings. Companies with high net income but low CFO may be using income recognition techniques that are suspect. The ability of a firm to generate cash from operations on a consistent basis is one indication of the financial health of the firm. For most firms, CFO is the "life blood" of the firm. Analysts search for trends in CFO to indicate future cash conditions and the potential for cash flow troubles.

Cash flow from investing activities (CFI) is an indication of how the firm is investing its cash. The analyst must consider the ability of the firm to continue to grow and expand activities and CFI is a good indication of the attitude of management in this area. Analysis of this component of total cash flow indicates the type of capital expenditures being made by management to either expand or maintain productive activities. CFI is also an indicator of the firm's financial flexibility and ability to generate sufficient cash to respond to unanticipated needs and opportunities. A decreasing CFI may be a sign of a slowdown in growth of the firm.

Cash flow from financing activities (CFF) presents the feasibility of financing, the sources of financing, and an indication of the types of sources management supports. Continued debt financing may signal a future cash flow problem. The dependency of a firm on external sources of financing (either borrowing or equity financing) may present troubles in the future such as debt servicing and maintaining dividend policy. Analysts also use CFF as an indication of the quality of earnings. It offers insights into the financial habits of management and potential future policies.

5. a. CF from operating activities = $260 - 85 - 12 - 35 = \$128$

   b. CF from investing activities = $-8 + 30 - 40 = -\$18$

   c. CF from financing activities = $-32 - 37 = -\$69$

6. a.

	Profit Margin	×	Asset Turnover	×	Interest Burden	×	Leverage Ratio	×	Tax Burden	=	Return on Equity
1993	1232/8529		8529/11751		1074/1232		11751/5030		671/1074	=	671/5030
	0.144	×	0.726	×	0.872	×	2.336	×	0.625	=	0.133
1989	1177/4594	×	4594/6657		1153/1177		6657/3044		703/1153		703/3044
	0.256		0.690	×	0.980	×	2.187	×	0.610	=	0.231

where:

Profit margin   = EBIT/Sales
Asset turnover   = Sales/Assets
Interest burden   = Earnings before taxes/EBIT
Leverage ratio   = Assets/Equity
Tax burden   = Net Income/Pretax income
Return on equity   = Net Income/Equity

b. The two components contributing to the change (decline) in Disney's ROE between 1989 and 1993 were the decrease in the profit margin and the lower ratio of earnings before taxes/EBIT (interest burden). The reasons for the changes were as follows:

Profit Margin. (1) Euro Disney losses and reserve provision (writeoff) in 1993, as compared with no effect in 1989. (2) Deterioration in the theme park margins because of lower attendance, which in turn, likely stemmed from a weak economy and higher prices. (3) Deterioration in consumer product margins as the business mix shifted away from licensing and royalty income. (4) Growth that was more rapid than the company average in the film entertainment business, which has the lowest operating margin of any of the business segments.

Interest Burden. (1) Interest expense increased faster than EBIT as Disney's borrowings expanded. (2) Interest expense appears to have also increased faster than borrowings, indicating several possibilities: (a) the rate Disney is paying on borrowings has increased, (b) the mix has shifted toward more costly borrowings, or (c) other interest-bearing liabilities exist that are not included in the borrowings category.

7. a. Average number of days receivables are outstanding

    $= 365 \times$ (Receivables/Sales)

    $= 365 \times 1390/8529$

    $= 59.5$ days.

    The "average number of days receivables are outstanding" is the number of days worth of sales for which the firm has yet to collect cash payment. It is days sales still booked as accounts receivable. If this ratio is high (for example, by comparison to industry norms) it may indicate that the firm has problem accounts or is too lenient in its credit policy.

    b. Cash flow from operations ratio:

    $=$ Cash flow from operations/Current liabilities

    $= 2145/2821$

    $= 0.76$ times.

    The "cash flow from operations" ratio is a liquidity measure. The higher the ratio, the safer. This ratio helps to assess a firm's ability to operate as a going concern, i.e., to meet short term needs for cash flow.

    c. Long-term debt = $2,386 million and market value of equity is $20,536 million. The long-term debt to capital ratio is therefore

    $$\frac{2386}{2386 + 20,536} = .1041$$

19-3

The debt-to-capital measures the degree of a firm's financial leverage. The higher the ratio, the riskier the firm's position and the less flexibility the firm will have to withstand adversity.

d. Times interest earned (also called interest coverage ratio):

= Earnings before interest and taxes/Interest

= (1074 + 158)/158 = 7.80

The "times interest earned" ratio indicates the degree of protection available to creditors by measuring the extent to which earnings meet or "cover" interest costs.

8 a. ROE = profit margin × interest burden × asset turnover × leverage × tax burden.

Using the definitions below, ROE for Eastover (EO) and Southampton (SHC) in 1990 are:

profit margin	=	$\dfrac{\text{EBIT}}{\text{Sales}}$	SHC: EO:	145/1793 795/7406	= =	8.1% 10.7%
interest burden	=	$\dfrac{\text{Pretax income}}{\text{EBIT}}$	SHC: EO:	137/145 600/795	= =	0.95 0.75
asset turnover	=	$\dfrac{\text{Sales}}{\text{Assets}}$	SHC: EO:	1793/2104 7406/8265	= =	0.85 0.90
leverage	=	$\dfrac{\text{Assets}}{\text{Equity}}$	SHC: EO:	2104/1167 8265/3864	= =	1.80 2.14
Tax burden	=	$\dfrac{\text{Net income}}{\text{Pretax income}}$	SHC: EO:	91/137 394/600	= =	0.66 0.66
ROE	=	$\dfrac{\text{Net income}}{\text{Equity}}$	SHC: EO:	91/1167 394/3864	= =	7.8% 10.2%

b. The differences in the components of ROE for Eastover and Southampton for 1990 are as follows:

Profit margin	EO has a higher margin
Interest burden	EO has a higher interest burden because its pretax profits are a lower percentage of EBIT
Asset turnover	EO is more efficient at turning over its assets
Leverage	EO has higher financial leverage
Tax Burden	No major difference here between the two companies
ROE	EO has a higher ROE than SHC, but this is only in part due to higher margins and a better asset turnover -- greater financial leverage also plays a part.

c. The sustainable growth rate can be calculated by multiplying ROE times the plowback ratio. For 1990, the sustainable growth rates for Eastover and Southampton are as follows:

	ROE	×	plowback ratio*	=	sustainable growth rate
Eastover	10.2%		0.36		3.7%
Southampton	7.8%		0.58		4.5%

The sustainable growth rates derived in this manner are not likely to be representative of future growth, since 1990 was probably not a "normal" year. For Eastover, earnings had not yet recovered to 1987-88 levels; earnings retention of only 0.36 seems low for a company in a capital intensive industry. Southampton's earnings fell by over 50 percent in 1990 and its earnings retention will probably be higher than 0.58 in the future. There is a danger, therefore, in basing a projection on just one year's results, especially for companies in a cyclical industry like forest products.

*Using data in table 19E,

Plowback	=	(1 – payout ratio)
EO	=	(1 – 1.20/1.56) = (1 – .64) = .36
SHC	=	(1 – 1.04/2.46) = (1 – .42) = .58

9. a. The formula for constant growth discounted dividend model is shown below:

$$Price = \frac{D_0(1 + g)}{k - g}$$

For Eastover:

$$Price = \frac{1.20 \times 1.08}{.11 - .08} = 43.20$$

This compares with its current stock price of $28. On this basis, it appears that Eastover is undervalued.

b. The formula for the two-stage discounted dividend model is as follows:

$$Price = D_1/(1+k) + D_2/(1+k)^2 + D_3/(1+k)^3 + P_3/(1+k)^3$$

For Eastover: $g_1 = .12$ and $g_2 = .08$

$D_0 = 1.20$			
$D_1 = 1.20$	×	1.12 =	1.34
$D_2 = 1.20$	×	$(1.12)^2$ =	1.51
$D_3 = 1.20$	×	$(1.12)^3$ =	1.69
$D_4 = D_3$	×	(1.08) =	1.82

$$P_3 = \frac{D_4}{k - g_2} = 1.82 / (.11 - .08) = 60.67$$

$$Price = 1.34/1.11 + 1.51/(1.11)^2 + 1.69/(1.11)^3 + 60.67/(1.11)^3 = 48.03$$

This approach indicates that Eastover is even more undervalued than was the case with the constant growth approach.

c. Advantages of the constant growth model include (1) logical, theoretical basis, (2) simple to compute, and (3) inputs can be estimated. Disadvantages include (1) very sensitive to inputs of growth, (2) g and k difficult to estimate accurately, (3) only valid for $g < k$, (4) constant growth is an unrealistic assumption, (5) assumes growth will never slow down, (6) dividend payout must remain constant, (7) not usable for firms not paying dividends

Improvements offered by the two-stage model include: (1) The two-stage model is more realistic. It accounts for low, high, or zero growth in the first stage, followed by constant long-term growth in the second stage. (2) The model can solve for stock value when the growth rate in the first stage exceeds the required rate of return.

10. a. In order to determine whether a stock is undervalued or overvalued, analysts often compute price-earnings ratios (P/Es) and price-book value ratios (P/Bs) and compare them to benchmarks for the market such as the S&P 500 index. The formulas for these calculations are:

$$\text{Relative P/E} = \frac{\text{P/E of specific company}}{\text{P/E of S\&P 500}}$$

$$\text{Relative P/B} = \frac{\text{P/B of specific company}}{\text{P/B of S\&P 500}}$$

To evaluate EO and SHC using a relative P/E model, Mulroney can calculate the five-year average P/E for each stock, and divide that number by the 5-year average P/E for the S&P 500. This gives the historical average relative P/E. Mulroney should then compare the historical average relative P/E to the current relative P/E (i.e., the current P/E on each stock, using 1992 estimated earnings per share, divided by the current P/E of the market, again using the 1992 estimate).

For the price/book model, Mulroney should make similar calculations, i.e., divide the five-year average price/book ratio for a stock by the five year average price/book for the S&P 500, and compare the result to the current relative price/book (using 1991 estimated book value).

The results are as follows:

	EO	SHC	S&P500
P/E model			
5 yr. avg. P/E	16.6	11.9	15.20
Relative 5 yr. P/E	1.09	0.78	
Current P/E	17.5	16.0	20.20
Current relative P/E	0.87	0.79	
Price/Book model			
5 yr. avg. price/book	1.52	1.10	2.10
Rel. 5 yr. price/book	0.72	0.52	
Current price/book	1.62	1.49	2.60
Current rel. price/book	0.62	0.57	

From this analysis, it is evident that EO is trading at a discount to its historical 5-year relative P/E ratio, whereas Southampton is trading right at its historical 5-year relative P/E. With respect to price/book, Eastover is trading at a discount to its historical relative price/book ratio, whereas SHC is trading modestly above its 5-year relative price/book ratio. As noted in the preamble to the problem, however, Eastover's book value is understated due to the very low historical cost basis for its timberlands. The fact that Eastover is trading below its 5-year average relative price to book ratio even though its book value is understated makes Eastover seem especially attractive on a price/book basis.

b.   Disadvantages of the relative P/E model include (1) the relative P/E measures only relative, not absolute value; (2) the accounting earnings estimate for the next year may not equal sustainable earnings; (3) accounting practices may not be standardized; (4) changing accounting standards may make historical comparisons difficult.

Disadvantages of relative P/B model include: (1) book value may be under or overstated -- particularly for a company like Eastover, which has valuable timberlands on its books carried at low historical cost; (2) book value may not be representative of earning power or future growth potential; (3) changing accounting standards make historical comparisons difficult.

11. The following table summarizes the valuation and ROE for Eastover and Southampton:

	Eastover	Southampton
Stock Price	$28	$48
Constant-growth model value	43	29
2-Stage growth model Value	48	35.50

	Eastover	Southampton
Current P/E	17.5	16.0
Current relative P/E	0.87	0.79
5-year average P/E	16.6	11.9
Relative 5 year P/E	1.09	0.78
Current P/B	1.62	1.49
Current relative P/B	0.62	0.57
5-year average P/B	1.52	1.10
Relative 5 year P/B	0.72	0.52
1990 ROE	10.2%	7.8%
Sustainable growth rate	3.7%	4.5%

Eastover seems to be undervalued under both discounted dividend models. Eastover also looks cheap on both a relative P/E and on a relative P/B basis. Southampton, on the other hand, looks expensive using discounted dividend models and is slightly overvalued using the relative price/book model. On a relative P/E basis, SHC looks to be fairly valued. Southampton does have a slightly higher sustainable growth rate, but not appreciably so, and its ROE is less than Eastover's.

The current P/E for Eastover is based on relatively depressed current earnings, yet the stock still comes out as attractive on this basis. In addition, the price/book ratio for Eastover is overstated due to the low historical cost basis used for the timberland assets. This makes Eastover seem all the more attractive on a price/book basis. Based on this analysis, Mulroney selected Eastover over Southampton.

12.   a.

	Profit Margin	×	Asset Turnover	×	Interest Burden	×	Financial Leverage	×	Tax burden	=	Return on equity
	$\dfrac{EBIT}{Sales}$	×	$\dfrac{Sales}{Assets}$	×	$\dfrac{Pretax}{EBIT}$	×	$\dfrac{Assets}{Equity}$	×	$\dfrac{Net}{Pretax}$	=	$\dfrac{Net}{Equity}$
1991:	$\dfrac{8622}{56,458}$		$\dfrac{56,458}{47,384}$		$\dfrac{6971}{8622}$		$\dfrac{47,384}{12,512}$		$\dfrac{3927}{6971}$		$\dfrac{3927}{12,512}$
	0.153	×	1.191	×	0.809	×	3.787	×	0.563	=	0.314
1981:	$\dfrac{1312}{10,886}$		$\dfrac{10,886}{9180}$		$\dfrac{1080}{1312}$		$\dfrac{9180}{3234}$		$\dfrac{660}{1080}$		$\dfrac{660}{3234}$
	0.121	×	1.186	×	0.823	×	2.839	×	0.611	=	0.204

b.   Philip Morris' return on equity increased from 20.4% to 31.4% over the years from 1981 to 1991. The primary reasons for the increase were a higher profit margin and greater financial leverage. Asset turnover was effectively constant over the period, the tax burden was lower and interest burden had an adverse impact on ROE. The increase in the profit margin was likely due to aggressive pricing on the part of Philip Morris management. The increase in financial leverage was due mainly to the reduction in equity stemming from the adoption of the FAS 106 accounting change and the repurchase of common shares.

c.   The expected sustainable growth rate can be calculated from the 1981 data as follows:

Sustainable growth	=	ROE × (1 – Payout ratio)
	=	20.4% × (1 –.379)
	=	12.7%

The 12.7% estimate of future growth implied by the sustainable growth methodology was much lower than the actual 20.4% growth rate in earnings achieved over the period. This discrepancy occurred despite management's decision to raise the dividend payout ratio from 37.9% in 1981 to 45.0% in 1991.

The sustainable growth methodology will yield a reliable estimate of future growth if a company's profitability (ROE) remains in equilibrium. This was not the case for Philip Morris during the decade of the 1980s. The company raised its level of profitability over this period by margin expansion and it incurred greater financial leverage. As a result, actual earnings growth was higher than the sustainable growth formula would predict while this change was occurring.

Note: It is only a coincidence that the ROE in 1981 equaled the actual growth rate of 20.4%

13. a. Net income can increase even when CF from operations falls. This can happen if there is a buildup in net working capital -- for example increases in accounts receivable or inventories, or reductions in accounts payable. Lower depreciation expenses also will increase net income but can lower CF through the impact on taxes owed.

   b. Cash flow from operations may be a good indicator of a firm's quality of earnings since it shows whether the firm is actually generating the cash necessary to pay bills and dividends without resorting to new financing. Cash flow is less susceptible to choice of accounting rules than is net income.

14. a [= sales – cash expenses – increase in A/R. Ignore depreciation, since it is a non-cash item and its impact on taxes already is accounted for.]

15. c [Assumng positive inflation, earnings are lower because the cost of goods sold is assessed at current cost rather than the historical cost for the goods produced when the level of prices was lower.]

16. a [Cost of goods sold is understated so income is higher, and assets (inventory) are valued at most recent cost so they are valued higher.]

17. a [Since goods still in inventory are valued at recent versus historical cost.]

18. c [The other items are not included with operating activities.]

19. b [The cash dividend has no effect on interest payments, earnings, or debt, but will reduce equity, at least minimally.]

20.

		1996	1999
(1) Operating margin =	$\dfrac{\text{Operating income} - \text{Depreciation}}{\text{Sales}}$	$\dfrac{38 - 3}{542} = 6.5\%$	$\dfrac{76 - 9}{979} = 6.8\%$
(2) Asset turnover =	$\dfrac{\text{Sales}}{\text{Total Assets}}$	$\dfrac{542}{245} = 2.21$	$\dfrac{979}{291} = 3.36$
(3) Interest Burden =	$\dfrac{[\text{Op Inc} - \text{Dep}] - \text{Int Expense}}{\text{Operating Income} - \text{Depreciation}}$	$\dfrac{38 - 3 - 3}{38 - 3} = .914$	1
(4) Financial Leverage	$\dfrac{\text{Total Assets}}{\text{Shareholders Equity}}$	$\dfrac{245}{159} = 1.54$	$\dfrac{291}{220} = 1.32$
(5) Tax rate =	$\dfrac{\text{Income taxes}}{\text{Pre-tax income}}$	$\dfrac{13}{32} = 40.63\%$	$\dfrac{37}{67} = 55.22\%$

Using the Du Pont formula,

ROE = $[1 - (5)] \times (3) \times (1) \times (2) \times (4)$

ROE(1996) = $.5937 \times .914 \times .065 \times 2.21 \times 1.54 = .12$ or 12%

ROE(1999) = $.4478 \times 1 \times .068 \times 3.36 \times 1.32 = .135$ or 13.5%

b. (i)   Asset turnover measures the ability of a company to minimize the level of assets (current or fixed) to support its level of sales. The asset turnover increased substantially over the period, thus contributing to an increase in the ROE.

(ii)   Financial leverage measures the amount of financing other than equity, including short and long-term debt. Financial leverage declined over the period thus adversely affected the ROE. Since asset turnover rose substantially more than financial leverage declined, the net effect was an increase in ROE.

CHAPTER 20:
OPTIONS MARKETS: INTRODUCTION

1.

	Cost	Payoff	Profit
Call option, X = 100	5 1/4	5	− 1/4
Put option, X = 100	3/4	0	− 3/4
Call option, X = 105	1 3/4	0	− 1 3/4
Put option, X = 105	2 1/4	0	− 2 1/4
Call option, X = 110	3/8	0	− 3/8
Put option, X = 110	5 3/4	5	− 3/4

2. In terms of dollar returns:

Stock price:	80	100	110	120
All stocks (100 shares)	8,000	10,000	11,000	12,000
All options (1000 shares)	0	0	10,000	20,000
Bills + options	9,360	9,360	10,360	11,360

In terms of rate of return, based on a $10,000 investment:

All stocks	−20%	0%	10%	20%
All options	−100%	−100%	0%	100%
Bills + options	−6.4%	−6.4%	3.6%	13.6%

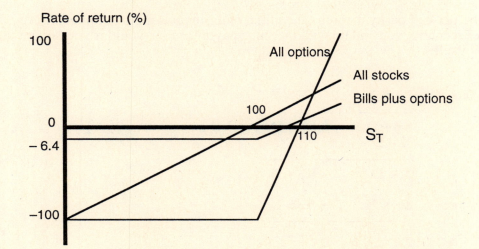

3. a. From put-call parity, $P = C - S_0 + X/(1 + r_f)^T$

   $P = 10 - 100 + 100/(1.10)^{1/4} = \$7.645$

   b. Purchase a straddle, i.e., both a put and a call on the stock. The total cost of the straddle would be $\$10 + \$7.645 = \$17.645$, and this is the amount by which the stock price would have to move in either direction for the profit on the call or put to cover the investment cost (not including time value of money considerations). Accounting for time value, the stock price would need to swing in either direction by $\$17.645 \times (1.10)^{1/4} = \$18.07$.

4. a. From put-call parity, $C = P + S - X/(1+r)^T$

   $C = 4 + 50 - 50/(1.10)^{1/4} = \$5.18$

   b. Sell a straddle, i.e., sell a call *and* a put to realize premium income of $\$4 + \$5.18 = \$9.18$. If the stock price ends up at $\$50$, both the options will be worthless and your profit will be $\$9.18$. This is your maximum possible profit since, at any other stock price, you will need to pay off on either the call or the put. The stock price can move by $\$9.18$ in either direction before your profits become negative.

   c. Buy the call, sell (write) the put, lend $\$50/(1.10)^{1/4}$. The payoff is as follows:

Position	Initial Outlay	Final Payoff	
		$S_T < X$	$S_T > X$
Call (long)	$C = 5.18$	0	$S_T - 50$
Put (short)	$-P = -4.00$	$-(50 - S_T)$	0
Lending position	$50/(1.10)^{1/4} = 48.82$	50	50
TOTAL	$C - P + \dfrac{50}{1.10^{1/4}} = 50$	S_T	S_T

   By the put-call parity theorem, the initial outlay equals the stock price, S_0, or $\$50$. In either scenario, you end up with the same payoff as you would if you bought the stock itself.

5. a.

Outcome:	$S_T \leq X$	$S_T > X$
Stock	$S_T + D$	$S_T + D$
Put	$X - S_T$	0
Total	$X + D$	$S_T + D$

   b.

Outcome:	$S_T \leq X$	$S_T > X$
Call	0	$S_T - X$
Zeros	$X + D$	$X + D$
Total	$X + D$	$S_T + D$

The total payoffs of the two strategies are equal whether or not S_T exceeds X.

c. The stock-plus-put portfolio costs $S_0 + P$ to establish. The call-plus-zero portfolio costs $C + PV(X + D)$. Therefore,

$$S_0 + P = C + PV(X + D)$$

which is identical to equation 20.2.

6. a. Butterfly Spread

Position	$S < X_1$	$X_1 < S < X_2$	$X_2 < S < X_3$	$X_3 < S$
Long call (X_1)	0	$S - X_1$	$S - X_1$	$S - X_1$
Short 2 calls (X_2)	0	0	$-2(S - X_2)$	$-2(S - X_2)$
Long call (X_3)	0	0	0	$S - X_3$
Total	0	$S - X_1$	$2X_2 - X_1 - S$	$(X_2 - X_1) - (X_3 - X_2) = 0$

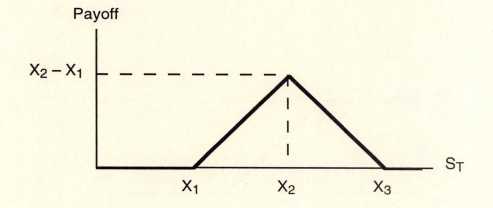

b. Vertical combination

Position	$S < X_1$	$X_1 < S < X_2$	$X_2 < S$
Long call (X_2)	0	0	$S - X_2$
Long put (X_1)	$X_1 - S$	0	0
Total	$X_1 - S$	0	$S - X_2$

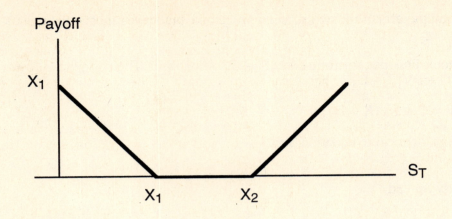

7. Bearish spread

Position	$S < X_1$	$X_1 < S < X_2$	$X_2 < S$
Buy Call (X_2)	0	0	$S - X_2$
Sell Call (X_1)	0	$-(S - X_1)$	$-(S - X_1)$
Total	0	$X_1 - S$	$X_1 - X_2$

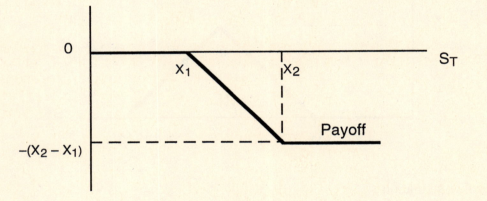

8. a. By writing covered call options, Jones takes in premium income of $30,000. If the price of the stock in January is less than or equal to $45, he will have his stock plus the premium income. But the *most* he can have is $450,000 + $30,000 because the stock will be called away from him if its price exceeds $45. (We are ignoring interest earned on the premium income from writing the option over this short time period.) The payoff structure is:

Stock price	Portfolio value
less than $45	10,000 times stock price + $30,000
more than $45	$450,000 + $30,000 = $480,000

This strategy offers some extra premium income but leaves substantial downside risk. At an extreme, if the stock price fell to zero, Jones would be left with only $30,000. The strategy also puts a cap on the final value at $480,000, but this is more than sufficient to purchase the house.

b. By buying put options with a $35 exercise price, Jones will be paying $30,000 in premiums to insure a minimum level for the final value of his position. That minimum value is $35 × 10,000 – $30,000 = $320,000. This strategy allows for upside gain, but exposes Jones to the possibility of a moderate loss equal to the cost of the puts. The payoff structure is:

Stock price	Portfolio value
less than $35	$350,000 – $30,000 = $320,000
more than $35	10,000 times stock price – $30,000

c. The net cost of the collar is zero. The value of the portfolio will be as follows:

Stock price	Portfolio value
less than $35	$350,000
between $35 and $45	10,000 times stock price
more than $45	$450,000

If the stock price is less than or equal to $35, the collar preserves the $350,000 in principal. If the price exceeds $45, the value of Jones' portfolio can rise to a cap of $450,000. In between, his proceeds equal 10,000 times the stock price.

The best strategy in this case would be (C) since it satisfies the two requirements of preserving the $350,000 in principal while offering a chance of getting $450,000. Strategy (A) seems ruled out since it leaves Jones exposed to the risk of substantial loss of principal.

Our ranking would be: (1) C   (2) B   (3) A

9.   a.

Protective Put	$S_T < 780$	$S_T > 780$
Stock	S_T	S_T
Put	$780 - S_T$	0
Total	780	S_T

Bills and Call	$S_T < 840$	$S_T > 840$
Bills	840	840
Call	0	$S_T - 840$
Total	840	S_T

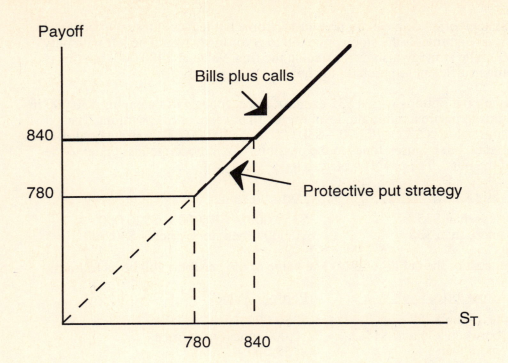

b. The bills plus call strategy has a greater payoff for some values of S_T and never a lower payoff. Since its payoffs are always at least as attractive and sometimes greater, it must be more costly to purchase.

c. The initial cost of the stock plus put position is 906; that of the bills plus call position is 930.

	$S_T = 700$	$S_T = 840$	$S_T = 900$	$S_T = 960$
Stock	700	840	900	960
+Put	80	0	0	0
Payoff	780	840	900	960
Profit	−126	−66	−6	54
Bill	840	840	840	840
+Call	0	0	60	120
Payoff	840	840	900	960
Profit	−90	−90	−30	+30

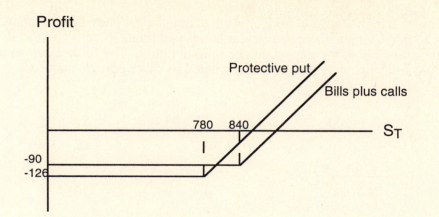

Profit

Protective put

Bills plus calls

-90
-126

780   840

S_T

d. The stock and put strategy is riskier. It does worse when the market is down and better when the market is up. Therefore, its beta is higher.

e. Parity is not violated because these options have different exercise prices. Parity applies only to puts and calls with the same exercise price and expiration date.

10. The farmer has the option to sell the crop for a guaranteed minimum price to the government if the market price is too low. If the support price is denoted P_S and the market price P_m then the farmer has a put option to sell the crop (the asset) at an exercise price of P_S even if the price of the underlying asset, P, is less than P_S.

11. The bondholders have in effect made a loan which requires repayment of B dollars, where B is the face value of bonds. If, however, the value of the firm, V, is less than B, the loan is satisfied by the bondholders taking over the firm. In this way, the bondholders are forced to "pay" B (in the sense that the loan is cancelled) in return for an asset worth only V. It is as though the bondholders wrote a put on an asset worth V with exercise price B. Alternatively, one may view the bondholders as giving the right to the equityholders to reclaim the firm by paying off the B dollar debt. They've issued a call to the equity holders.

12. The manager get a bonus if the stock price exceeds a certain value and get nothing otherwise. This is the same as the payoff to a call option.

13. a. If one buys a call option and writes a put option on a T-bond, the total payoff to the position at maturity is $S_T - X$, where S_T is the price of the T-bond at the maturity date, time T. This is equivalent to the profits on a forward or futures position with futures price X. If you choose an exercise price, X, equal to the current T-bond futures price, the profit on the portfolio will replicate that of market-traded futures.

b. Such a position will increase the portfolio duration, just as adding a T-bond futures contract would increase duration. As interest rates fall, the portfolio gains additional value, so duration is longer than it was before the synthetic futures position was established.

c. Futures can be bought and sold very cheaply and quickly. They give the manager flexibility to pursue strategies or particular bonds that seem attractively priced without worrying about the impact on portfolio duration. The futures can be used to make any adjustments to duration necessitated by other portfolio actions.

14. a.

	$S < 100$	$100 < S < 105$	$S > 105$
Written Call	0	0	$-(S - 100)$
Written Put	$-(100 - S)$	0	0
Total	$S - 100$	0	$105 - S$

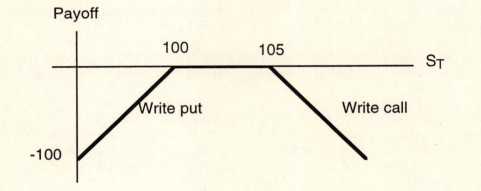

b. Proceeds from writing options:

Call	=	$1 3/4
Put	=	3/4
Total	=	$2 1/2

If IBM sells at $102, both options expire out of the money, and profit = $2.50. If IBM sells at $115 the call written results in a cash outflow of $10 at maturity, and an overall profit of $2.50 – $10 = –$7.50.

c. You break even when *either* the put *or* the call written results in a cash outflow of $2.50. For the put, this would require that 2.50 = 100 – S, or S = $97.50. For the call this would require that $2.50 = S – 105, or S = $107.50.

d. The investor is betting that IBM stock price will have low volatility. This position is similar to a straddle.

15. The put with the higher exercise price must cost more. Therefore, the net outlay to establish the portfolio is positive. The payoff and profit diagram is:

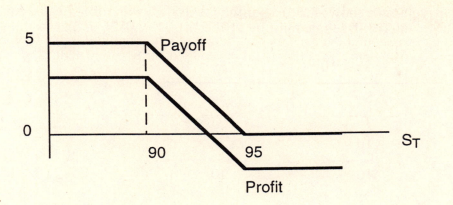

16. Buy the X = 62 put (which should cost more but does not) and write the X = 60 put. Your net outlay is zero, since the options have the same price. Your proceeds at maturity may be positive, but cannot be negative.

	$S_T < 60$	$60 \leq S_T \leq 62$	$S_T > 62$
Buy put (X = 62)	$62 - S_T$	$62 - S_T$	0
Write put (X = 60)	$-(60 - S_T)$	0	0
TOTAL	2	$62 - S_T$	0

Payoff = Profit (because net investment = 0)

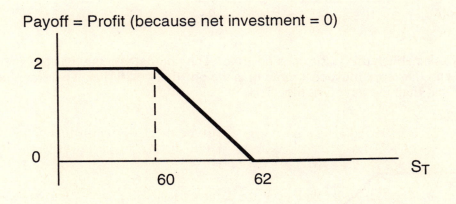

17. According to put-call parity (assuming no dividends), the present value of a payment of $100 can be calculated using the options with January maturity and exercise price of $100.

$$
\begin{aligned}
PV(X) \quad &= \quad S + P - C \\
PV(100) \quad &= \quad 104\ 5/16 \ + \ 3/4 \ - \ 5\ 1/4 \\
&= \quad 104.3125 \ + \ 0.75 \ - \ 5.25 \\
&= \quad 99.8125
\end{aligned}
$$

18. The following payoff table shows that the portfolio is riskless with time-T value equal to $10. Therefore, the risk-free rate must be $10/$9.50 − 1 = .0526 or 5.26%.

	$S_T < 10$	$S_T > 10$
Buy stock	S_T	S_T
Write call	0	$-(S_T - 10)$
Buy put	$10 - S_T$	0
Total	10	10

19. From put-call parity, $C - P = S - X/(1+r)^T$

If the options are at the money, then $S = X$ and therefore, $C - P = X - X/(1+r)^T$, which must be positive. Therefore, the right-hand side of the equation is positive, and we conclude that $C > P$.

20. a.b.

	$S_T < 100$	$100 < S_T < 110$	$S_T > 110$
Buy put (X=110)	$110 - S_T$	$110 - S_T$	0
Write put (X=100)	$-(100 - S_T)$	0	0
Payoff at expiration	10	$110 - S_T$	0

The net outlay to establish this position is positive. The put that you buy has a higher exercise price and therefore must cost more than the one that you write. Therefore, net profits will be less than the payoff at time T.

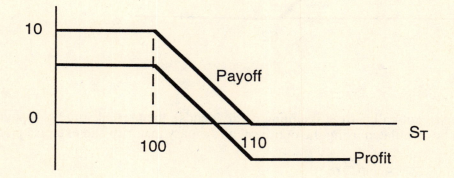

c. The value of this portfolio generally decreases with the stock price. Its beta therefore is negative.

21. a. <u>Joe's strategy</u>

	Cost	Payoff	
		$S < 400$	$S > 400$
Stock index	400	S	S
Put option (X=400)	20	$400 - S$	0
Total	420	400	S
Profit = payoff − 420		−20	$S - 420$

<u>Sally's Strategy</u>

	Cost	Payoff	
		$S < 390$	$S > 390$
Stock index	400	S	S
Put option (X=390)	15	$390 - S$	0
Total	415	390	S
Profit = payoff − 415		−25	$S - 415$

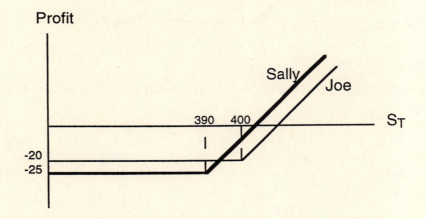

b. Sally does better when the stock price is high, but worse when the stock price is low. (The break-even point occurs at S = $395, when both positions provide losses of $20.)

c. Sally's strategy has greater systematic risk. Profits are more sensitive to the value of the stock index.

22. This strategy is a bearish spread. The initial proceeds are $9 − $3 = $6. The ultimate payoff is either negative or zero:

	$S_T < 50$	$50 < S_T < 60$	$S_T > 60$
Buy call (X = 60)	0	0	$S_T − 60$
Write call (X = 50)	0	$−(S_T − 50)$	$−(S_T − 50)$
TOTAL	0	$−(S_T − 50)$	−10

Breakeven occurs when the payoff offsets the initial proceeds of $6, which occurs at a stock price of $S_T = 56.

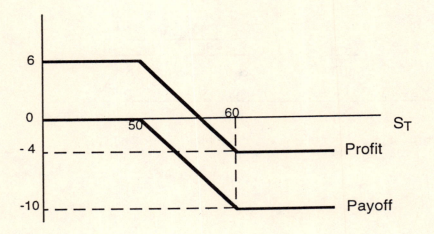

23. Buy a share of stock, write a call with X = 50, write a call with X = 60, and buy a call with X = 110.

	$S_T < 50$	$50 < S_T < 60$	$60 < S_T < 110$	$S_T > 110$
Buy share of stock	S_T	S_T	S_T	S_T
Write call (X = 50)	0	$−(S_T − 50)$	$−(S_T − 50)$	$−(S_T − 50)$
Write call (X = 60)	0	0	$−(S_T − 60)$	$−(S_T − 60)$
Buy call (X = 110)	0	0	0	$S_T − 110$
TOTAL	S_T	50	$110 − S_T$	0

The investor is making a volatility bet. Profits will be highest when volatility is low and the stock price ends up in the interval between $50 and $60.

24. a. (i)

    b. (ii)   [Profit = 40 − 25 + 2.50 − 4.00]

    c. (ii)   [Conversion premium is $200, which is 25% of $800]

    d. (i)

    e. (ii)   [2 × $(55–45) − 2 × $5 − $4]

    f. (i)

CHAPTER 21: OPTION VALUATION

1. Put values also must increase as the volatility of the underlying stock increases. We see this from the parity relation as follows:

$$P = C + PV(X) - S + PV(Dividends).$$

Given a value of S and a risk-free interest rate, if C increases because of an increase in volatility, so must P to keep the parity equation in balance.

2. a. Put A must be written on the lower-priced stock. Otherwise, given the lower volatility of stock A, put A would sell for less than put B.

b. Put B must be written on the stock with lower price. This would explain its higher value.

c. Call B. Despite the higher price of stock B, call B is cheaper than call A. This can be explained by a lower time to expiration.

d. Call B. This would explain its higher price.

e. Call A must be written on the stock with higher volatility -- this would explain the higher option premium.

3.

X	Hedge ratio
115	85/150 = 0.567
100	100/150 = 0.667
75	125/150 = 0.833
50	150/150 = 1.000
25	150/150 = 1.000
10	150/150 = 1.000

As the option becomes more in the money, its hedge ratio increases to a maximum of 1.0.

4.

S	d_1	$N(d_1)$
45	−.0268	.4893
50	.5000	.6915
55	.9766	.8356

5. a. When S_T is 130, P will be 0.

   When S_T is 80, P will be 30.

   The hedge ratio is $(P^+ - P^-)/(S^+ - S^-) = (0 - 30)/(130 - 80) = -3/5.$

b.

Riskless Portfolio	S = 80	S = 130
3 shares	240	390
5 puts	150	0
Total	390	390

Present value = 390/1.10 = 354.545

c. The portfolio cost is 3S + 5P = 300 + 5P, and it is worth $354.545 . Therefore P must be 54.545/5 = $10.91.

6. The hedge ratio for the call is $(C^+ - C^-)/(S^+ - S^-) = (20 - 0)/(130 - 80) = 2/5$.

Riskless Portfolio	S = 80	S = 130
2 shares	160	260
5 calls written	0	−100
Total	160	160

−5C + 200 = 160/1.10. Therefore, C = 10.91.

Does P = C + PV(X) − S?

10.91 = 10.91 + 110/1.10 − 100
10.91 = 10.91

7. $d_1 = .3182$ $N(d_1) = .6248$
$d_2 = -.0354$ $N(d_2) = .4859$
$Xe^{-rT} = 47.56$
C = 8.131

8. a. C falls to 5.5541
   b. C falls to 4.7911
   c. C falls to 6.0778
   d. C rises to 11.5066
   e. C rises to 8.7187

9. According to the Black-Scholes model, the call option should be priced at

$55 \times N(d_1) - 50 \times N(d_2) = 55 \times .6 - 50 \times .5 = \$8$

Because the option actually sells for more than $8, implied volatility is higher than .30.

10. Less. The change in the call price would be $1 only if (i) there were 100% probability that the call would be exercised, and (ii) the interest rate were zero.

11. Holding firm-specific risk constant, higher beta implies higher total stock volatililty. Therefore, the value of the put option will increase as beta increases.

12. Holding beta constant, the high firm-specific risk stock will have higher total volatility. The option on the stock with higher firm-specific risk will be worth more.

13. Lower. The call option will be less in the money. Both d_1 and $N(d_1)$ are lower when X is higher.

14. More. The option elasticity exceeds 1.0. In other words, the option is effectively a levered investment and the rate of return on the option will be more sensitive to interest rate swings.

15. Implied volatility has increased. If not, the call price would have fallen.

16. Implied volatility has increased. If not, the put price would have fallen.

17. The hedge ratio approaches one. As S increases, the probability of exercise approaches 1.0. $N(d_1)$ approaches 1.0.

18. The hedge ratio approaches –1.0. As S decreases, the probability of exercise approaches 1. $N(d_1) -1$ approaches –1 as $N(d_1)$ approaches 0.

19. The hedge ratio of the straddle is the sum of the hedge ratios of the individual options: .4 + (–0.6) = –0.2.

20. a. The delta of the collar is calculated as follows:

	Delta
Stock	1.0
Call written	$- N(d_1) = -.35$
Put purchased	$N(d_1) - 1 = -.40$
Total	.25

If the stock price increases by $1, the value of your position will increase by $.25. The stock will be worth $1 more, the loss on the purchased put will be $.40, and the call written will represent a *liability* that increases by $.35.

b. If S becomes very large, then the delta of the collar approaches zero. Both $N(d_1)$ terms approach 1. Intuitively, for very large stock prices, the value of the portfolio is simply the (present value of the) exercise price of the call, and is unaffected by small changes in the stock price. As S approaches zero, the delta also approaches zero: both $N(d_1)$ terms approach 0. For very small stock prices, the value of the portfolio is simply the (present value of the) exercise price of the put, and is unaffected by small changes in the stock price.

21.

Put	X	Delta
A	10	−.1
B	20	−.5
C	30	−.9

22. a.   A. Calls have higher elasticity than shares. For equal dollar investments, a call's capital gain potential will be higher than that of the underlying stock.

b.   B. Calls have hedge ratios less than 1.0, so the shares have higher profit potential. For an equal number of shares controlled, the dollar exposure of the shares is greater than that of the calls, and the profit potential is therefore higher.

23. S = 100; current value of portfolio
X = 100; floor promised to clients (0% return)
σ = .25; volatility
r = .05; risk-free rate
T = 4 years; horizon of program

a.   Using the Black-Scholes formula, we find that

d_1 = .65, $N(d_1)$ = .7422, d_2 = .15, $N(d_2)$ = .5596, and

put value = 10.27. Therefore, total funds to be managed are $110.27 million: $100 million of portfolio value plus the $10.27 million fee for the insurance program.

The put delta is $N(d_1) - 1 = .7422 - 1 = -.2578$. Therefore, sell off 25.78% of the equity portfolio, placing the remaining funds in bills. The amount of the portfolio in in equity is therefore $74.22 million, while the amount in bills is $110.27 − $74.22 = $36.05 million.

b.   At the new portfolio value, the put delta becomes −.2779, meaning that you must reduce the delta of the portfolio by .2779 − .2578 = .0201. You should sell an additional 2.01% of the original equity position and use the proceeds to buy bills. Since the stock price is now at only 97% of its original value, you need to sell $97 million × .0201 = $1.950 million worth of stock.

24. a.

Stock Price	Put Payoff
110	0
90	10

The hedge ratio is −0.5. A portfolio comprised of one share and two puts would provide a guaranteed payoff of $110, with present value $110/1.05 = $104.76. Therefore,

$S + 2P = 104.76$
$100 + 2P = 104.76$
$P = \$2.38$

b. The protective put strategy = 1 share + 1 put = $100 + $2.38 = $102.38

c. Our goal is a portfolio with the same exposure to the stock as the hypothetical protective put portfolio. As the put's hedge ratio is –0.5, we want to hold 1 – 0.5 = 0.5 shares of stock, which costs $50, and place our remaining funds ($52.38) in bills, earning 5% interest.

Stock Price:	90	110
Half share	45	55
Bills	55	55
Total	100	110

This payoff is exactly the same as that of the protective put portfolio. Thus, the stock plus bills strategy replicates both the cost and payoff of the protective put.

25. When $r = 0$, one should never exercise a put early. There is no "time value cost" to waiting to exercise, but there is a "volatility benefit" from waiting. To show this more rigorously, consider this portfolio: lend $X and short one share of stock. The cost to establish the portfolio is $X - S_0$. The payoff at time T (with zero interest earnings on the loan) is $X - S_T$. In contrast, a put option has a payoff at time T of $X - S_T$ *if* that value is positive, and zero otherwise. The put's payoff is *at least* as large as the portfolio's, and therefore, the put must cost at least as much to purchase. Hence, $P \geq X - S_0$, and the put can be sold for more than the proceeds from immediate exercise. We conclude that it doesn't pay to exercise early.

26. a. Xe^{-rT}

   b. X

   c. 0

   d. 0

   e. It obviously is optimal to exercise immediately a put on a stock that has fallen to zero. The value of the American put equals the exercise price. Any delay in exercise lowers value by the time value of money.

27. Step 1: Calculate the option values at expiration. The two possible stock prices are $120 and $80. Therefore, the corresponding two possible call values are $20 and $0.

   Step 2: Find that the hedge ratio is $(20 - 0)/(120 - 80) = .5$. Therefore, form a riskless portfolio by buying one share of stock and writing two calls. The cost of the portfolio is $S - 2C = 100 - 2C$.

   Step 3: Show that the payoff of the riskless portfolio must equal $80. Therefore, find the value of the call by solving

   $100 - 2C = $80/1.10$
   C = 13.636

Notice that we never used the probabilities of a stock price increase or decrease. These are not needed to value the call option.

28. The hedge ratio is $(30-0)/(130-70) = .5$. Form the riskless portfolio by buying one share of stock and writing two call options. The portfolio costs $S - 2C = 100 - 2C$. The payoff of the riskless portfolio is $70. Therefore, $100 - 2C = 70/1.10$, which implies that $C = \$18.182$, which is greater than the value in the lower-volatility scenario.

29. The hedge ratio for a put with $X = 100$ would be $(0 - 20)/(120 - 80) = -.5$. Form the riskless portfolio by buying one share of stock and buying two put options. The portfolio costs $S + 2P = 100 + 2P$. The payoff of the riskless portfolio is $120. Therefore, $100 + 2P = 120/1.10$, which implies that $P = \$4.545$. According to put-call parity, $P + S = C + PV(X)$. Our estimates of option value satisfy this relationship: $4.545 + 100 = 13.636 + 100/1.10$.

30. If one assumes that the only possible exercise date is just prior to the ex-dividend date, the relevant parameters for the Black-Scholes formula are:

$S_0 = 60$ $r = .5\%$ per month
$X = 55$ $\sigma = 7\%$
$T = 2$ months

In this case, $C = \$6.04$.

If instead, one precommits to foregoing early exercise, one must reduce the stock price by the present value of the dividends. Therefore, we use

$S_0 = 60 - 2e^{-(.005 \times 2)} = 58.02$ $r = .5\%$ per month
$X = 55$ $\sigma = 7\%$
$T = 3$ months

In this case, $C = \$5.05$. The pseudo-American option value is the higher of these two values, $6.04.

31. True. The call option has an elasticity greater than 1.0. Therefore, the call's percentage returns are greater than those of the underlying stock. Hence the GM calls will respond more than proportionately when the GM stock price changes along with broad market movements. Therefore, the beta of the GM calls is greater than the beta of GM stock.

32. True. The elasticity of a call option is higher the more out of the money is the option. (Even though the delta of the call is lower, the value of the call is also lower. The *proportional* response of the call price to the stock price increases. You can confirm this with numerical examples.) Therefore, the rate of return of the call with the higher exercise price will respond more sensitively to changes in the market index. It will have the higher beta.

33. As the stock price increases, conversion becomes ever-more assured. The hedge ratio approaches 1.0. The convertible bond price will move one-for-one with changes in the price of the underlying stock.

CHAPTER 22: FUTURES MARKETS

1. a. The closing price for the spot index was 957.94. The dollar value of stocks is thus $250 × 957.94 = \$239,485$. The closing futures price for the March contract was 963.30, which has a dollar value of $963.30 × \$250 = \$240,825$ and therefore requires a margin of \$24,082.50.

    b. The futures price increases by $970 - 963.30 = 6.70$. The credit to your margin account would be $6.70 × \$250 = \$1,675$, which is a percent gain of $\$1,675/\$24,082.50 = .0696 = 6.96\%$. Note that the futures price itself increased by only $.696\%$.

    c. Following the reasoning in part (b), any change in F is magnified by a ratio of 1/(margin requirement). This is the leverage effect. The return will be -10%.

2. There is little hedging or speculative demand for cement futures, since cement prices are fairly stable and predictable. The trading activity necessary to support the futures market would not materialize.

3. The ability to buy on margin is one advantage of futures. Another is the ease of altering one's holdings of the asset. This is especially important if one is dealing in commodities, for which the futures market is far more liquid than the spot market.

4. Short selling results in an immediate cash inflow, whereas the short futures position does not:

Action	Initial CF	Final CF
Short Sale	$+P_0$	$-P_T$
Short Futures	0	$F_0 - P_T$

5. a. False. For any given level of the stock index, the futures price will be lower when the dividend yield is higher. This follows from spot-futures parity :
    $F_0 = S_0(1 + r - d)^T$.

    b. False. The parity relationship tells us that the futures price is determined by the stock price, the interest rate, and the dividend yield; it is *not* a function of beta.

    c. True. The short futures position will profit when the market falls. This is a negative beta position.

6. a. $F = S_0(1 + r) = 150 × (1.06) = 159$
    b. $F = S_0(1 + r)^3 = 150 × (1.06)^3 = 178.65$
    c. $F = 150 × (1.08)^3 = 188.96$

7. As S increases, so will F. You should buy the futures. A long position in futures is better than buying the stock since you get the advantage of buying on margin.

8. a. Take a short position in T-bond futures, to offset interest rate risk. If rates increase, the loss on the bond will be offset to some extent by gains on the futures.

   b. Again, a short position in T-bond futures will offset the interest rate risk.

   c. You wish to protect your cash outlay when the bond is purchased. If bond prices increase, you will need extra cash to purchase the bond. Thus, you want to take a long futures position that will generate a profit if prices increase.

9. $F = S_0(1 + r - d) = 950(1 + .06 - .02) = 988$

10. The put-call parity relation states that
$$P = C - S + X/(1 + r)^T$$
If $F = X$, then $P = C - S + F/(1 + r)^T$
But spot-futures parity tells us that $F = S(1 + r)^T$. Substituting, we find that
$$P = C - S + [S(1 + r)^T]/(1 + r)^T = C - S + S, \text{ which implies that } P = C.$$

11. According to the parity relation, the proper price for December futures is:

$$F_{Dec} = F_{June}(1 + r)^{1/2} = 346.30 \times (1.05)^{1/2} = 354.85.$$

The actual futures price for December is too high relative to the June price. You should short the December contract and take a long position in the June contract.

12. a. $120 \times (1.06) = 127.20$
    b. The stock price falls to $120 \times (1 - .03) = 116.40$
       The futures price falls to $116.4 \times (1.06) = 123.384$
       The investor loses $(127.20 - 123.384) \times 1000 = \$3816$
    c. The percentage loss is $3,816/12,000 = .318 = 31.8\%$

13. a. The initial futures price is $F_0 = 950 \times (1 + .005 - .002)^{12} = 984.77$
       In one month, the futures price will be $F_0 = 960 \times (1 + .005 - .002)^{11} = 992.16$
       The increase in the futures price is 7.39, so the cash flow will be $7.39 \times \$250 = \$1,847.50$
    b. The holding period return is $\$1847.50/\$15,000 = .123 = 12.3\%$

14. a. The call option is distinguished by its asymmetric payoff. If the Swiss franc rises in value, the firm can buy francs for a given number of dollars to service its debt, and thereby put a cap on the dollar cost of its financing. If the franc falls, the firm will benefit from the change in the exchange rate.

   The futures and forward contracts have symmetric payoffs. The dollar cost of the financing is locked in regardless of whether the franc appreciates or depreciates. The major difference from the firm's perspective in futures vs. forwards is in the mark-to-market feature of futures, which means that the firm must be ready for the cash management issues surrounding cash inflows or outflows as the currency values and futures prices fluctuate.

   b. The call option gives the firm the ability to benefit from depreciation in the franc, but at a cost equal to the option premium. Unless the firm has some special expertise in currency speculation, it seems that the futures or forward strategy, which locks in a dollar cost of financing without an option premium may be the better strategy.

15. The treasurer would like to buy the bonds today, but cannot. As a proxy for this purchase, T-bond futures contracts can be purchased. If rates do in fact fall, the treasurer will have to buy back the bonds for the sinking fund at prices higher than the prices at which they could be purchased today. However, the gains on the futures contracts will offset this higher cost to some extent.

16. The important distinction between a futures contract and an options contract is that the futures contract is an obligation. When an investor purchases or sells a futures contract, the investor has an obligation to accept or deliver, respectively, the underlying commodity on the expiration date. In contrast, the buyer of an option contract is not obligated to accept or deliver the underlying commodity but instead has the right, or choice, to accept delivery (for call holders) or make delivery (for put holders) of the underlying commodity anytime during the life of the contract.

   Futures and options modify a portfolio's risk in different ways. Buying or selling a futures contract affects a portfolio's upside risk and downside risk by a similar magnitude. This is commonly referred to as symmetrical impact. On the other hand, the addition of a call or put option to a portfolio does not affect a portfolio's upside risk and downside risk to a similar magnitude. Unlike futures contracts, the impact of options on the risk profile of a portfolio is asymmetrical.

17. The parity value of F is $950 \times (1 + .05 - .02) = 978.50$. The actual futures price is 980, too high by 1.50.

Arbitrage Portfolio	CF now	CF in 1 year
Buy index	-950	$S_T + (.02 \times 950)$
Short futures	0	$980 - S_T$
Borrow	950	-950×1.05
Total	0	1.50

18. a. The current yield on the bonds (coupon divided by price) plays the role of the dividend yield.

    b. When the yield curve is upward sloping, the current yield will exceed the short rate. Hence, distant futures prices will be lower than near-term futures prices.

19.a.

Action	Cash Flows		
	Now	T_1	T_2
Long futures with T_1 maturity	0	$P_1 - F(T_1)$	0
Short futures with T_2 maturity	0	0	$F(T_2) - P_2$
At T_1 buy asset. Sell at T_2	0	$-P_1$	$+P_2$
At T_1, borrow $F(T_1)$	0	$F(T_1)$	$-F(T_1) \times (1+r)^{(T_2-T_1)}$
Total	0	0	$F(T_2) - F(T_1) \times (1+r)^{(T_2-T_1)}$

    b. Since the T_2 cash flow is riskless and no net investment was made, any profits would represent an arbitrage opportunity.

    c. The zero-profit no-arbitrage restriction implies that

$$F(T_2) = F(T_1) \times (1+r)^{(T_2-T_1)}$$

20. The futures price is the agreed-upon price for deferred delivery of the asset. If that price is fair, then the *value* of the agreement ought to be zero; that is, the contract will be a zero-NPV agreement for each trader.

21. Because long positions equal short positions, futures trading *must* entail a "canceling out" of bets on the asset. Moreover, no cash is exchanged at the inception of futures trading. Thus, there should be minimal impact on the spot market for the asset, and futures trading should not be expected to reduce capital available for other uses.

CHAPTER 23: FUTURES MARKETS: A CLOSER LOOK

1. a. $950 \times (1.06) - 10 = 997$

    b. $950 \times (1.03) - 10 = 968.50$

    c. The futures price is too low. Buy futures, short the index, and invest the proceeds of the short sale in T-bills.

	CF Now	CF in 6 months
Buy futures	0	$S_T - 948$
Short index	950	$-S_T - 10$
Buy bills	−950	978.50
TOTAL	0	20.50

    The arbitrage profit equals the mispricing of the contract.

2. a. The value of the underlying stock is $\$250 \times 900 = \$225,000$.
       $\$25/225,000 = .00011 = .011\%$ of the value of the stock.

    b. $40 \times .00011 = \$.0044$, less than half of one cent.

    c. $.30/.0044 = 68$. The transaction cost in the stock market is 68 times the transaction cost in the futures market.

3. a. From parity, $F_0 = 800 \times (1 + .03) - 10 = 814$. Actual F_0 is 812, so the futures price is 2 below the "proper" level.

    b. Buy the relatively cheap futures and sell the relatively expensive stock.

	CF Now	CF in 6 months
Sell shares	+800	$- (S_T + 10)$
Buy futures	0	$S_T - 812$
Lend $800	−800	$+ 824$
TOTAL	0	2

    c. If you do not receive interest on the proceeds of the short sales, then the $800 you receive will not be invested but will simply be returned to you. The proceeds from the strategy in part (b) are now negative: an arbitrage opportunity no longer exists.

	CF Now	CF in 6 months
Sell shares	+800	$- (S_T + 10)$
Buy futures	0	$S_T - 812$
Place $800 in margin account	−800	$+ 800$
TOTAL	0	−22

    d. If we call the original futures price F_0, then the proceeds from the long-futures, short-stock strategy are:

	CF Now	CF in 6 months
Sell shares	+800	$- (S_T + 10)$
Buy futures	0	$S_T - F_0$
Place $800 in margin account	−800	$+ 800$
TOTAL	0	$790 - F_0$

Therefore, F_0 can be as low as 790 without giving rise to an arbitrage opportunity. On the other hand, if F_0 is higher than the parity value, 814, an arbitrage opportunity (buy stocks, sell futures) will open up. There is no short-selling cost in this case. Therefore, the no-arbitrage band is $790 \leq F_0 \leq 814$.

4. a. Call p the fraction of proceeds from the short sale to which we have access. Ignoring transaction costs, the lower bound on the futures price that precludes arbitrage is $S_0(1 + rp) - D$, which is the usual parity value, except for the factor p. The factor p arises because only this fraction of the proceeds from the short sale can be invested in the risk-free asset. We can solve for p as follows: $900 (1 + .022p) - 10.80 = 901$, which can be rearranged to show that $p = .596$.

b. With $p = .9$, the no-arbitrage lower bound on the futures price is $900(1 + .022 \times .9) - 10.80 = 907.02$. The actual futures price is 901. The departure from the bound is therefore 6.02. This departure also equals the potential profit from an arbitrage strategy. The strategy is to short the stock, which currently sells at 900 [investor receives 90% of the proceeds, 810; the remainder, 90, remains in margin account until the short position is covered in 6 months], buy futures, and lend:

	CF Now	CF in 6 months
Buy futures	0	$S_T - 901$
Short stock	810	$90 - S_T - 10.80$
Lend	−810	$810(1.022) = 827.82$
TOTAL	0	6.02

The profit is $6.02 \times \$250$ per contract, or \$1,505.

5. a. Short. If the stock value falls, you need futures profits to offset the loss.

b. Each contract is for \$250 times the index, currently valued at 900. Therefore, each contract controls \$225,000 worth of stock, and to hedge a \$4.5 million portfolio, you need $\frac{4,500,000}{225,000} = 20$ contracts.

c. Now your stock swings only .6 as much as the market index. Hence, you need .6 as many contracts as in (b): $0.6 \times 20 = 12$ contracts.

6. a. The strategy would be to sell Japanese stock index futures to hedge the market risk of Japanese stocks, and also to sell yen futures to hedge the currency exposure.

b. Some possible practical difficulties with this strategy include:

- Contract size on futures may not match size of portfolio
- Stock portfolio may not closely track index portfolios on which futures trade
- Cash flow management issues from marking to market
- Potential mispricing of futures contracts (violations of parity)

7. The dollar is depreciating relative to the Swiss franc. To induce investors to invest in the U.S., the U.S. interest rate must be higher.

8. a. From parity, $F_0 = 1.60 \times \dfrac{1.04}{1.08} = 1.541$.

    b. Suppose that $F_0 = \$1.58/\text{pound}$. Then dollars are relatively too cheap in the forward market, or equivalently, pounds are too expensive. Therefore, you should borrow the present value of £1, use the proceeds to buy pound-denominated bills in the spot market, and sell £1 forward:

Action Now	CF in $	Action at period-end	CF in $
Sell 1 pound forward for $1.58	0	Unwind: Collect $1.58, deliver 1 pound	$1.58 − E_1
Buy £1/1.08 in spot market, and invest at the British risk-free rate	−1.60/1.08 = −$1.481	Exchange one pound for E_1	E_1
Borrow $1.481	$1.481	Repay loan; U.S. interest rate = 4%	−$1.54
Total	0	Total	$ .04

9. Borrowing in the U.S. offers 4%. Borrowing in the U.K. and covering interest rate risk with futures or forwards offers a rate of return of: $(1+r_{UK})F_0/E_0 = 1.07(1.58/1.60) = 1.0566$, or 5.66%. It appears to be advantageous to borrow in the U.S. where the rates are lower, and to lend in the U.K. An arbitrage strategy involves simultaneous lending and borrowing with the covering of any interest rate risk:

Action Now	CF in $	Action at period-end	CF in $
Lend 1 pound in U.K.	−$1.60	Be repaid, and exchange proceeds for dollars	$(1.07) E_1$
Borrow in U.S.	$1.60	Repay loan	−1.60(1.04)
Sell forward 1.07 pounds for $1.58 each.(Sell forward the proceeds from the U.K. loan.)	0	Unwind	$1.07 (1.58 − E_1)$
Total	0	Total	$.0266

10. a. The hedged investment involves converting the $1 million to foreign currency, investing in that country, and selling forward that foreign currency to lock in the dollar value of the investment. Because the interest rates are for 90-day periods, we assume they are quoted as bond equivalent yields, annualized using simple interest. Therefore, to express rates on a per quarter basis, we simply divide by 4:

	Japanese government	German government
Convert $1 million to local currency	$1,000,000 × 133.05 = ¥133,050,000	$1,000,000 × 1.5260 = DM1,526,000
Invest in local currency for 90 days	¥133,050,000 × (1 + .076/4) = ¥135,577,950	DM1,526,000 × (1 + .086/4) = DM1,558,809
Convert to $ at 90-day forward rate	135,577,950/133.47 = $1,015,793	1,558,809/1.5348 = $1,015,643

b. The results in either currency are nearly identical. This near-equality reflects the interest rate parity theorem. This theory asserts that the pricing relationships between interest rates and spot and forward exchange rates must make covered (that is, fully hedged and riskless) investments in any currency equally attractive.

c. The 90-day return in Japan was 1.5793%, which represents a bond-equivalent yield of 1.5793% × 365/90 = 6.405%. The 90-day return in Germany was 1.5643%, which represents a bond-equivalent yield of 1.5643% × 365/90 = 6.344%. The estimate for the 90-day risk-free U.S. government money market yield would be in this range.

11. Muni yields, which are below T-bond yields because of their tax-exempt status, are expected to close in on Treasury yields. Because yields and prices are inversely related, this means that muni prices will perform poorly compared to Treasuries. Therefore you should establish a spread position, buying Treasury-bond futures and selling municipal bond futures. The net bet on the general level of interest rates is approximately zero. You have simply made a bet on relative performances in the two sectors.

12. Salomon holds bonds worth $5.354 million. If the interest rate increases to 5.1% semiannually, the value of the unhedged bonds will fall to $100 million/$(1.051)^{60}$ = $5,056,349, a capital loss of $297,651. The T-bonds to be delivered on the bond contract are selling at $90.80 at the current 4.5% semiannual yield. If the yield increases to 4.6%, the price will fall to $89.115; since the face value of the contract is $100,000, the loss is $1,685 per contract. Therefore, you need 297,651/1,685 = 177 contracts held *short* to hedge.

13. $F_0 = S_0(1 + r)^T = 350 (1.10) = 385$

If F = 390, you could earn arbitrage profits as follows:

	CF Now	CF in 1 year
Buy gold	− 350	S_T
Short futures	0	390 − S_T
Borrow	350	− 385
	0	5

The forward price must be 385 in order for this arbitrage strategy to yield no profits.

14. If a bad harvest this year means a worse than average harvest in future years, then the futures prices will rise in response to this year's harvest, although presumably the two-year price will change by less than the one-year price. The same reasoning holds if corn is stored across the harvest. Next year's price is determined by the available supply at harvest time, which is the actual harvest plus the stored corn. A smaller harvest now means less stored corn for next year which can lead to higher prices.

Suppose first that corn is never stored across a harvest, and second that the quality of a harvest has nothing to do with the quality of past harvests. Under these circumstances, there is no link between the current price of corn and the expected future price of corn. The quantity of corn stored will fall to zero before the next harvest, and thus the quantity of corn and the price in a year will depend solely on the quantity of next year's harvest, which has nothing to do with this year's harvest.

15. The required rate of return on an asset with the same risk as corn is $1 + .5(1.8 - 1) = 1.4\%$ per month. Thus, in the absence of storage costs, three months from now corn would have to sell for $\$2.75 \times (1.014)^3 = \$2.867$. The future value of the 3 month's storage costs is $\$.03 \times FA(1\%, 3) = \$.091$, where FA stands for the future value factor of a level annuity with a given interest rate and number of payments. Thus, the expected price would have to be $\$2.867 + \$.091 = \$2.958$ to induce storage. Because the expected spot price is only $\$2.94$, don't store it.

16. Situation A. The market value of the portfolio to be hedged is $20 million. The market value of the bonds controlled by one futures contract is $63,330. If we were to equate the market values of the portfolio and the futures contract, we would sell $20,000,000/63,330 = 315.806$ contracts. However, we must adjust this "naive" hedge for the price volatility of the bond portfolio relative to the futures contract. Price volatilities will differ according to both the durations of the bonds and the yield volatility of the bonds. In this case, the yield volatilities may be assumed equal, because any yield spread between the Treasury portfolio and the Treasury bond underlying the futures contract is likely to be stable. However, the duration of the Treasury portfolio is lower than that of the futures contract. Adjusting the naive hedge for relative duration and relative yield volatility, we obtain the adjusted hedge position:

$$315.806 \times \frac{7.6}{8.0} \times 1.0 = 300 \text{ contracts}$$

Situation B. Here we need to hedge the purchase price of the bonds, and require a long hedge. The market value of the bonds to be purchased is $20 million $\times .93 = \$18.6$ million. The duration ratio is 7.2/8.0, and the relative yield volatility is 1.25. Therefore, the hedge requires the treasurer to go long in the following number of contracts:

$$\frac{18,600,000}{63,330} \times \frac{7.2}{8.0} \times 1.25 = 330 \text{ contracts}$$

17. If the exchange of currencies were structured as 3 separate forward contracts, the forward prices would be:

Year	Forward exchange rate × $1 million marks	= Number of dollars to be delivered
1	$.65 \times (1.05/1.08)$	$.6319 million
2	$.65 \times (1.05/1.08)^2$	$.6144 million
3	$.65 \times (1.05/1.08)^3$	$.5973 million

Instead, we deliver the same number, F*, of dollars each year. The present value of this obligation is determined as follows:

$$\frac{F^*}{1.05} + \frac{F^*}{1.05^2} + \frac{F^*}{1.05^3} = \frac{.6319}{1.05} + \frac{.6144}{1.05^2} + \frac{.5973}{1.05^3} = 1.6751$$

F* equals $.6151 million per year

18. a. The swap rate moved in favor of firm ABC. It was supposed to receive 1 percent more per year than it could receive in the current swap market. Based on notional principal of $10 million, the loss is $.01 \times \$10$ million = $100,000 per year.

    b. The market value of that fixed annual loss is obtained by discounting at the current rate on 3-year obligations, 7%. The loss is $100,000 \times$ Annuity factor(7%, 3) = $262,432.

    c. If ABC had become insolvent, XYZ would not be harmed. XYZ would be happy to see the swap agreement cancelled. However, the swap agreement ought to be treated as an asset of ABC when the firm is reorganized.

19. If one buys the cap and writes a floor, one reproduces a conventional swap, which is costless to enter. Therefore, the proceeds from writing the floor must be the same as from buying the cap, $0.30.

20. The firm receives a fixed rate that is 2% higher than the market rate. The extra payment of $.02 \times \$10$ million has present value equal to

$200,000 \times$ Annuity factor(5, 8%) = $798,542.

CHAPTER 24: PERFORMANCE EVALUATION

1. a. Arithmetic average: $\bar{r}_{ABC} = 10\%$ $\bar{r}_{XYZ} = 10\%$

   b. Dispersion: $\sigma_{ABC} = 7.07\%$, $\sigma_{XYZ} = 13.91\%$. XYZ has greater dispersion. (We used 5 degrees of freedom to calculate standard deviations.)

   c. Geometric average:

   $r_{ABC} = (1.2 \times 1.12 \times 1.14 \times 1.03 \times 1.01)^{1/5} - 1 = .0977 = 9.77\%$

   $r_{XYZ} = (1.3 \times 1.12 \times 1.18 \times 1.0 \times .90)^{1/5} - 1 = .0911 = 9.11\%$

   Despite the equal arithmetic averages, XYZ has a lower geometric average. The reason is that the greater variance of XYZ drives the geometric average further below the arithmetic average.

   d. In terms of "forward looking" statistics, the arithmetic average is the better estimate of expected return. Therefore, if the data reflect the probabilities of *future* returns, 10% is the expected return of *both* stocks.

2. a. Time-weighted average returns are based on year-by-year rates of return.

Year	Return [(capital gains + dividend)/price]
1995-1996	$[(120 - 100) + 4]/100 = 24.00\%$
1996-1997	$[(90 - 120) + 4]/120 = -21.67\%$
1997-1998	$[(100 - 90) + 4]/90 = 15.56\%$

   Arithmetic mean: $(24 - 21.67 + 15.56)/3 = 5.96\%$

   Geometric mean: $(1.24 \times .7833 \times 1.1556)^{1/3} - 1 = .0392 = 3.92\%$

   b.

Date	Cash flow	Explanation
1/1/95	−300	Purchase of three shares at $100 each.
1/1/96	−228	Purchase of two shares at $120 less dividend income on three shares held.
1/1/97	110	Dividends on five shares plus sale of one share at $90.
1/1/98	416	Dividends on four shares plus sale of four shares at $100 each.

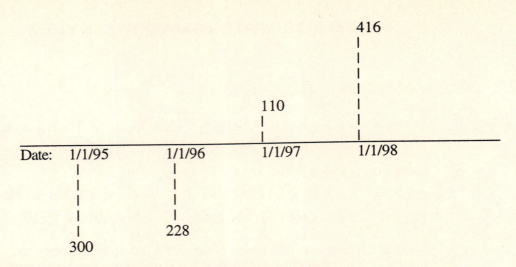

Date: 1/1/95   1/1/96   1/1/97   1/1/98

416

110

300

228

Dollar-weighted return = Internal rate of return = –.1607%.

3.

Time	Cash flow ($)	Holding period return
0	3(–90) = –270	
1	100	(100–90)/90 = 11.11%
2	100	0
3	100	0

a.   Time-weighted geometric average rate of return = $(1.1111 \times 1.0 \times 1.0)^{1/3} - 1 =$ .0357 = 3.57%

b.   Time-weighted arithmetic average rate of return = (11.11 + 0 + 0)/3 = 3.70%. The arithmetic average is always greater than or equal to the geometric average; the greater the dispersion, the greater the difference.

c.   Dollar-weighted average rate of return = IRR = 5.46%. [You can find this using a financial calculator by setting n = 3, PV = (–)270, FV = 0, PMT = 100, and solving for the interest rate.] The IRR exceeds the other averages because the investment fund was the largest when the highest return occurred.

4.   a.

	E(r)	σ	β
Portfolio A	12	12	.7
Portfolio B	16	31	1.4
Market index	13	18	1.0
Risk-free asset	5	0	0.0

The alphas for the two portfolios are:

$\alpha_A = 12 - [5 + 0.7(13 - 5)] = 1.4\%$

$\alpha_B = 16 - [5 + 1.4(13 - 5)] = -0.2\%$

Ideally, you would want to take a long position in A and a short position in B.

b. If you will hold only one of the two portfolios, then the Sharpe measure is the appropriate criterion:

$$S_A = \frac{12 - 5}{12} = .583$$

$$S_B = \frac{16 - 5}{31} = .355$$

Portfolio A is preferred using the Sharpe criterion.

5. a.

		Stock A	Stock B
(i)	Alpha is the intercept of the regression	1%	2%
(ii)	Appraisal ratio $= \alpha/\sigma(e)$	.0971	.1047
(iii)	Sharpe measure* $= (r_p - r_f)/\sigma$	.4907	.3373
(iv)	Treynor measure** $= (r_p - r_f)/\beta$	8.833	10.5

* To compute the Sharpe measure, note that for each stock, $r_p - r_f$ can be computed from the right-hand side of the regression equation, using the assumed parameters $r_M = 14\%$ and $r_f = 6\%$. The standard deviation of each stock's returns is given in the problem.

** The beta to use for the Treynor measure is the slope coefficient of the regression equation presented in the problem.

b. (i) If this is the only risky asset, then Sharpe's measure is the one to use. A's is higher, so it is preferred.

(ii) If the stock is mixed with the index fund, the contribution to the *overall* Sharpe measure is determined by the appraisal ratio; therefore, B is preferred.

(iii) If it is one of many stocks, then Treynor's measure counts, and B is preferred.

6. We need to distinguish between market timing and security selection abilities. The intercept of the scatter diagram is a measure of stock selection ability. If the manager tends to have a positive excess return even when the market's performance is merely "neutral" (i.e., has zero excess return) then we conclude that the manager has on average made good stock picks. Stock selection must be the source of the positive excess returns.

Timing ability is indicated by the curvature of the plotted line. Lines that become steeper as you move to the right of the graph show good timing ability. The steeper slope shows that the manager maintained higher portfolio sensitivity to market swings (i.e., a higher beta) in periods when the market performed well. This ability to choose more market-sensitive securities in anticipation of market upturns is the essence of good timing. In contrast, a declining slope as you move to the right means that the portfolio was more sensitive to the market when the market did poorly and less sensitive when the market did well. This indicates poor timing.

We can therefore classify performance for the four managers as follows:

	Selection Ability	Timing Ability
A.	Bad	Good
B.	Good	Good
C.	Good	Bad
D.	Bad	Bad

7. a.

Bogey:	$.60 \times 2.5\% + .30 \times 1.2\% + .10 \times 0.5\%$	$= 1.91\%$
Actual:	$.70 \times 2.0\% + .20 \times 1.0\% + .10 \times 0.5\%$	$= \underline{1.65\%}$
*Under*performance:		.26%

b. *Security Selection*

Market	(1) Differential return within market (Manager – index)	(2) Manager's portfolio weight	(3) = (1) × (2) Contribution to performance
Equity	−0.5%	.70	−0.35%
Bonds	−0.2%	.20	−0.04
Cash	0.0	.10	0.
Contribution of security selection			−0.39%

c. *Asset Allocation*

Market	(1) Excess weight: Manager – benchmark	(2) Index return	(3) = (1) × (2) Contribution to performance
Equity	.10	2.5%	.25%
Bonds	−.10	1.2	−.12
Cash	0	0.5	.0
Contribution of asset allocation			.13%

Summary

Security selection	− .39%
Asset allocation	.13%
Excess performance	− .26%

8. a. Total value added

Manager return	$= .30 \times 20 + .10 \times 15 + .40 \times 10 + .20 \times 5$	$= 12.50\%$
Benchmark (bogey)	$= .15 \times 12 + .30 \times 15 + .45 \times 14 + .10 \times 12$	$= \underline{13.80}$
Added value	$=$	− 1.30%

b. Added value from country allocation

Country	(1) Excess weight: Manager – benchmark	(2) Index return minus bogey	(3) = (1) × (2) Contribution to performance
UK	.15	−1.8%	−.27%
Japan	−.20	1.2	−.24
U.S.	−.05	0.2	−.01
Germany	.10	−1.8	−.18
Contribution of country allocation			−.70%

c. Added value from stock selection

Market	(1) Differential return within country (Manager – index)	(2) Manager's country weight	(3) = (1) × (2) Contribution to performance
UK	8%	.30	2.4%
Japan	0	.10	0.
U.S.	− 4	.40	−1.6
Germany	− 7	.20	−1.4
Contribution of stock selection			−0.6%

9. *Support*: A manager could be a better performer in one type of circumstance. For example, a manager who does no timing, but simply maintains a high beta, will do better in up markets and worse in down markets. Therefore, we should observe performance over an entire cycle. Also, to the extent that observing a manager over an entire cycle increases the number of observations, it would improve the reliability of the measurement.

Contradict: If we adequately control for exposure to the market (i.e., adust for beta), then market performance should not affect the relative performance of individual managers. It is therefore not necessary to wait for an entire market cycle to pass before you evaluate a manager.

10. It does, to some degree, if those manager groups can be made sufficiently homogeneous with respect to style.

11. a. The manager's alpha is $10 - [6 + .5(14 - 6)] = 0$

b. From Black-Jensen-Scholes and others, we know that, on average, portfolios with low beta have had positive alphas. (The slope of the empirical security market line is shallower than predicted by the CAPM -- see Chapter 13.) Therefore, given the manager's low beta, performance could be sub-par despite the estimated alpha of zero.

12. a. The following briefly describes one strength and one weakness of each manager.

1. **Manager A**

Strength. Although Manager A's one-year total return was slightly below the international index return (–6.0 percent versus –5.0 percent, respectively), this manager apparently has some country/security return expertise. This large local market return advantage of 2.0 percent exceeds the 0.2 percent return for the international index.

Weakness. Manager A has an obvious weakness in the currency management area. This manager experienced a marked currency return shortfall, with a return of –8.0 percent versus –5.2 percent for the index.

2. **Manager B**

Strength. Manager B's total return exceeded that of the index, with a marked positive increment apparent in the currency return. Manager B had a –1.0 percent currency return versus a –5.2 percent currency return on the international index. Based on this outcome, Manager B's strength appears to be some expertise in the currency selection area.

Weakness. Manager B had a marked shortfall in local market return. Therefore, Manager B appears to be weak in security/market selection ability.

b. The following strategies would enable the fund to take advantage of the strengths of the two managers and simultaneously minimize their weaknesses.

1. **Recommendation:** One strategy would be to direct Manager A to make no currency bets relative to the international index and to direct Manager B to make only currency decisions, and no active country or security selection bets.

Justification: This strategy would mitigate Manager A's weakness by hedging all currency exposures into index-like weights. This would allow capture of Manager A's country and stock selection skills while avoiding losses from poor currency management. This strategy would also mitigate Manager B's weakness, leaving an index-like portfolio construct and capitalizing on the apparent skill in currency management.

2. **Recommendation:** Another strategy would be to combine the portfolios of Manager A and Manager B, with Manager A making country exposure and security selection decisions and Manager B managing the currency exposures created by Manager A's decisions (providing a "currency overlay").

Justification: This recommendation would capture the strengths of both Manager A and Manager B and would minimize their collective weaknesses.

13. a.   Indeed, the one year results were terrible, but one year is a poor statistical base on which to draw inferences. Moreover, this fund was told to adopt a long-term horizon. The Board specifically instructed the investment manager to give priority to long term results.

    b.   The sample of pension funds had a much larger share in equities than did Alpine. Equities performed much better than bonds. Yet Alpine was told to hold down risk, investing at most 25% of its assets in common stocks. (Alpine's beta was also somewhat defensive). Alpine should not be held responsible for an asset allocation policy dictated by the client.

    c.   Alpine's alpha measures its risk-adjusted performance compared to the market's.

$$\alpha = 13.3 - [7.5 + .9(13.8 - 7.5)] = .13\%, \text{ actually above zero.}$$

    d.   Note that the last 5 years, particularly the last one, have been bad for bonds, the asset class that Alpine had been encouraged to hold. Within this asset class, however, Alpine did much better than the index fund (bottom two lines). Moreover, despite the fact that the bond index underperformed both the actuarial return and T-bills, Alpine outperformed both. Alpine's performance *within* each asset class has been superior on a risk-adjusted basis. Its overall disappointing returns were due to a heavy asset allocation weighting towards bonds, which was the Board's — not Alpine's — choice.

    e.   A trustee may not care about the time-weighted return, but that return is more indicative of the manager's performance. After all, the manager has no control over the cash inflow of the fund.

14.   Method I does nothing to separate the effects of market timing versus security selection decisions. It also uses a very questionable "neutral position," the composition of the portfolio at the beginning of the year.

    Method II is not perfect, but is the best of the three techniques. It at least tries to focus on market timing by examining the returns on portfolios constructed from bond market *indexes* using actual weights in various indexes versus year-average weights. The problem with the method is that the year-average weights need not correspond to a client's "neutral" weights. For example, what if the manager were optimistic over the whole year regarding long-term bonds? Her average weighting could reflect her optimism, and not a neutral position.

    Method III uses net purchases of bonds as a signal of bond manager optimism. But such net purchases can be due to withdrawals or contributions to the fund rather than the manager's decisions. (Note that this is an open-ended mutual fund.) Therefore, it is inappropriate to evaluate the manager based on whether net purchases turn out to be reliable bullish or bearish signals.

15. a.   Treynor $= (17 - 8)/1.1 = 8.2$

16. d.   Sharpe $= (24 - 8)/18 = .888$

17. a. <u>Treynor measures</u>

Market: $(12 - 6)/1 = 6$
Porfolio X: $(10 - 6)/.6 = 6.67$

<u>Sharpe measures</u>

Market: $(12 - 6)/13 = .462$
Porfolio X: $(10 - 6)/18 = .222$

Portfolio X outperforms the market based on the Treynor measure, but underperforms based on the Sharpe measure.

b. The two measures of performance are in conflict because they use different measures of risk. Portfolio X has less systematic risk than the market based on its lower beta, but more total risk (volatility) based on its higher standard deviation. Therefore, the portfolio outperforms the market based on the Treynor measure but underperforms based on the Sharpe measure.

18. b.

19. b.

20. c.

21. a.

22. c.

23. b.

24. b.

25. d.

26. a. ii.
    b. i.

27. a. [Dollar-weighted return = 11.7%; time-weighted return = 12.5%]

28. b.

29. a.

30. a.

CHAPTER 25: INTERNATIONAL DIVERSIFICATION

1. d.

2. a.

3. c.

4. a.   10,000/2 = 5,000 pounds

   5,000/40 = 125 shares

   b. To fill in the table, we use the relation:

   $$1 + r_{US} = (1 + r_{UK}) E_1/E_0$$

Price per Share (Pounds)	Pound-Denominated Return (%)	Dollar-Denominated Return (%) For Year-End Exchange Rate		
		1.80	2.00	2.20
35	−12.5	−21.25	−12.5	−3.75
40	0	−10.00	0	10.00
45	12.5	1.25	12.5	23.75

   c. The dollar-denominated return equals the pound-denominated return in the scenario that the exchange rate remains unchanged over the year.

5. The standard deviation of the pound-denominated return (using 3 degrees of freedom) is 10.21%. The dollar-denominated return has a standard deviation of 13.10% (using 9 degrees of freedom), greater than the pound standard deviation. This is due to the addition of exchange rate risk.

6. First we calculate the dollar value of the 125 shares of stock in each scenario. Then we will add the profits from the forward contract in each scenario.

| | Dollar Value of Stock at given exchange rate | | |
Exchange Rate:	1.80	2.00	2.20
Share Price in Pounds			
35	7,875	8,750	9,625
40	9,000	10,000	11,000
45	10,125	11,250	12,375
Profits on Forward Exchange:	1,500	500	-500
$[= 5000(2.10 - E_1)]$			

| | Total Dollar Proceeds at given exchange rate | | |
Exchange Rate:	1.80	2.00	2.20
Share Price in Pounds			
35	9,375	9,250	9,125
40	10,500	10,500	10,500
45	11,625	11,750	11,875

Finally, calculate the dollar-denominated rate of return, recalling that the initial investment was $10,000.

| | Rate of return (%) for given exchange rate | | |
Exchange Rate:	1.80	2.00	2.20
Share Price in Pounds			
35	−6.25	−7.50	−8.75
40	5.00	5.00	5.00
45	16.25	17.50	18.75

b. The standard deviation is now 10.24%. This is lower than the unhedged dollar-denominated standard deviation.

7. Currency Selection

EAFE: $[.30 \times (−10\%)] + (.10 \times 0) + (.60 \times 10\%) = 3\%$

Manager: $[.35 \times (−10\%)] + (.15 \times 0) + (.50 \times 10\%) = 1.5\%$

Loss of 1.5% relative to EAFE.

Country Selection

EAFE: $(.30 \times 20) + (.10 \times 15) + (.60 \times 25) = 22.5\%$

Manager: $(.35 \times 20) + (.15 \times 15) + (.50 \times 25) = 21.75\%$

Loss of 0.75% relative to EAFE

Stock Selection

$(18 − 20) \times .35 + (20 − 15) \times .15 + (20 − 25) \times .50 = − 2.45\%$

Loss of 2.45% relative to EAFE.

8. $1 + r_{US} = (1 + r_{UK})F/E_0 = 1.08 \times 1.85/1.75 = 1.1417$, implying $r_{US} = 14.17\%$.

9. You can now purchase $10,000/1.75 = 5,714.29$ pounds, which will grow with 8% interest to 6,171.43 pounds. Therefore, to lock in your return, you need to sell forward 6,171.43 pounds at the forward exchange rate.

10. a. The primary rationale is the opportunity for diversification. Factors that contribute to low correlations of stock returns across national boundaries are:

    i.   imperfect correlation of business cycles
    ii. imperfect correlation of interest rates
    iii. imperfect correlation of inflation rates
    iv. exchange rate volatility

    b. Obstacles to international investing are:

    i. <u>Availability of information</u>, including insufficient data on which to base investment decisions. Interpreting and evaluating data that are different in form and/or content than the routinely available and widely understood U.S. data is difficult. Much foreign data also are reported with a considerable lag.

    ii. <u>Liquidity</u>, in terms of the ability to buy or sell, in size and in a timely manner, without affecting the market price. Most foreign stock exchanges offer (relative to U.S. norms) limited trading and involve greater price volatility. Moreover, only a (relatively) small number of individual foreign stocks enjoy liquidity comparable to that of U.S. stocks, although this situation is improving steadily.

    iii. <u>Transaction costs</u>, particularly when viewed as a combination of commission plus spread plus market impact costs, are well above U.S. levels in most foreign markets. This, of course, adversely affects realized returns.

    iv. <u>Political risk</u>.

    v. <u>Foreign currency risk</u>, although this can be hedged to a great extent.

    c. The asset-class performance data for this particular period reveal that non-U.S. dollar bonds provided a small incremental return advantage over U.S. dollar bonds, but at a considerably higher level of risk. Both categories of fixed income assets outperformed the S&P 500 Index measure of U.S. equity results in both risk and return terms, certainly an unexpected outcome (with its roots in the disastrous 1973-74 results for U.S. equities). Within the equity area, non-U.S. stocks, as represented by the EAFE Index, outperformed U.S. stocks by a considerable margin at only slightly more risk. In contrast to U.S. equities, this asset category performed as it should relative to fixed income assets, providing more return for the higher risk involved.

    Concerning the Account Performance Index, its position on the graph reveals an aggregate outcome that is superior to the sum of its component parts. To some extent, this is due to the beneficial effect on performance available from multi-market diversification and the differential covariances involved. In this case, the portfolio manager(s) (apparently) achieved a positive alpha, adding to total portfolio return by their actions. The inclusion of international (i.e., non-U.S.) securities in a portfolio that would otherwise have held only domestic (U.S.) securities clearly worked to the advantage of this fund over this time period.

11. The return on the German bond is the sum of the coupon income + the gain or loss from the premium or discount in the forward rate relative to the spot exchange rate + any capital gain or loss on the bond. Over the six-month period, the return is:

Coupon   + forward premium/discount   + capital gain

$$= \frac{7.50\%}{2} \qquad + \qquad (-.75\%) \qquad\qquad + \text{ Price change in \%}$$

$$= 3.00\% + \% \text{ capital gain}$$

The expected semi-annual return on the U.S. bond is 3.25%. There is no expected capital gain or loss on the U.S. bond, since it is selling at par and its yield is expected to remain unchanged.

Therefore, to provide an equal return, the German bond must provide a capital gain of .25% (i.e., 1/4 point relative to par value of 100) over and above any expected capital gain on the U.S. bond.

12. a. We exchange $1 million for foreign currency at the current exchange rate and sell forward the amount of foreign currency we will accumulate 90 days from now. For the yen investment, we initially receive 1 million/.0119 = 84.034 million yen, invest it for 90 days to accumulate 84.034 × (1 + .0252/4) = 84.563 million yen (since the money market interest rates are quoted as annual percentage rates). If we sell this number of yen forward at the forward exchange rate of .0120 yen per dollar, we will end up with 84.563 million × .0120 = $1.0148 million, for a 90-day dollar interest rate of 1.48%.

   Similarly, the dollar proceeds from the 90-day Canadian dollar investment will be

   [$1 million / .7284] × [1 + (.0674/4)] × .7269 = $1.0148 million

   which results in a 90-day dollar interest rate of 1.48%, the same as that in the yen investment.

   b. The dollar-hedged rate of return on default-free government securities in both Japan and Canada is 1.48%. Therefore, the 90-day interest rate available on U.S. government securities also must be 1.48%. This corresponds to an APR of 5.92%, which is greater than the APR in Japan, and less than the APR in Canada. This result makes sense, as the relationship between forward and spot exchange rates indicates that the U.S. dollar is expected to depreciate against the yen and appreciate against the Canadian dollar.

13. a. The market value of equity of each firm increases by $10 million. Outstanding equity of the two firms is now $220 million.

   b. The value of the equity held by the noncorporate sector remains at $200 million. $20 million is held in the corporate sector.

   c. Firm A balance sheet before the issue and purchase is

Assets		Liabilities and net worth	
Plant, equipment, etc.	$100 million	Stockholders' equity	$100 million

   After the issue of stock and purchase of shares of firm B, the balance sheet is

Assets		Liabilities and net worth	
Plant, equipment, etc.	$100 million	Stockholders' equity	$110 million
Shares in firm B	10 million		

   The results for firm B are identical.

   d. The weights in both firms would increase since the S&P 500 is a value-weighted index and the market capitalization of each firm is now higher.

14. a. The following arguments could be made in favor of active management:

   Economic diversity: the diversity of the Otunian economy across various sectors may offer the opportunity for the active investor to employ "top down," sector timing strategies.

   High transaction costs: very high transaction costs may discourage trading activity by international investors and lead to inefficiencies which may be exploited successfully by active investors.

   Good financial disclosure and detailed accounting standards: good financial disclosure and detailed accounting standards may provide the well-trained analyst an opportunity to perform fundamental research analysis to identify inefficiently priced securities.

   Capital restrictions: restrictions on capital flows may discourage foreign investor participation and serve to segment the Otunian market, thus creating exploitable market inefficiencies for the active investor.

   Developing economy and securities market: developing economies and markets are often characterized by inefficiently priced securities and by rapid economic change and growth; these characteristics may be exploited by the active investor.

   Settlement problems: long delays in settling trades by non-residents may serve to discourage international investors, leading to inefficiently priced securities which may be exploited by active management.

The following arguments could be made in favor of indexing:

Economic diversity: economic diversity across a broad sector of industries implies that indexing may provide a diverse representative portfolio which is not subject to the risks associated with concentrated sectors.

High transaction costs: indexing would be favored by the implied lower levels of trading activity and thus costs.

Settlement problems: indexing would be favored by the implied lower levels of trading activity and thus settlement requirements.

Financial disclosure and accounting standards: wide public availability of reliable financial information presumably leads to greater market efficiency, reducing the value of both fundamental analysis and active management and favoring indexing.

Restrictions of capital flows: indexing would be favored by the implied lower levels of trading activity and thus smaller opportunity for regulatory interference.

b. A recommendation for active management would focus on short-term inefficiencies in, and long term prospects for, the developing Otunian markets and economy, inefficiencies and prospects which would not be easily found in more developed markets.

A recommendation for indexing would focus on the factors of economic diversity, high transaction costs, settlement delays, capital flow restrictions, and lower management fees.

CHAPTER 26: THE PROCESS OF PORTFOLIO MANAGEMENT

1. a. An appropriate investment policy statement for the endowment fund will be organized around the following major, specific aspects of the situation:
    1. The primacy of the current income requirement;
    2. The inability to accept significant risk as to 85% of the original capital;
    3. The 10-year time horizon present within the fund's infinite life span;
    4. The unique and dominating circumstance represented by the June 30, 1998, capital payout requirement; and
    5. The requirements of the "spending rule".

    VIZ:

    "The endowment fund's investment assets shall be managed in a Prudent Man context to provide a total return of at least 8% per year, including an original $500,000 (5%) current income component growing at 3% annually. Meeting this current income goal is the primary return objective. Inasmuch as $8,500,000 of capital must be distributed in cash on June 30, 1998, no significant risk can be taken on whatever sum is required to guarantee this payout; a normal risk capacity shall be assumed with respect to remaining investment assets. The fund's horizon is very long term as to assets not required for the 1998 distribution. The Investment Committee's 'spending rule' shall be taken into account in determining investment strategy and annual income distributions."

    b. The account circumstances will affect the initial asset allocation in the following major ways:
    1. The aggregate portfolio will have much larger than normal holdings of U.S. Treasury and Treasury-related securities. Maximum use of discount Treasuries and related zero-coupon securities will be made to minimize the risk and the amount of total assets that must be "frozen" in order to assure the availability of $8,500,000 on June 30, 1998.
    2. The aggregate portfolio will have much smaller than normal holdings of equity securities, given the need to "lock up" the 1998 distribution requirement in virtually riskless form. The initial mix here might well be 15% zeros, 55% discount Treasuries, and only 30% equities; in a normal situation, 60-70% in equities would not be uncommon.
    3. The equity portfolio will emphasize a growth orientation. Excess income over the current income requirement will be added to equity. Not only must building of future value and income come from the rather small equity component of the portfolio, but it must also serve an inflation protection need as well. Since it does not appear that meeting the annual current income target will be difficult initially, there is plenty of room for lower-yielding issues to be included in the equity mix.
    4. The aggregate portfolio risk level will be well below average. The 1998 payout requirement dictates a zero risk posture on a large part of the total,

while the Prudent Man environment will act to prevent overzealous risk-taking in the "remainder" portion.

5.   The fund's tax exempt status maximizes allocation flexibility, both as to income aspects and as to planning for future capital growth.

6.   A 10-year horizon must be accommodated as to a major portion of total capital funds, while a very long term horizon applies to the rest.

2.   a. Liquidity

3.   b. Employees

4.   b. Organizing the management process itself.

5.   d.   high income bond fund

6.   a.   An approach to asset allocation that GSS could use is the one detailed in the chapter. It consists of the following steps:

1.   Specification of the asset classes to be included in the portfolio. The major classes usually considered are:
- Money market instruments (usually called cash)
- Fixed income securities (usually called bonds)
- Stocks
- Real estate
- Precious metals
- Other

2.   Specify capital market expectations. This step consists of using both historical data and economic analysis to determine your expectations of future rates of return over the relevant holding period on the assets to be considered for inclusion in the portfolio.

3.   Derive the efficient portfolio frontier. This step consists of finding portfolios that achieve the maximum expected return for any given degree of risk.

4.   Find the optimal asset mix. This step consists of selecting the efficient portfolio that best meets your risk and return objectives while satisfying the constraints you face.

b.   A guardian investor typically is an individual who wishes to preserve the purchasing power of his assets. Extreme guardians would be exclusively in AAA short term credits. GSS should first determine how long the time horizon is and how high the return expectations are. Assuming a long horizon and 8-10% return (pretax) expectations, the portfolio could be allocated 30-40% bonds, 30-40% stocks, and modest allocations to the other asset groups.

7. A.(I) Key constraints are important in devloping a satisfatocry investment plan in Green's situation, as in all investment situations. In particular, those constraints involving investment horizon, liquidity, taxes, and unique circumstances are especially important to Green. His investment policy statement fails to provide an adequate treatment of the following key constraints:

1. **Horizon.** At age 63 and enjoying good health, Green still has an intermediate to long investment horizon ahead. When considered in the light of his wish to pass his wealth onto his daughter and grandson, the horizon extends further. Despite his apparent personal orientation toward short-term income considerations, planning should reflect a long-term approach.

2. **Liquidity.** With spending exceeding income and cash resources down to $10,1000, Green is about to experience a liquidity crisis. His desire to maintain the present spending level requires reorganizing his financial situation. This may involve using some capital and reconfiguring his investment assets.

3. **Tax considerations.** Green's apparent neglect of this factor is a main cause of his cash squeeze and requires prompt attention as part of reorganizing his finances. He should get professional advice and adopt a specific tax strategy. In the United States, such a strategy should include using municipal securities and possibly other forms of tax shelter/

4. **Unique circumstances.** Green's desire to leave a $1,000,000 estate to benefit his daughter and grandson is a challenge whose effects are primary to reorganizing his finances. Again the need for professional advice is obvious. The form of the legal arrangements, for example, may determine the form the investment take. Green is unlikely to accept any investment advice that does not address this expressed goal.

Other constraints. Three other constraints are present. First, Green does not mention the need to protect himself against inflation's effects. Second, he does not appear to realize the inherent contraditcions involved in saying he needs a "maximum return" with "an income element large enough "to meet his considerable spending needs. He also wants "low risk," a minimum "possibility of large losses" and preservation of the $1,000,000 value of his investments. Thirs, his statements are unclear about whether he intends to leave $1,000,000 or some larger sum that would be the inflation-adjusted future equivalent of to today's $1,000,000 value.

(ii) Appropriate return and risk objectives for Green are as follows:

Return. In managing Green's portfolio, return emphasis should reflect his need for maximizing current income consistent with his desire to leave and estate at least equal to the $1,000,000 current value of his invested assests. Given his inability to reduce spending and his constraining tax situation, this may require a total return approach. To meet his spending needs, Green may have to supplement an insufficient yield in certain years with some of his investment gains. He should also consider inflation protection and a specific tax strategy in determining assest allocation. These are important needs in this situation given the intermediate to long investment horizon and his estate-disposition plans.

Risk. Green does not appear to have a high tolerance for risk, as shown by his concern about capital preservation and the avoidance of large losses. Yet, he should have a moderate degree of equity exposure to protect his estate against inflation and to provide growth in income over time. A long time horizon and the size of his assets reflect his ability to accept such risk. He clearly needs counseling in this area because the current risk level is too high given his preferences.

B.(i) The following shows the calculation of the expected total return associated with the fund for *each* of the two different asset mixes, given the three scenarios in Table 2.

Table 2 shows projected returns for each of the three economic scenarios. The "Degearing" scenario is for a stable economic environment: economic growth is 2.5 percent a year and the inflation rate is 3.0 percent. This scenario provides positive returns for all three asset classes, and stocks outperform both bonds and Treasury bills. The other two scenarios- "Disinflation" and "Inflation"-posit less stable conditions in which stocks do poorly. Bonds also generate losses in the "Inflation" scenario, but provide considerable downside protection under "Disinflation" conditions.

The calculations for the multiple scenario analysis (see below) show that of the three asset classes, bonds offer the highest expected real return, 2.25 percent, over the forecast horizon. Over the same horizon, stocks are projected to generate a negative real return of -0.125 percent. Stocks are adversely affected under the "Disinflation" scenario and show losses under the "Inflation" scenario. Given the probabilities assigned to the three scenarios, the stock/bond/cash mix of 40/20/20 provides a superior real return (1.10 percent) to that from the alternative 60/30/10 mix (0.73 percent). This analysis reveals that equities do not automatically produce the highest expected returns even when the preponderant economic probability is for a stable environment accompanied by slow growth. If other less favorable outcomes have a reasonable probability of occurring, higher equity exposures may not produce a commensurately higher return. The multiple scenario forecasting methodology provides a valuable tool for effectively exploring the impact of various possibilities via a "what if" approach.

26- 4

	Return	Real Total Returns			
		Degearing	Disinflation	Inflation	Expected
T-bills		(1.50x0.5) +	(1.5x0.25) +	(0.5x0.25) =	1.250%
Bonds		(3.25x0.5) +	(6.5x0.25) +	(-4.0x0.25) =	2.250
Stocks		(5.25x0.5) +	(-9.0x0.25) +	(-2.0x.25) =	-0.125

	Real Portfolio Returns	
	40/40/20 Mix	60/30/10 Mix
T-bills	1.250 x 0.2 = 0.25%	1.250 x 0.1 = 0.125%
Bonds	2.250 x 0.4 = .90	2.250 x 0.3 = 0.675
Stocks	-0.125 x 0.4 = -0.05	-0.125 x 0.6 = -0.725
Total	1.10%	0.725%

An alternate calculation approach is set forth below. This approach involves finding the portfolio returns under each scenario and then finding the final expected returns using the probabilities:

Real Return 40/40/20 Mix

Degearing: (5.25 x 0.40) + (3.25 x 0.40) + (1.5 x 0.20)   = 3.7%
Disinflation: (-9.00 x 0.40) + (6.50 x 0.40) + (1.5 x 0.20)   = -0.7
Inflation: (-2.00 x 0.40) + (-4.00 x 0.40) + (0.5 x 0.20) = -2.3

Expected Return = [(3.7% x 0.5) (-0.7% x 0.25) + (-2.3% x 0.25)] = 1.1%

The same alternate procedure applies to the 60/30/10 mix.

(ii) **Justification:** The answer to part I provides much of the justification for the Fund's 40/40/20 asset mix. Given the three economic scenarios, each having a reasonable chance of occurring, the expected portfolio real returns are 1.10 percent for the existing mix versus 0.725 percent for the 60/30/10 mix. Therefore, the 40/40/20 mix is superior. Although using the scenarios may fail to capture subsequent events, the 40/40/20 mix provides the lowest risk exposure. The return superiority, if any, represent added value. Perversely, the more stocks in the portfolio, the worse the outcomes under the circumstances captured by the scenarios.

Explanation: The explanation, also captured in the answer to Part I, lies primarily in the fact stocks generate losses in both the "Disinflation" and the "Inflation" scenarios. Increasing the proportion in stocks increases the portfolio's exposure to their relatively poor performance.

26- 5

Bonds offer the highest expected real returns over the investment horizon, followed by cash equivalents such as Treasury bills, whose return is positive under each scenario. Stocks'superiority of returns under the "Degearing" scenario is insufficient, even with that scenario given a 0.50 probability of being the dominant set of circumstances, to overcome the "Disinflation" outcome for that asset class.

(iii)   Based on the Introduction and the answer to Question 1, Green's key needs are:

1. a portfolio offering a long horizon,
2. tax awareness (if not tax shelter)
3. control over the timing of gain realization,
4. an emphasis on production of current income,
5. a smooth and dependable flow of investment income and,
6. a below-average risk level, especially as to the possibility of large losses.

Green owns no real estate, receives no private pension income, and has only a small, partly- taxable government benefit payment. He also has no major noninvestment resources and depends entirely on his investment income for his spending. He does not intend to reduce his spending level. Although Green seems ambivalent about inflation, he hopes to leave his present worth to his daughter and grandson for their future financial protection. These factors provide the background for evaluating the appropriateness of the Fund as a primary investment asset.

In the Fund's favor are the following positive characteristics:

1. **Diversifying agent.** If the Fund were part of a portfolio rather than Green's only investment, it would serve as an excellent diversifying agent.

2. **Adequate return.** Green has owned the Fund shares for six years, over which period (via distributions of both income and gains) he has realized a return on cost averaging 8 percent a year and has also recorded a $100,000 unrealized gain from Fund value value growth beyond the distributions. This is an average but a satisfactory result.

3. **Conservative orientation.** Based on the Question 2.A scenario exercise and existing 40/40/20 asset allocation, the Fund's management team appears to have a conservative orientation, which meets Green's expressed preference.

Despite the positive aspects of the Fund, most of the evidence suggests that the Fund is inappropriate as a primary investment asset for Green for the following reasons:

26- 6

1. **Risky strategy to achieve Green's goals.** The "all eggs in one basket," single-asset nature of Green's investment is a high-risk strategy, which is clearly inappropriate to Green's circumstances. The 55 percent out-of-U.S. exposure Green holds via the Fund appears excessive compared with any known needs or goals.

2. **Nonoptimal asset mix of Fund for Green.** Although the Fund's broad global diversification might maximize return and minimize volatility with respect to it own particular asset allocation, its composition is unlikely to meet Green's complex set of specific return needs. The asset mix that is optimal for the Fund is not necessarily optimal for Green.

3. **Excessive Volatility.** Much of the distribution flow from the Fund depends on capital gains.Given Green's spending pattern, the volatility of this flow is likely to be excessive in terms of Green's needs for income stability and dependability.

4. **Lack of focus on after-tax returns and control.** The Fund's management focuses on producing total returns, but Green's need is for maximum after-tax returns and for some control over the timing of gain realizations. Under present circumstances, gain realizations are random, uncontrollable events for Green, who must pay taxes on the gain distributions as they occur.

5. **Lack of focus on income needs.** The Fund cannot give the single-minded attention to income type, amount, regularity, and tax nature that this aspect of Green's situation needs.

6. **Inflation.** The global nature of the Fund's investment means that inflation in the United States, which affects Green directly, probably does not get the concentrated attention that planning for Green must give it.

On balance, the Fund is an appropriate primary investment for Green, except as a diversifying piece of a much larger, balanced portfolio.

C.   Description of Adjustment

1. **Historical real interest rate.** The historical real interest rate should be adjusted to remove distortion caused by the U.S. government's "pegging" of interest rates at artificially low levels in the 1940s and early 1950s, when Treasury-bill rates averaged a 0.53 percent return (1941-50). If the government had not pegged interest rates during this period, the rate
probably would have been higher than observed, and the "true" long-term average rates would be higher. This situation suggests an *upward adjustment* to historical real interest rates.

2. **Bond maturity premium.** The observed bond maturity premium should be adjusted to remove bias caused by the pronounced upward trend in inflation and nominal interest rates during the period 1926-87, when investors systematically experienced capital losses on long-term bond holdings. Arnott-Sorenson estimated the loss on long-term bonds at 0.8 percent a year. Therefore, an *upward adjustment* to the long-term bond maturity premium is also indicated to remove the trend.

Justification: The justification for each of these adjustments is that the data contain systematic, long-lasting artificial biases. Such biases must be removed if these data items are to be useful for forming valid expectations.

D.   Adjustments are justified when existing or prospective circumstances relating to the economic or market factors to be considered differ from those reflected in the historical data. Key circumstances to consider when forming expectations about future returns are:

1. **Current yield curve and rate of inflation.** In deriving expected returns, an investor might adjust the historical returns of different asset classes to consider the current yield curve and inflation rate. Over time, prospective returns may converge on historical experience, but the expectations embedded in current data must also be considered in deriving best expectations of the future.

2. **"Halo" or markdown effect.** A halo effect may develop around an asset class that has done unusually well over a prolonged period, resulting in a historical record needing adjustment. Market participants do not easily forget bad investment experience with a particular asset class. Therefore, investors might want to adjust historical returns on an asset class that has done badly over a prolonged period to eliminate any embedded bias.

3. **Distinct period.** The historical return data since 1926 include many distinct eras with different capital market and inflation experiences. An investor might want to reflect the possibility that the forecast period might differ substantially from the historical norm or might closely resemble a subperiod.

4. **New dimensions in environment.** The environment of today's capital markets has dimensions to it such that history may be of little use. These dimensions include the savings/investment and import/export disequilibria in the U.S. economy, the globalization and integration of capital markets, and rapid innovation in financial instruments. An investor may want to consider these dimensions in forecasting future returns.

5. **Different growth prospects.** If the economic growth prospects today differ from history, an investor should consider this circumstance when forming expectations about future returns.

6. **Unavailability of complete or comparable data.** The lack of availability of complete or comparable data on a given asset class (e.g., real estate, venture capital, and non-U.S. investments) does not justify ignoring them. An investor might use available results plus knowledge of the risk/return characteristics of that asset class to derive useful expected return data and, thus, include that class in the universe of available asset classes.

7. **Link between risk tolerance and value of capital assets.** Sharpe points out that a direct link exists between the collective risk tolerance of investors and the per capita value of capital assets. An increase in this measure should cause risk premia (maturity, default, equity) to decline, and vice versa. An investor who believes market participants have not considered this may want to adjust historical risk premia appropriately.

8.   A.   An Investment Policy Statement for Fairfax based *only* on the information provided in the Introduction is shown below.

Overview. Fairfax is 58 years old and has seven years to go until a planned retirement. She has a fairly lavish lifestyle but few money worries: Her large salary pays all current expenses, and she has accumulated $2 million in cash equivalents from savings in previous years. Her health is excellent, and her health insurance coverage will continue after retirement and is employer paid. While Fairfax's job is a high-level one, she is not well versed in investment matters and has had the good sense to connect with professional counsel to get started on planning for her investment future, a future that is complicated by ownership of a $10 million block of company stock that while listed on the NYSE, pays no dividends and has a zero-cost basis for tax purposes. All salary, investment income (except interest on municipal bonds), and realized capital gains are taxed to Fairfax at a 35 percent rate; this rate and a 4 percent inflation rate are expected to continue into the future. Fairfax would accept a 3 percent real, after-tax return from the investment portfolio to be formed from her $2 million in savings ("the Savings Portfolio") if that return could be obtained with only modest portfolio volatility (i.e., less than a 10 percent annual decline). She is described as being conservative in all things.

Objectives

• **Return Requirement.** Fairfax's need for portfolio income begins seven years from now, at the date of requirement when her salary stops. The investment focus for her Savings Portfolio should be on growing the portfolio's value in the interim in a way that provides protection against loss of purchasing power. Her 3 percent real, after-tax return preference implies a gross total return requirement of at least 10.8 percent, assuming her investments are fully taxable (as is the case now) and assuming 4 percent inflation and a 35 percent tax rate. For Fairfax to maintain her current lifestyle, she would have to generate $500,000 x $(1.04)^7$ or $658,000, in annual income, inflation adjusted, when she retires. If the market value of Reston's stock does not change, and if she has been able to earn a 10.8 percent return on the Savings Portfolio (or 7 percent nominal after-tax return=$2,000,000 x $(1.07)^7$=$3,211,500). she should accumulate $13,211,500 by retirement age. To generate $658,000, a return on $13,211,500 of 5.0 percent would be needed.

- **Risk Tolerance.** From the information provided, Fairfax is quite risk averse, indicating she does not want to experience a decline of more than 10 percent in the value of the Savings Portfolio in any given year. This would indicate that the portfolio should have below average risk exposure to minimize its downside volatility. In terms of overall wealth, she could afford to take more than average risk, but because of her preferences and the nondiversified nature of the total portfolio, a below-average risk objective is appropriate for the Savings Portfolio.

    It should be noted, however, that truly meaningful statements about the risk of Fairfax's total portfolio are tied to assumptions about the volatility of Reston's stock, if it is retained, and about when and at what price the Reston stock will be sold. Because the Reston holding constitutes 83% of Fairfax's total portfolio, it will largely determine the risk she actually experiences as long as it remains intact.

Constraints

- **Time Horizon.** Two time horizons are applicable to Fairfax's life, perhaps 25-30 years from now. The first time horizon represents the period during which Fairfax should set up her financial situation in preparation for the balance of the second time horizon, her retirement period of indefinite length. Of the two horizons, the longer term to the expected end of her life is the dominant horizon because it is over this period that the assets must fulfill their primary function of funding her expenses, in an annuity sense, in retirement.

- **Liquidity.** With liquidity defined either as income needs or as cash reserves to meet emergency needs, Fairfax's liquidity requirement is minimal. $500,000 of salary is available annually, health cost concerns are nonconsistent, and we know of no planned needs for cash from the portfolio.

- **Taxes.** Fairfax's taxable income (salary, taxable investment income, and realized capital gains on securities) is taxed at a 35 percent rate. Careful tax planning and coordination of tax policy with investment planning is required. Investment strategy should include seeking income that is sheltered from taxes and holding securities for lengthy time periods to produce larger after-tax-returns. Sale of the Reston stock will have sizeable tax consequences because

Fairfax's cost basis is zero; special planning will be needed for this. Fairfax may want to consider some form of charitable giving, either during her lifetime or at death. She has no immediate family, and we know of no other potential gift or bequest recipients.

- **Laws and Regulations.** Fairfax should be aware of and abide by any securities (or other) laws or regulation relating to her "insider" status at Reston and her holding of Reston stock. Although there is no trust instrument in place, if Fairfax's future investing is handled by an investment advisor, the responsibilities associate with the Prudent Person Rule will come into play, including the responsibility for investing in a diversified portfolio. Also, she has a need to seek estate planning legal assistance, even though there are no apparent gift or bequest recipients.

- **Unique Circumstances and/or Preferences.** Clearly, the value of the Reston stock dominates the value of Fairfax's portfolio. A well-defined exit strategy needs to be developed for the stock as soon as is practical and appropriate. If the value of the stock increases, or at least does not decline before it is liquidated, Fairfax's present lifestyle can be sustained after retirement with the combined portfolio. A significant and prolonged setback for Reston Industries, however, could have disastrous consequences. Such circumstances would require a dramatic downscaling of Fairfax's lifestyle or generation of alternate sources of income to maintain her current lifestyle. A worst-case scenario might be characterized by a 50 percent drop in the market value of Reston's stock and sale of that stock to diversify the portfolio, where the sale proceeds would be subject to a 35 percent tax rate. The net proceeds of the Reston part of the portfolio would be $10,000,000 x .5 x (1-.35)=$3,250,000. When added to the Savings Portfolio, total portfolio value would be $5,250,000. For this portfolio to generate $658,000 in income, a 12.5% return would be required.

> *Synopsis.* The policy governing investment in Fairfax's Savings Portfolio shall put emphasis on realizing a 3 percent real, after-tax return from a mix of high-quality assets aggregating less than average risk. Ongoing attention shall be given to Fairfax's tax planning and legal needs, her progress toward retirement, and the value of her Reston stock. The Reston stock holding is a unique circumstance of decisive significance in this situation: Developments should be monitored closely, and protection against the effects of a worst-case scenario should be implemented as soon as possible.

> B. A critique of the Coastal Advisors proposal, created for investment of the Savings Portfolio investment,
> Including three weaknesses related to the Investment Policy Statement in Part A, follows.

> *Critique.* The Coastal proposal produces a real, after-tax expected return of approximately 5.17 percent, which is above the 3 percent level sought by Fairfax. The expected return of the proposal can be calculated by subtracting the tax

exempt yield from the total current yield (4.9 percent - .55 percent = 4.35 percent) and converting this to an after-tax yield [4.35 percent x (1-. 35) = 2.82 percent]. The tax exempt income is then added back in (2.82 percent + .55 percent = 3.37 percent). The appreciation portion of the return (5.8 percent) is then added to the after tax yield to get the nominal portfolio return (3.37 percent + 5.80 percent = 9.17 percent). Finally, the 4 percent inflation factor is subtracted to produce the expected real after tax return (9.17 percent – 4.0 percent = 5.17 percent). This result can also be obtained by determining these calculations for each of the individual holdings, weighting each result by the portfolio percentage and then adding to a total portfolio result.

From the data available, it is not possible to determine specifically the inherent degree of portfolio volatility. Despite meeting the return criterion, the allocation is neither realistic nor, in its detail, appropriate to Fairfax's situation in the context of an investment policy usefully applicable to her. The primary weaknesses are the following:

- **Allocation of Equity Assets.** Exposure to equity assets will be necessary to achieve the return requirements of Fairfax; however, greater diversification of these assets among other equity classes is needed to produce a more efficient, potentially less volatile portfolio that would meet her risk tolerance parameters as well as her return requirements. An allocation that focuses the equity investments in U.S. *large-cup* and/or *small-cup* holdings and includes smaller international and Real Estate Investment Trust exposure is more likely to achieve the return and risk tolerance goals. If more information were available concerning the returns and volatility of the Reston stock, an argument could be made that this holding is the U.S. equity component of her portfolio. But the lack of this information precludes taking it into account for the Savings Portfolio allocation and creates the need for broader equity diversification.

- **Cash allocation.** Within the proposed fixed-income component, the allocation to cash (15 percent) is excessive given the limited liquidity need and low returns the asset class offers.

- **Corporate/Municipal Bond Allocation.** The corporate bond allocation (10 percent) is inappropriate given Fairfax's tax situation and the superior after tax yield on municipal bonds relative to corporate (5.5 percent vs. 4.8 percent).

- **Venture Capital Allocation.** The allocation to venture capital is questionable given Fairfax's policy statement which reveals that she is quite risk averse and dislikes volatility. Although venture capital may provide diversification benefits, venture capital returns historically have been more volatile than other risky assets such as large- and small-cap stocks in the United States. Hence, even a small percentage allocation to venture capital may prove vexing.

- **Lack of Risk/Volatility Information.** The proposal concentrates on return expectations and ignores risk/volatility implications. Specifically, the proposal should have addressed the expected volatility of the entire portfolio to see if it falls within the risk tolerance parameters of Fairfax.

C. (i) Fairfax has stated that she is seeking a 3 percent real, after-tax return. Table II provides nominal, pre-tax figures, which must be adjusted for both taxes and inflation to ascertain which portfolios meet
Fairfax's return guideline. A simple solution is for the candidate to subtract the municipal bond return component from the stated return, then subject the resulting figure to a 35 percent tax rate, and add back tax-exempt municipal bond income. This produces a nominal, after-tax return. Then subtract 4 percent inflation to arrive at the real, after-tax return. For example, Allocation A has a real after-tax return of 3.4 percent, calculated by $[.099 - (.072) \times (.4)] \times [1-.35] + [(.072) \times (.4)] - [.04] = 3.44$ percent = 3.4 percent. Alternatively, it can be calculated by multiplying the taxable returns by their allocations, summing these products, adjusting for the tax rate, adding the result to the product of the nontaxable (municipal bond) return and its allocation, and deducting the inflation rate from this sum. For Allocation A, $[(.045) \times (.10) + (.13) \times (.2) + (.15) \times (.1) + (.15) \times (.1) + (.1) \times (.1)] \times [1 - .35] + [(.072) \times (.4)] - [.04] = 3.46$ percent = 3.5 percent.

Allocation

Return Measure	A	B	C	D	E
Nominal Return	9.9%	11.0%	8.8%	14.4%	10.3%
Real After-Tax Return	3.5%	3.1%	2.5%	5.4%	3.4%

Table II also provides after-tax returns that could be adjusted for inflation and then used to ascertain the portfolios that meet Fairfax's return guidelines.

Allocations A, B, D, and E meet Fairfax's real, after-tax return objectives.

(ii) Fairfax has stated that a worst case return of –10 percent in any 12-month period would be acceptable. The expected return less two times the portfolio risk (expected standard deviation) is the relevant risk tolerance measure. In this case, three allocations meet the criterion: A, C, and E.

Allocation

Parameter	A	B	C	D	E
Expected Return	9.9%	11.0%	8.8%	14.4%	10.3%
Exp. Std. Deviation	9.4%	12.4%	8.5%	18.1%	10.1%
Worst Case Return	-8.9%	-13.8%	-8.2%	-21.8%	-9.9%

D.   I.   The Sharpe Ratio for Allocation D, using the cash equivalent rate of 4.5 percent as the risk-free rate, is (.144-.045)/.181=.547.

        II.   The two allocations with the best Sharpe Ratios are A and E with ratios of 0.574 each.

E.   The recommended allocation is A. The allocations that meet both the minimum real, after-tax objective and the maximum risk tolerance objective are A and E. These allocations have identical Sharpe Ratios. Both allocations have large exposures to municipal bonds. But Allocation E also has a large position in REIT stocks, whereas Allocation A's counterpart large equity allocation is to a diversified portfolio of large and small cap domestic stocks. Because of the diversification value of the large and small stock representation in A as opposed to the specialized or nondiversified nature of REIT stocks and their limited data history, there can be more confidence that the expectational data for the large- and small- cap stock portfolios will be realized than for the REIT portfolio.

9.   A.   The key elements that should determine the foundation's grant-making (spending) policy are:

1. Average expected inflation over a long horizon;
2. Average expected nominal return on the endowment portfolio over the same long horizon; and
3. The 5%-of-asset-value payout requirement imposed by the tax authorities as a condition for ongoing U.S. tax exemption, a requirement that is expected to continue indefinitely.

To preserve the real value of its assets and to maintain its spending in real terms, the foundation cannot pay out more, on average over time, than the real return it earns from its investment portfolio, since no fun-raising activities are contemplated. In effect, the portion of the total return, representing the inflation rate must be retained and reinvested if the foundation's principal is to grow with inflation and, thus, maintain its real value and the real value of future grants. At present there is no conflict between this concept and the 5% nominal "must payout" rate of spending mandated by tax considerations, then the real return of the portfolio will have to equal or exceed 5% in order to preserve the foundation's tax exempt status and maintain its real value of principal and future payouts.

B.   Objectives

Return Requirement: Production of current income, the Committee's focus before Mr. Franklin's gift, is no longer a primary objective, given the enlargement of the asset base and the Committee's understanding that investment policy must accommodate long-term as well as short-term goals. The need for a minimum annual payout equal to 5% of assets must be considered, as well as the need to maintain the real value of these assets. A total return objective is appropriate, in amount equal to the grant rate plus the inflation rate but not less than the 5% required for maintenance of the Foundation's U.S. tax-exempt status.

Risk Tolerance: The increase in the Foundation's financial flexibility arising from Mr.Franklin's gift and the Committee's spending policy change have increased its ability to assume risk. The organization has a more or less infinite expected life span and, in the context of this long-term horizon, has the ability to accept the consequence of short-term fluctuations in asset values. Moreover, adoption of a clear-cut spending rule will permit cash flows to be planned with some precision, adding stability to annual budgeting and reducing the need for precautionary liquidity. Overall, the Foundation's risk tolerance is above average and oriented to long-term considerations.

Constraints

Liquidity Requirements: Liquidity needs are low, with the little likelihood of unforeseen demands requiring either forced asset sales or immense cash. Such needs as exist, principally for annual grant-making, are known in advance and relatively easy to plan for in a systematic way.

Time Horizon: The foundation has a virtually infinite life; the need to plan for future as well as current, financial demand justifies a long-term horizon with perhaps a five year cycle of planning and review.

Taxes: Tax-exempt under present U.S. law, if the annual minimum payout requirement (currently 5% of asset value) is met.

Legal and Regulatory: Governed by state law and Prudent Person standards; ongoing attention must be paid to maintaining the tax-exempt status by strict observance of IRS and any related Federal regulations.

Unique Circumstances: The need to maintain real value after grants is a key consideration, as its the 5% of assets requirement for ongoing tax exemption. The real return achieved must meet or exceed the grant rate, with the 5% level a minimum requirement.

Narrative: Investment actions shall take place in a long-term-tax-exempt context, reflect above average tolerance, and emphasize production of real total returns at or above a nominal level sufficient to meet the annual 5% of previous year-end asset value nor exceed the real rate of return earned in the endowment portfolio in the preceding year, except as the Investment Committee may authorize under exceptional circumstances.

C.   To meet requirements of this question, it is first necessary to identify a spending rate that is
both sufficient (i.e., 5% in nominal terms or higher) and feasible (i.e., prudent and attainable under the circumstances represented by the Table 4 data and the empirical evidence of historical risk and return for the various asset classes). The real return from the recommended allocation should be shown to equal or exceed the minimum payout requirement (i.e., equal to or greater than 5% in nominal terms) but not in excess of the real return component.

The allocation philosophy will reflect the Foundation's need for real returns at or above the grant rate, its total return orientation, its above average risk tolerance, its low liquidity requirements, and its tax exempt status. While the Table 4 data and historical experience provide needed inputs to the process, several generalizations are also appropriate:

1.   Allocations to fixed income instrument will be less than 50% as bonds have provided inferior real returns in the past, and while forecasted real returns from 1993 to 2000 are higher, they are still lower than for stocks. Real return needs are high and liquidity needs are low. Bonds will be included primarily for diversification and risk education purposes. he ongoing cash flow from bond portfolios of this size should easily provide for all normal working capital needs.

2.   Allocations to equities will be greater than 50%, and this asset class will be the portfolio's " work horse asset." Expected and historical real returns are high, the horizon is long, risk tolerance is above average, and taxes are not a consideration.

3.   Within the equity universe there is room in this situation for small cap as well as large cap issues, for international as well as domestic issues and, perhaps, for venture capital investment as well. Diversification will

contribute to risk reduction, and total return could be enhanced. All could be included.

4.   Given its value as an alternative to stocks and bonds as a way to maintain real return and provide diversification benefits, real estate could be included in this portfolio. In a long term context, real estate has provided good inflation protection, helping to protect real return production.

As an example of an appropriate, modestly aggressive allocation is shown below. Table 4 contains an array of historical and expected return data which was used to develop real return forecasts. In this case, the objective was to reach a spending level in real terms as close to 6% as possible, a level appearing to meet the dual goals of the Committee that is also both sufficient and feasible. The actual expected real portfolio return is 5.8%

Asset Class	7-Year Forecast of Real Returns	Recommended Allocation	Real Return Contribution
Cash (U.S.)			
T-bills	0.7%	*0%	
Bonds:			
Intermediate	2.3	5	.115%
Long Treasury	4.2	10	.420
Corporate	5.3	10	.530
International	4.9	10	.490
Stocks			
Large Cap	5.5	30	1.650
Small Cap	8.5	10	.850
International	6.6	10	.660
Venture Capital	12.0	*5	.600
Real Estate	5.0	**10	.500
Total Exp. Return		100%	5.815%

*No cash is included because ongoing cash flow from the portfolio should be sufficient to meet all normal working capital needs.

**Whiles these asset classes were not referenced in Table 4, an estimate of their returns is in other readings. They also provide additional diversification.

10.   A.   Derivatives can be used in an attempt to bridge the 90-day time gap in the following three ways:

1.   The foundation could <u>buy (long) calls</u> on equity index such as the S & P 600 Index and on Treasury bonds, notes, or bills. This strategy would

require the foundation to make an immediate cash outlay for the "premiums" on the calls. If the foundation were to buy calls on the entire $45 million, the cost of these calls could be substantial, particularly if their strike prices were close to current stock and bond prices (i.e. the calls were close to being "in the money").

2.   The foundation would <u>write or sell (short) puts</u> on an equity index and on Treasury bonds, notes, or bills. By writing puts, the foundation would receive an immediate cash inflow equal to the "premiums" on the puts (less brokerage commissions). If stock and bond prices rise as the committee expects, the puts would expire worthless, and the foundation would keep the premiums, thus hedging part or all of the market increase. If the prices fall, however, the foundation loses the difference between the strike price and the current market price, less the value of the premiums.

3.   The foundation could <u>buy (long) equity and fixed-income futures.</u> This is probably the most practical way for the foundation to hedge its expected gift. Futures are available on the S & P 500 Index and on Treasury bonds, notes, and bills. No cash outlay would be required. Instead, the foundation could use some of its current portfolio as a good faith deposit or "margin" to take the long positions. The market value of the futures contracts will, in general, mirror changes in the underlying market values of the S & P 500 Index and Treasuries. Although no immediate cash outlay is required, any gains (losses) in the value of the contracts will be added (subtracted) from the margin deposit daily. Hence, if markets advance as the committee expects, the balances in the foundation's futures account should reflect the market increase.

B.   There are both positive and negative factors to be considered in hedging the 90 day gap before the expected receipt of the Franklin gift.

POSITIVE FACTORS

1.   The foundation could establish its position in stock and bond markets using derivatives <u>today,</u> benefit in any subsequent increases in market values in the S & P Index and Treasury instruments in the 90 day period. In effect, the foundation would have a <u>synthetic</u> position in those markets beginning today.

2.   The cost of establishing the synthetic position is relatively low, depending on the derivative strategy used. If calls are used, the cost is limited to the premiums paid. If futures are used, the losses on the futures contracts would be similar to the amounts that would be lost if the foundation invested the gift today. Writing the puts is the riskiest strategy because

26- 18

there is an open ended loss if the market declines, but here again the losses would be similar if the foundation invested today and stock and bond markets declined.

3. Derivative markets (for the types of contracts under consideration here) are liquid.

NEGATIVE FACTORS

1. The Franklin gift could be delayed or not received at all. This would create a situation in which the foundation would have to unwind its position and could experience losses, depending on market movements in the underlying assets.

2. The committee might be wrong in its expectation that stock and bond prices will rise in the 90-day period. If prices decline on stocks and bonds, the foundation would lose part or all of the premium on the calls and have losses on the futures contracts and the puts written. The risk of loss of capital is a serious concern. (Given that the current investment is primarily bonds and cash, the foundation may not be knowledgeable enough to forecast stock prices over the next 90 days.)

3. Because there is a limited choice of option and futures derivative contract compared to the universe that the committee might wish to invest in, there could be a mismatch between the specific equities and bonds the foundation wishes to invest in and the contracts available in size for $45 million. Unless the 90 day period exactly matches the 90 day period before expiration dates on the contracts, there may be a timing mismatch.

4. The cost of the derivatives is (potentially) high. For example, if the market in general shares the committee's optimistic outlook, the premiums paid for calls would be expensive and the premiums received on puts would be lean. The opportunity cost on all derivative strategies would be large if the committee is wrong on the outlook for one or both market.

5. There may exist regulatory restrictions on the use of derivatives by endowment funds.

EVALUATION

The negative factors appear to outweigh the positive factors if the outlook for the market is neutral; therefore, the committee's decision on using derivatives to bridge the gap for 90 days will have to be related to the strength of its conviction that stock and bond prices will rise in that period. The certainty of receiving the gift in 90 days is also a factor. The committee should certainly beware that there is a cost to establish the derivative positions, especially if its expectations do not work out. The committee might want to consider a partial hedge of the $45 million.

11. I would advise them to exploit all available retirement tax shelters, like 403b, 401k, Keogh plans, IRAs, etc. Since they will not be taxed on the interest earned on these accounts until they withdraw the funds, they should avoid investing in tax-preferred instruments like municipal bonds.
    If they are very risk-averse, they should consider investing a large proportion of their funds in inflation-indexed CDs, which offer a riskless real rate of return.

12. C.B. SNOWS WIDOW

A. Income:
(An item marked REAL is expected to increase at the rate of inflation. An item marked nominal is expected to remain fixed.)

Income from Trust Assets:

	Pre-tax	Aftertax
Money market fund ($75,000x14.7%)(Nominal)	$11,025	$7,718
Munis ($105,000x8%)	8,400	8,400
Highway Cartage common ($120,000x7.9%)(REAL	9,480	6,636
Total income from Trust assets	28,905	22,754
Social Security ($600 per mo x 12) (REAL)	7,200	6,120
(Tax on Soc. Sec. = .15x$7,200)		
Total Income	36,105	28,874

Expenses:

Household (REAL)	19,600
Mortgage on new second home ($45,000@17.5%)(NOMINAL)	7,938*
Country Club dues ($125 per mo x 12)(REAL)	1,500
Total Expenses	29,038

*Interest tax savings will be used to pay maintenance fee.

Conclusion:
Her requirements cannot be met for this year without selling some assets. Furthermore, inflation will cause her expenses, which are $21, 100 REAL plus

$7,938 NOMINAL, to increase more rapidly than her after-tax income, which is $12,756 REAL plus $16,118 NOMINAL.

B.   Mrs. Snow's objectives seem to be:
1.   To maintain her current standard of living.
2.   To leave as much of her assets as possible for her daughter, subject to the first objective being met.

C.   Mrs. Snow should use $45,000 of the $300,000 Trust to pay off her mortgage immediately since the after-tax rate of interest on the mortgage of 12.25% per year (.7x17.5%) exceeds what she could earn on alternative fixed-income investments. With no mortgage payment to make, her required real after-tax income would be $21,000 per year.
Her Social Security income is $7,200 per year. By investing all of her remaining $255,000 in low coupon municipal bonds, she could avoid paying any income taxes on her Social security benefits and maintain the real value of her Trust assets for her daughter. The current yield on the munis would have to be sufficient to cover the difference between her needs of $21,100 per year and her Social Security benefits of $7,200 per year, i.e., $13,900 per year. This implies a current yield of 5.45% per year (13,900/255,000).

13.   A.   George More's accumulation at age 65:

	n	I	PV	FV	PMI
TIAA	25	3	100,000	?	1,500 FV=$265,067
CREF	25	6	100,000	?	1,500 FV=$511,484

B.   Expected retirement annuity:

	n	I	PV	FV	PMI
TIAA	15	3	264,067	0	? PMT=$22,120
CREFF	15	6	511,484	0	? PMT=$52,664

D.   In order to get a TIAA annuity of $30,000 per year his accumulation at age 65 would have to be:

n	I	PV	FV	PMI
15	3	?	0	30,000 PV=358,138

His annual contribution would have to be:

n	I	PV	FV	PMI
25	3	100,000	-358,138	? PMT=$4,080

This is an increase of $2,580 per year over his current contribution of $1,500 per year.

14.   A.   Joe's accrued benefit is currently $21,000 per year starting at age 65: .015 x 35 x $40,000.

Its PV at age 65 is $21,000(annuity factor, 8%,15)=$179,749, and its PV at age 60 is $122,334.

B.   An actuarially fair annuity starting one year from now would be $12,460 per year.

15.   A.   FPI faces a dilemma. On the one hand, it needs to improve returns in order to "catch up" on its underfunding; this necessity implies that more risk should be taken. On the other hand, FPI can't afford to have the underfunding get worse, it would get worse, which it would if FPI incurs more risk that is not productive of higher returns in the short run. Alternatively, the firm might be tempted to, as the chairman suggests, raise the actuarial assumption of what future return levels will be, thereby making the asset base automatically more productive simply by declaring it to be so. Future returns are not generated by actuaries or by chairmen; however, but by markets, by asset-class exposures within markets, and by long-term relationships between economic and market factors-all taking place in the context of funding, allocation, and payout decisions unique to FPI's pension plan.

Of primary importance is that the return expected must be consistent with what the various alternative investment instruments available to the plan can reasonably be shown to offer in terms of long-run productivity, with risk considered. In general, FPI's existing portfolio is not allocated in a manner that makes the most of likely long-run economic/market conditions: (1) The portfolio holds only domestic securities. (2) Asset allocation, at 50 percent stocks and 50 percent bonds, appears to have been more a comfortable accident than a though-out strategy. (3) It holds only large-capitalization equities. (4) It holds only high-quality, long-maturity corporate bonds.

The possibility exists, then, that the portfolio could be improved in terms of expected returns terms without necessarily raising the risk level. Improving it enough to meet the chairman's 10 percent level, however, may not be possible, which is the first thing to be determined.

The data in Table 1 make it apparent that, although U.S. stock and bond returns have been above the plan's long-term return assumption of 9 percent during the past decade, they have also been well above their long-term historical norms. The forecast data indicate a consensus that future returns will be more in line with the long-term record than with the exceptional levels recorded from 1984 to 1993. Accordingly, the chairman's observation should not be turned into a recommendation to increase the rate of return assumption; on the contrary, given the tendency of rates to regress to the mean over long periods of time, a more appropriate recommendation would be to lower the assumed rate of return toward the 8 percent level and allocate the plan's assets accordingly.

The FPI plan might have been better funded than it is if the asset allocation decision had been given more attention or had been more expansive in asset-class terms in the past. The allocation shown below is an example of a more appropriate mix, in light of what we know about the company's needs and goals. Even with the consensus forecast numbers lowered considerably from recent experience, this allocation provides enhanced opportunity to improve returns without, relative to the present mix, significantly increasing the level of total portfolio risk. Improved diversification through a broader range of asset classes represents a more realistic and opportunistic approach to the plan's market exposures and appears to offer a better prospect, of meeting the plan's obligations over time than does the current allocation.

To effect a change to a more rational and better diversified asset mix from the existing 50 percent large-capitalization U.S. stocks/50 percent long-duration U.S. corporate bond mix, a number of additional asset types are available: intermediate-maturity Treasury bonds, non-U.S. bonds(AAA), small-capitalization U.S. stocks, non-U.S. stocks, and U.S. real estate. Of these, several offer (based on consensus expected returns) levels of return that are comparable to or higher than current levels, at levels of risk that when diversification benefits are considered, are the same or only slightly higher than that of the existing mix. For example, the following allocation moves the portfolio to 70 percent equity/30 percent fixed-income assets with similar riskiness as currently for the total portfolio.

Asset Class	Percent of Total	1994-2000 Expected Return	Weighted Expected Return
Fixed income			
Intermediate Treasury	10%	5.0%	0.50%
U.S. corporate AAA	10	6.5	0.65
Non-U.S. AAA	10	6.5	0.65
Subtotal	30%		1.80%
Equity			
U.S. large cap	40%	8.5%	3.40%
U.S. small cap	10	10.5	1.05
Non-U.S.	10	9.5	0.95
U.S. real estate	10	7.5	0.75
Subtotal	70%		6.15%
Total	100%		7.95%

The chairman's desire to raise the long-term return assumption cannot be supported by present return levels or levels that can reasonably be expected. What he sees in the rearview mirror does not carry through to the road ahead. From a practical standpoint, in fact, the return assumption should be lowered toward 8 percent, not raised from 9 percent to 10 percent. To recommend an increase in the return assumption at this time would be both imprudent and unreasonable.

B.   A U.S. pension plan's discount rate is the rate applied in determining the present value of its pension obligations. Because the time period involved is obviously long-term, the discount rate should bear some rational relationship to the long-term rates of interest present in the market at the time of the calculation. The usual model for the discount rate is the rate at which high-quality, long-term bonds (often the long Treasury, but the rate on long corporates is also used) are quoted, reflecting consensus expectations of long-run inflation plus a real rate of return. Based on the consensus forecast in Table 1 and present capital market conditions, a discount rate of 6-7 percent would be reasonable. FPI's current using 8 percent discount rate is already out of line with such conditions. FPI should, therefore, seriously consider adopting a lower rate. Thus, the capital market conditions would be those that render the existing rate unrealistic as reflected in prevailing long-term rates.

C.   In the United States, every ERISA-qualified defined-benefit pension plan has a "Projected Benefit Obligation (PBO)," which represents the discounted present value of the retirement benefits that the plan is obligated by law to make, given certain assumptions about future rates of pay and work-force factors. If the "plan assets at fair market value" exceed the PBO, the plan is said to be "overfunded." Conversely , if the plan assets are less than the PBO, the plan is said to be (as in this case) "underfunded." Given that FPI's plan is underfunded by $200 million, whereas its assets total $750 million, its PBO must be $950 million. Amortization of this shortfall will add to FPI's financial burdens. In more general terms, an underfunded situation exists whenever the fair value of the assets "securing" a liability are insufficient to extinguish the liability.

D.   Reducing the discount rate applied to FPI's pension benefit obligations would have the effect of raising FPI's discounted present value. Because the market value of the assets available to liquidate this obligation is unchanged, the underfunded situation would be made worse by a discount-rate reduction. The size of the gap between the PBO and the value of the assets, now $200 million, would be increased, as would the size of the amortization requirement.

16.   A.   1.   Using historical data – The use of long-term historical asset class data (returns, standard deviations and correlation characteristics) is the traditional method for determining an optimal asset allocation focused on maximizing portfolio return while minimizing portfolio risk. As discussed by Ambachtsheer, the usefulness of such long-term data will be enhanced by careful adjustment and updating to reflect important structural changes over the period that the data was being generated.

Strengths of this method include:
- its appropriateness for setting long-term strategic targets.
- Its simplicity and ability to accommodate as many asset classes for which valid data is available.
- The avoidance of forecaster bias.

Weaknesses of this method include:

- Unless adjusted, the raw historical data may not represent a valid model of future return, variability or correlation experience and, hence, represent a poor base for optimization.
- Asset class characteristics often deviate from long-term trendlines over business cycles and for even longer periods of time. Accordingly, use of this method is inappropriate for short-and intermediate-term allocation applications.
- Particularly when setting risk/return objectives for individuals, the concepts of standard deviation and correlation as risk and diversification measures may impede understanding and acceptance.

2. <u>Multiple scenario forecasting</u> – This method involves establishing a set of economic/market expectations based on different possible scenarios that have had probabilities assigned to their occurrence. The mix of scenarios may include those based on past experience as well as those based on econometric modeling.

Strengths of this method include:

- This method fosters recognition of the likelihood of error in the "most likely" forecast because it forces assessment of the probabilities of occurrence for <u>other</u> scenarios, including especially the "worst case" scenario.
- Its time independence allows short- or intermediate-term expectations or situations to be included in the allocation process.
- It forces the forecaster to focus on the key variables affecting the forecast and to consider the forecast from a variety of points of reference.
- It reduces a complex task to workable proportions and provides an excellent mechanism for communicating common-based information across an organization.

Weaknesses of the method include:
- The likelihood of forecaster bias, in which "hopes" enter the process and the range of scenario content fails to capture the extremes of the distribution possibilities.

- The large number of explicit assumptions and relationships required to be specified.
- The possibility that errors may come into play as, for example, in establishing levels of probability for each scenario's occurrence.

3. Asset/Liability forecasting – This method allocates assets in a manner aimed at matching the duration of the liabilities for which the assets are maintained.

Strengths of this method include:

- A higher probability (than in either the historical data or multiple scenario approaches) that a policy goal of surplus maintenance can be achieved.
- Minimizes complexity of portfolio structure and associated costs, since assets are typically allocated to bonds of the appropriate liability-matching durations.
- Given the few variables involved, forecasting liability growth is typically more accurate than forecasting returns, etc.

Weaknesses of the method include:
- a reduction in potential returns because portfolio structures are not optimal from a long-term return/risk standpoint.
- The difficulty of achieving a perfect "hedge" where asset liability "returns" are matched.
- Techniques for measuring liability durations are still new and in need of refinement.

B. 1.   In creating a set of long-term asset allocation ranges for the PTC pension portfolio, consideration must be given to the characteristics of each asset class to be part of the mix, including expected returns, standard deviations and correlations. In addition, specific plan risk/return objectives and constraints, including the structure and duration of plan liabilities, must be taken into account.
For PTC, the following are the major considerations:

- A long time horizon is available; no near-term cash needs exist and the work force if of a relatively young age.
- The plan's risk-assuming capacity is above-average.
- The plan has a total return objective, expressed in real terms, accompanied by a goal of growing surplus over time.
- Liabilities are sensitive to inflation as benefits are tied to final wage levels and retirement benefits are adjusted to reflect inflation experience.
- 30% of liabilities are now in non- U.S. $ form, and this liability category is expected to grow at a faster rate than domestic liabilities in the future.
- The plan is tax-exempt but subject to ERISA regulations.

Given the background here, an appropriate weighting of asset classes for long-term planning purposes will be found in the following allocation range table:

	Range	Mid-Point
U.S. Stocks	30-50	40%
Non-U.S. Stocks	15-25	20
Equity Real Estate	5-15	10
U.S. Bonds	10-25	15
Non- U.S. Bonds	5-15	10
Cash equivalents	0-10	5
		100%

Summarized by Asset Class:

	Range	Mid-Point
Equities, including U.S. And non-U.S. Stocks plus Equity Real Estate	50-90%	70%
Bonds, U.S. and non-U.S.	25-40	25
Cash Equivalents	0-10	5
		100%

Summarized by Geographic Exposure:

	Range	Mid-Point
U.S. Investment	60-75%	70%
Non-U.S. Investments	25-40	30
		100%

2. Justification for the above asset allocation range set will be found in the following discussion:

U.S. Stocks – A sizeable allocation to domestic stocks is mandated by the plan's total return objective, its reliance on real returns, its long horizon, its tax-exempt status, and the large size of its U.S.

Non-U.S. Stocks- This allocation is warranted by the presence in the plan liabilities of a growing non-U.S. $ component and by the general considerations cited above. In addition, the immediate diversification and long-term return enhancement aspects of such exposure are other factors of justification. In the context of the long term, hedging is not an appropriate strategic move for PTC given the growing non-$ liabilities. In the short run, tactical hedging may be considered from time to time as a source of added return.

Equity Real Estate- Given the importance of inflation protection to the plan and the past success of real estate in protecting value in periods of high inflation, a meaningful allocation to this asset class is justified. In addition, the diversification benefits of including real estate equities in this portfolio are a further plus, as are the likely level and stability of the asset's income stream.

U.S. Bonds- The justification for U.S. bond holdings is their role as a deflation hedge, their diversification value and the stability of their interest earnings in a situation where liquidity will be kept to a minimum. In an emergency, they also represent a ready source of cash.

Non-U.S. Bonds- As is the case with non-U.S. stocks, this asset class exposure is justified by its diversification benefits, and its usefulness in relation to the non-U.S. liabilities. In addition, the deflation-hedge role of bonds is of some value, as is their steady income and their availability as a source of cash in an emergency.

Cash Equivalents- Although the plan contemplates minimal liquidity reserves, residual cash is always present and some deflation and income continuity benefits are present. By identifying this asset class as a specific element in the allocation process, the optimization solution will more accurately identify appropriate allocations to the other asset classes at alternative risk/return levels.

C.(I)   The two primary asset class statistics required to develop optimal asset allocations, in addition to returns, are standard deviations and correlations between asset classes. The roles they play are as follows:

Standard deviations are the widely accepted measure of risk associated with asset returns. Because higher-returning assets have higher commensurate risk over the long-run, utilizing this risk measure serves to limit exposure to the highest-returning and thus riskiest asset in the asset allocation process. Such a measure is required to determine and optimal solution such that return is maximized over the long term within acceptable levels of return variance over shorter time periods.

Correlations are the measure of co-movement between assets or asset classes over time. They are a critical input in the asset allocation process allowing for proper measurement of risk associated with portfolios comprised of investments providing different returns during the same time period. Lower asset correlations will lead to lower portfolio standard deviations. Using valid correlation data is critical to identifying the impact on portfolio risk associated with combining less-than-perfectly correlated assets or asset classes.

NOTE: Consider structurally-adjusted historical returns as a weaker, but legitimate identification of a missing key asset class statistic.

(II)   Calculation of expected asset-class returns:

U.S. Stocks	(.3 x 7%) + (.5 x 12%) + (.2 x 8%)	= 9.7%
Non-U.S. Stocks	(.3 x 4%) + (.5 x 10%) + (.2 x 0%)	= 8.0%
Real Estate	(.3 x 0%) + (.5 x 9%) + (.2 x 14%)	= 7.3%
U.S. Bonds	(.3 x 15%) + (.5 x 8%) + (.2 x 3%)	= 9.1%
Non-U.S. Bonds	(.3 x 10%) + (.5 x 9%) + (.2 x 2%)	= 7.9%
Cash Equivalents	(.3 x 3%) + (.5 x 5%) + (.2 x 9%)	= 5.2%

(III)   A tactical asset allocation developed for use over short-to-intermediate time periods should focus on expected asset class returns for such periods. Assuming no significant differences between long-term and three-year risk and correlation measures, returns derived above in Part C.II suggest the deviations to incorporate now relative to the strategic long-term asset allocation identified in Part B. Because the scenario probabilities slightly favor a deflationary environment over a high inflation environment, the results suggest the following adjustments:

-     A lower equity weight compared to long-term targets is taken in exchange for higher bond exposure, given that expected bond returns both within the U.S. sector and non-U.S. sector are nearly as high as equity returns and would likely be even more attractive on a risk-adjusted basis. This is consistent with maintaining a higher relative bond exposure as a deflationary hedge. Within the bond segment, preference is given to increasing the U.S. bond proportion (+10%) vs. the non-U.S. bond proportion (+5%) because of the large difference in expected returns under the deflation scenario vs. the very small difference under the slow growth/low inflation scenario (which difference is reversed under the rapid growth/high inflation scenario). The allocation to cash is not changed; its return differentials are unattractive except in the low-probability rapid growth/high inflation scenario.

A lower exposure to real estate relative to the long term target would be desirable, given the lower expected performance of the asset class during deflationary times, and given its low expected return relative to both stock and bonds. However, real estate exposures may be difficult to adjust in the short run due to liquidity constraints; it is assumed that this would be the case here, and its level has, therefore, not been adjusted.

With in the reduced equity exposure, U.S. stocks have been adjusted in the same proportion as non-U.S. stocks (-10 from the 40% equals 30% vs. –5 from 20% equals 15%) despite better relative U.S. return expectations (except in the rapid growth/high inflation case) out of a desire to continue to provide via non-U.S. equity exposure an offset to the company's non-U.S. pension benefit liabilities. Taken together, non-U.S. equity and bond exposure is thus maintained at the 30% level before and after this overall tactical shift.

Summary of suggested adjustments:

	Strategic Allocation	Adjustment	Preferred Tactical Allocation
U.S. Stocks	40	-10%	*30%
Non- U.S. Stocks	20	-5%	15
Equity Real Estate	10	N.C.	10
U.S. Bonds	15	+10%	*25
Non-U.S. Bonds	10	+55	15
Cash Equivalents	5	N.C.	5
	100%		100%

*An acceptable alternative allocation would be 35% U.S. stocks and 20% U.S. Bonds.

D.   1.   Futures and options may be used to increase and decrease asset class exposures. For example, (1) exposures could be increased by buying futures or selling put options on an equity index or a particular type of bond; or (2) exposure could be decreased by selling futures or buying put options on an equity index or bond. The choice of instrument and the specific characteristics of that instruments are dependent on the underlying investments in the plan's asset class exposure, and the level of risk reduction the plan sponsor is trying to achieve. Derivative securities cannot be used to alter exposure to all asset classes (e.g., real estate) due to lack of availability.

Strengths, or reasons for using derivatives, include:

-   Their cost-effectiveness compared to trading underlying securities in that transactions costs are low. (Cost effectiveness is also dependent, though, on the relative pricing of the derivative);
-   The ability to act immediately with no market impact on the underlying position. (There is, however, a possible impact within the derivatives market.)

Weaknesses, or reasons against using derivatives, include;
-   Rollover problems, in that the expiration of the derivatives position will not likely match the investor's timetable regarding exposure changes. Therefore, the investor is exposed to additional price-change risk.
-   The lack of availability of derivatives in some asset classes, notably real estate.
-   Exposures to pricing inefficiencies between the derivatives and the underlying markets.
-   Inefficiencies in derivatives markets in some foreign equity markets which increases risk related to price volatility or exposure mismatch.
-   Currency risk associated with foreign derivatives used to hedge underlying foreign positions with currency exposure.

17.   A.   Historically the primary investment benefits of owning unlevered real estate have been risk reduction and attractive real return. Both contentions are based on real estate's historical average along with its low correlation with other asset classes.

Attractive real returns are based in part on the ability of real estate owners to adjust income streams by recovering increased costs at the time of lease roll-over and/or through various types of escalator clauses designed to maintain market rents. Property value may be maintained or increased by increased income originating from escalator clauses or the renewal of leases in strong leasing environments. The ability of real estate assets to adjust income streams during periods of high inflation and provide capital gains argues for including real estate as both a source of diversification and a hedge against inflation.

Several sources report a low standard deviation of returns fore real estate as an asset class compared to common stock. More importantly, the reported small covariability or negative correlation of real estate returns with other asset classes makes real estate attractive due to the portfolio risk reduction possibilities attributable to this diversification effect.

The ability of real estate to provide attractive real returns and a hedge against inflation may be negatively influenced by local conditions. Poor management and location specific factors such as overbuilding and/or the deterioration of the local economy can impair the leasing environment by lowering the income stream and result in lower property values. Under such conditions the reported inflation hedging characteristics of real estate are difficult to achieve.

Measurement of real estate returns is complicated by the limited availability of transactions based data and the need to rely on appraised values to calculate periodic returns, the standard deviations about these returns, and the covariance of these returns with other asset classes. This appraisal induced smoothing may understate both the actual standard deviations of returns and the covariance with other asset classes. If these data deficiencies are strong and occur simultaneously, then real estate returns may, at least in the short run, be materially misrepresented.

B.   Over the course of the next five years, the property will not support either of the two claims. The loss of the principal tenant in a depressed rental market will result in any new leases that can be negotiated being written at the market rate, well below the existing leases. Little improvement in rental rates or vacancy levels can be expected until supply and demand regain equilibrium. The volatility of annual income will change unfavorably and the valuation of the underlying property will be impaired. The usefulness of the property as a short term inflation hedge is doubtful. The lack of short term inflation protection does not affect the diversification aspects of the property. A high standard deviation of return does not determine a particular asset's covariance with other asset classes in the portfolio and, as such, does not impair the investment's ability to provide portfolio diversification.

Over the next 20 years, the property might well provide the inflation protection and diversification benefits claimed for real estate. The forecast depends on the assumptions made about the regional economy in general and the local real estate market in particular. The robust growth and diversification of the local economy plus the absence of new construction in the last several years should produce increased returns for existing properties that are well maintained. Under this set of assumptions this downtown office building should provide good inflation protection. Over the 20 year time frame stable rates of growth of population and employment and a low correlation of this office building's returns with returns from other asset classes should also make this property attractive from a risk reduction standpoint.

18.   A.   An appropriate Investment Policy Statement for the Defined Contribution (Profit Sharing) Plan would reflect the following facts:

1.   For the employees covered by it, the plan supplements coverage by the Defined Benefit (Pension) Plan;

2.   The covered employees largely comprise a unique, older group, but some participants do have a considerable time to go before normal retirement;

3.   Company contributions to the plan are no longer being made;

4.   Investments in the plan portfolio are not made in response to participant direction but rather are determined by company decisions in accordance with policy created by the Investment Committee;

5.   As the participants own the assets in the form of individual rights to proportionate shares of the total value on the date of withdrawal via termination or retirement, they (not the company) bear the full risk of fluctuation and/or loss and do so individually; and

6.   While, in principle, the participants should individually direct investment action in accordance with their own individual investment objectives, constraints, and preferences, this ideal situation does not exist in the situation described.

Given these facts, the corollary inferences that may be drawn from them, and other information provided in the preamble, an appropriate Investment Policy Statement for the plan would:

-       Emphasize positive real total return production and preservation of capital values as primary investment objectives. Since investment income is the only source of new money for the portfolio, and as it compounds until individual withdrawals occur production of a significant level of current income is desirable but not an end in itself, with some participants having many years of further involvement, growth of principal in addition to income is an important consideration as well.

-       Reflect the fact that the plan's investment horizon is not infinite; many participants are already "older" and some will be retiring sooner than later, making lump-sum withdrawal demands on the portfolio which its liquidity planning must take into account. Frequent cash flow analyses from the actuary are needed as part of that planning process.

-       Provide ongoing attention to both ERISA and Internal Revenue Service rules and requirements, as this is a qualified, tax-free situation whose integrity must be preserved for the participants.

-        Reflect the situation's unique aspects, namely the absence of external cash flows (the fund is "frozen"), a participant group which is not representative of the work force as a whole; and a liability set which is not

26- 33

reflective of the international involvements or requirements existing in the defined benefit (pension) plan (for example, there is no requirement for any non- U.S. return component).

B. An effective way to compare the elements of the two plans' policy statements is to place these elements in a common framework as follows:

	Pension Plan	Profit-sharing Plan
Objectives:		
Return	Seek high Inflation-adjusted total return. Maintain/increase plan surplus.	Seek moderate real returns with some growth of both income and principal.
Risk	Above-average capacity; aggressive posture acceptable.	Below-average capacity: no "deep Pocket" or further contributions.
Constraints:		
Time Horizon	Very long; work force average is young.	Medium, possibly very short as to individual participants but still long for others.
Liquidity	Minimal; contributions and income flows compound indefinitely.	Relatively high; some payouts are near, others are certain to follow and must be funded.
Legal/ Regulatory	ERISA: IRS regulations.	ERISA: IRS Regulations.
Tax	Tax-exempt.	Tax-exempt.

| Unique Circumstances | Need to plan for growing non-U.S. liability coverage and provide non-U.S. return component now. | No new participants; fund is "frozen" as to non-income cash flows; liquidity needs uncertain as to timing; no employee group with two plan coverages. |

The major differences between appropriate policies for the two plans are:

1.   The difference in risk objective, where the profit sharing plan is best served by an above-average level. In the pension case, PTC provides a "deep pocket" and a continuing flow of contributions that will cushion temporary declines in market values. The profit sharing plan has no inflow from contributions and all losses, temporary or permanent, in investment values are borne by the participants themselves.

Both plans will benefit from a real, total return objective, but the profit sharing plan's policy will also see capital preservation as part of a realistic return goal.

2.   The difference in time horizon, which reflects not only the difference in the age mix of the participants but also the fact that the profit sharing plan has a finite liquidation ahead while the pension plan will go on virtually indefinitely.

3.   The difference in provision which must be made for liquidity, which is significant in the profit sharing case but irrelevant for the pension plan.

4.   The fact that the pension plan must accommodate a sizeable and growing amount of non-U.S. $ liabilities while the profit sharing plan is free of such considerations is also an important policy-influencing difference between the two. However, the absence of specific non-$ liabilities in the profit sharing case should not preclude investment of a portion of participants' interests in international securities for the diversification and potential for return enhancement that so doing would provide.

5.   There are unique circumstances in both situations that must be accommodated in the investment policies, as noted above. However, tax and regulatory aspects are similar in each case.

C.   The grounds cited by the opposing Committee member are weak, inappropriate, and invalid in the context of the plan as it exists. The member's objection ignores the fact that the sole interests to be served here are those of the participants and that the sole question to be answered therefore is whether or not the addition of the international vehicle would improve their investment alternatives. Perhaps this Committee member has equated the requirements of the pension plan (where it is necessary to have a non-U.S. securities component specifically structured to reflect the plan's non-U.S. liabilities) with the absence of such requirements in the profit-sharing plan.

The issue for the profit-sharing plan is not requirements (there are none) but rather potential benefits to be gained by the use of a non-U.S. securities component. Neither the U.S. base of the participant set nor the solely U.S. nature of the liabilities is a valid reason for opposition; the decision for or against the Chairman's proposal should be made on the basis of relevant investment characteristics.

Those relevant investment considerations would include:

1.   Diversification Benefit

        Evidence is strong that the addition of securities (markets) not highly correlated with an investor's domestic securities (markets) reduces the risk of a portfolio, in the same way and for the same reasons that diversifying a portfolio of domestic securities (markets) reduces risk. That is, international diversification helps improve the risk-adjusted performance of a domestic-only securities portfolio due to the relatively low correlation between the non-U.S. and U.S. asset classes.

2.   Incremental Performance Potential

        Addition of an international securities component would provide the portfolio with access to an enhanced mix of return opportunities, adding exposure to many sets of economic and market conditions where only one set existed before. These additional exposures would not only improve diversification but would also provide potential for incremental return performance over time.

3.   ERISA

        ERISA guidelines on prudent investment for the sole benefit of plan participants mandate diversification; international exposure in appropriate form and proportions would help meet this mandate.

3.   Currency Risk

        While the introduction of a non-U.S. securities component does introduce currency risk, such risk can be actively managed through a hedging program, leaving all or most of the diversification benefit intact.

4.   Openness Matching

Grantham's "openness matching" concept argues that, to the extent that U.S. pensioners buy foreign goods as part of their total "market basket" of goods, the portfolio should include foreign stocks to hedge the foreign component of the basket. The proposal to add a non-U.S. component in the situation described would be consistent with this argument.

CHAPTER 27: RISK MANAGEMENT AND HEDGING

1. If the beta of the portfolio were 1.0, she would sell $1 million of the index. Because beta is 1.25, she needs to sell $1.25 million of the index

2. She must sell $1 million $\times \dfrac{8}{10}$ = $.8 million of T-bonds.

3. The farmer must sell forward 100,000 bushels $\times (1/.90)$ = 111,111 bushels of yellow corn. This requires selling 111,111/5,000 = 22.2 contracts.

4. Suppose the yield on your portfolio increases by 1.5 basis points. Then the yield on the T-bond contract is likely to increase by 1 basis point. The loss on your portfolio will be $1 million $\times \Delta y \times D^*$ = $1 million $\times .00015 \times 4$ = $600. The change in the futures price (per $100 par value) will be $95 \times .0001 \times 9$ = $.0855, or on a $100,000 par value contract, $85.50. Therefore you should sell $600/$85.50 = 7 contracts.

5. If yield changes on the bond and the contracts are each 1 basis point, the bond value will change by

$$\$10 \text{ million} \times .0001 \times 8 = \$8000.$$

The contract will result in a cash flow of

$$\$100,000 \times .0001 \times 6 = \$60.$$

Therefore, you should sell 8000/60 = 133 contracts. You *sell* because you need profits on the contract to offset losses as a bond issuer if interest rates increase.

6. a. $800 \times (1.01) = 808$

   b. $8 million/$(250 \times 800)$ = 40 contracts *short*.

   c. $40 \times 250 \times (808 - S_T)$ = 8,080,000 - 10,000 S_T

   d. The expected return on a stock is

   $$\alpha + r_f + \beta \, [E(r_M) - r_f]$$

   The CAPM predicts that $\alpha = 0$. In this case, however, if you believe that $\alpha = 2\%$ (i.e., .02), you forecast a portfolio return of

$$.02 + .01 + 1.0 \times (r_M - .01)$$
$$= .03 + [1 \times (r_M - .01)]$$

e. Because the market is assumed to pay no dividends, $r_M = (S_T - 800)/800 = S_T/800 - 1$, and the expected rate of return on the portfolio also can be written as

$$r_P = .03 + \left(1 \times [(S_T/800 - 1) - .01]\right)$$

The *dollar* value of the stock portfolio as a function of the market index is therefore $8 million $\times (1 + r_P)$, which equals

$$\$8 \text{ million} \times [.03 + S_T/800 - .01] = \$160,000 + 10,000 \, S_T$$

The dollar value of the short futures position will be (from part c)

$$8,080,000 - 10,000 \, S_T$$

The total value of the portfolio plus the futures proceeds is therefore

$$\begin{array}{l} 160,000 + 10,000 \, S_T \\ + \underline{8,080,000 - 10,000 \, S_T} \\ 8,240,000 \end{array}$$

The payoff is independent of the value of the stock index. Systematic risk has been eliminated by hedging (although firm-specific risk remains).

f. The portfolio-plus-futures position cost $8 million to establish. The expected end-of-period value is $8,240,000. The rate of return is therefore 3 percent.

g. The beta of the hedged position is 0. The fair return should be $r_f = 1\%$. Therefore, the alpha of the position is $3\% - 1\% = 2\%$, the same as the alpha of the portfolio. Now, however, one can take a position on the alpha without incurring systematic risk.

7. You would short $.50 of the market index contract and $.75 of the computer industry stock for each dollar held in IBM.

8. Salomon believes that the market assessment of volatility is too high. Therefore, it should sell options because its analysis suggests the options are overpriced with respect to true volatility. The delta of the call is .6, while that of the put is $.6 - 1 = -.4$. Therefore, it should sell puts to calls in the ratio of .6 to .4. For example, if it sells 2 calls and 3 puts, it will be delta neutral:

$$\text{Delta} = 2 \times .6 + 3 \times (-.4) = 0$$

9. Using a volatility of 32% and time to maturity $T = .25$ years, the hedge ratio for Exxon is $N(d_1) = .5567$. Because you believe the calls are underpriced (selling at too low implied volatility), you will buy calls and short .5567 shares for each call that you buy.

10. The calls are cheap (implied $\sigma = .30$) and the puts are expensive (implied $\sigma = .34$). Therefore, buy calls and sell puts. Using the "true" volatility of $\sigma = .32$, the call delta is .5567 and the put delta is $.5567 - 1 = -.4433$. Therefore buy $.5567/.4433 = 1.256$ puts for each call purchased.

11. a. To calculate the hedge ratio, suppose that the market increases by 1%. Then the stock portfolio would be expected to increase by $1\% \times 1.5 = 1.5\%$, or $.015 \times \$1,250,000 = \$18,750$. Given the option delta of .8, the option portfolio would increase by $\$18,750 \times .8 = \$15,000$ and Salomon's liability from writing these options would increase by this amount. The futures price would increase by 1%, from 1,000 to 1,010. The 10-point gain would be multiplied by $250 to provide a gain of $2,500 per contract. Therefore, Salomon would need to buy $\$15,000/\$2,500 = 6$ contracts to hedge its exposure.

    b. The delta of a put option is $.8 - 1 = -0.2$. Therefore, for every 1% the market increases, the index will rise by 10 points and the value of the put option contract will change by $\text{delta} \times 10 \times \text{contract multiplier} = -0.2 \times 10 \times 100 = -\$200$. Therefore, Salomon should write $\$12,000/\$200 = 60$ put contracts.

12. If the stock market increases 1%, the 1 million shares of stock on which the options are written would be expected to increase by $.75\% \times \$5 \times 1 \text{ million} = \$37,500$. The options would increase by $\text{delta} \times \$37,500 = .8 \times \$37,500 = \$30,000$. The futures price will increase by 10 points from 1,000 to 1,010, providing a profit per contract of $10 \times \$250 = \$2,500$. You need to sell $\$30,000/\$2,500 = 12$ contracts to hedge against the possibility of a market decline.

13. Although people will want to hedge this source of risk, the lack of correlation between security returns and the risk factor will make such hedging impossible. Because security returns are uncorrelated with the risk factor, the securities cannot serve to offset the uncertainty surrounding that factor. Hence there is no reason for investors to tilt their portfolios toward or away from any security for hedging in connection with the factor.

14. a. The stock is a good inflation hedge. Its real return increases when the inflation rate increases. This will offset the exposure I already suffer due to my fixed-income pension.

    b. If I produce gold and already benefit from inflation, I do not want this stock for hedging. It exaggerates my current exposure.

c. If retirees are more numerous, there will be a net hedging demand for stocks with high inflation betas that will drive up their prices and reduce their expected rates of return.

15. a. The industry factor is a statistically useful means to describe returns because it helps to explain movement in a nontrivial group of stocks. It is a common factor for all machine tool producers. However, there is no compelling reason to identify this industry return with a significant extramarket hedge factor. Investors can diversify away "industry-specific" risk if each industry is sufficiently small. On this score, a machine-tool factor would not be expected to appear in connection with the multifactor CAPM.

b. One would not expect the factor to command a risk premium. In the jargon of the APT, it would be a nonpriced factor. The industry factor would not be expected to command a risk premium by the usual principles of the CAPM, since industry-specific risk presumably can be diversified away. Neither does it seem that the machine-tool industry portfolio is a natural hedge for any significant source of extramarket risk. More generally, the APT allows for many factors (such as industry co-movements) that help to describe returns of various subsets of securities, but that do not serve to hedge a meaningful source of systematic risk.

16. Method 1: Sell short T-bonds to offset the risk of the P&G bonds. To determine how many T-bonds to sell, use the hedge ratio, which gives the ratio of the number of T-bonds to sell for each P&G bond held in the portfolio.

The yield beta tells us how much the P&G bond yield changes in relation to the yield on the T-bond. The regression equation indicates that the yield beta is 0.89, indicating that P&G yields are somewhat more stable than Treasury yields.

The hedge ratio is therefore

$$.89 \times \frac{.08286}{.08766} = .8413$$

Since Byron holds 10,000 P&G bonds ($10 million face value), he needs to sell short .8413 x 10,000 Treasury bonds, each with face value $1000.

Method 2: Sell T-bond futures contracts. Here, the yield beta is .47 so the hedge ratio is

$$.47 \times \frac{.08286}{.0902} = .4318$$

Byron needs to sell short .4318 of the benchmark T-bonds on which the contract is written for each P&G bond he holds. This means he needs to sell 4,318 bonds. Since each futures contract calls for delivery of 100 bonds (i.e., $100,000 face value), he would need to short 43.18 contracts.

A more advanced answer that goes beyond the material covered in the text would note that the actual delivery bond is not the benchmark 8% coupon bond. Since the conversion factor of the "cheapest to deliver" is 1.1257, the hedge ratio is increased to

$$43.18 \times 1.1257 = 48.6 \text{ contracts}$$

CHAPTER 28: THE THEORY OF ACTIVE PORTFOLIO MANAGEMENT

1. a. Define $R = r - r_f$. Note that we compute the estimates of standard deviation using 4 degrees of freedom (i.e., we divide the sum of the squared deviations from the mean by 4 despite the fact that we have 5 observations), since deviations are taken from the sample mean, not the theoretical population mean.

$$E(R_B) = 11.16\% \qquad\qquad E(R_U) = 8.42\%$$
$$\sigma_B = 21.24\% \qquad\qquad\qquad \sigma_U = 14.85\%$$
$$\rho = .75$$

Risk neutral investors would prefer the Bull Fund because its performance suggests a higher mean. Given the estimates of the variance of the series and the small number of observations, the difference in the averages is too small to determine the superiority of Bull with any confidence.

b. Using the reward to volatility (Sharpe) measure,

$$S_B = \frac{E(r_B) - r_f}{\sigma_B} = \frac{E(R_B)}{\sigma_B} = \frac{11.16}{21.24} = .5254$$

$$S_U = \frac{E(R_U)}{\sigma_U} = \frac{8.42}{14.85} = .5670$$

The data suggest that the Unicorn Fund dominates for a risk averse investor.

c. The decision rule for the proportion to be invested in the risky asset, given by the formula

$$y = \frac{E(r) - r_f}{\sigma} = \frac{E(R)}{.01A\sigma^2}$$

maximizes a mean variance utility of the form, $U = E(r) - .005A\sigma^2$ for which Sharpe's measure is the appropriate criterion for the selection of optimal risky portfolios. In any event, an investor with $A = 3$ would invest the following fraction in Unicorn:

$$y_U = \frac{8.42}{.01 \times 3 \times 14.85^2} = 1.2727$$

Note that the investor wants to borrow in order to invest in Unicorn. In that case, his portfolio risk premium and standard deviation would be:

$$E(r_P) - r_f = 1.2727 \times 8.42 = 10.72\% , \qquad \sigma_P = 1.2727 \times 14.85 = 18.90\%$$

and his utility level would be:

$$U(P) = r_f + 10.72 - .005 \times 3 \times 18.90^2 = r_f + 5.36.$$

If borrowing is not allowed, investing 100% in Unicorn would lead to:

$$E(r_P) - r_f = 8.42\%$$

$$\sigma_P = 14.85\%$$

$$U(P) = r_f + 8.42 - .005 \times 3 \times 14.85^2 = r_f + 5.11$$

Note that if Bull must be chosen, then

$$y_B = \frac{11.16}{.01 \times 3 \times 21.24^2} = .8246$$

$$E(r_P) - r_f = .8246 \times 11.16 = 9.20\%$$

$$\sigma_P = .8246 \times 21.24 = 17.51\%$$

$$U(P) = r_f + 9.20 - .005 \times 3 \times 17.51^2 = r_f + 4.60.$$

Thus, even with a borrowing restriction Unicorn (with the lower mean) is still superior.

2. $\sigma = 5.5\%$ and $r_f = 1\%$

Write the Black-Scholes formula from Chapter 21 as

$$C = SN(d_1) - PV(X) \, N(d_2)$$

In this application, where we express the value of timing per dollar of assets, we use $S = 1.0$ for the value of the stock; the present value of the exercise price also is 1. Note that

$$d_1 = \frac{\ln(S/X) + (r + \sigma^2/2)T}{\sigma\sqrt{T}} \quad \text{and } d_2 = d_1 - \sigma\sqrt{T}$$

When $S = PV(X)$, and $T = 1$, the formula for d_1 reduces to $d_1 = \sigma/2$ and $d_2 = -\sigma/2$.
Therefore, $C = N(\sigma/2) - N(-\sigma/2)$. Finally recall that $N(-x) = 1 - N(x)$. Therefore, we can write the value of the call as

$$C = N(\sigma/2) - [1 - N(\sigma/2)] = 2N(\sigma/2) - 1$$

Since $\sigma = .055$, the value is:

$$C = 2N(.0275) - 1.$$

Interpolating from the standard normal table (Table 21.2):

28-2

$$C = 2[.5080 + \frac{.0075}{.0200}(.5160 - .5080)] - 1$$

$$C = 1.0220 - 1 = .0220$$

Hence the added value of a perfect timing strategy is 2.2% per month.

3. a. Using the relative frequencies to estimate the conditional probabilities P_1 and P_2 for timers A and B, we find:

	Timer A	Timer B
P_1	78/135 = .58	86/135 = .64
P_2	57/92 = .62	50/92 = .54
$P^* = P_1 + P_2 - 1$	.20 >	.18

The data suggest that timer A is the better forecaster

b. Using the following equation to value the imperfect timing services of A and B,

$$C(P^*) = C(P_1 + P_2 - 1)$$
$$C_A(P^*) = 2.2\% \times .20 = .44\% \text{ per month}$$
$$C_B(P^*) = 2.2\% \times .18 = .40\% \text{ per month}$$

Timer A's added value is greater by 4 basis points per month.

4 a.

Alphas, α	Expected excess return
$\alpha_i = r_i - [r_f + \beta_i(r_M - r_f)]$	$E(r_i) - r_f$
$\alpha_A = 20 - [8 + 1.3(16 - 8)] = 1.6\%$	$20 - 8 = 12\%$
$\alpha_B = 18 - [8 + 1.8(16 - 8)] = -4.4$	$18 - 8 = 10\%$
$\alpha_C = 17 - [8 + 0.7(16 - 8)] = 3.4$	$17 - 8 = 9\%$
$\alpha_D = 12 - [8 + 1.0(16 - 8)] = -4.0$	$12 - 8 = 4\%$

Stocks A and C have positive alphas, whereas stocks B and D have negative alphas. The variances are

$$\sigma_e^2(A) = 3364 \qquad \sigma_e^2(C) = 3600$$
$$\sigma_e^2(B) = 5041 \qquad \sigma_e^2(D) = 3025$$

b.	To construct the optimal risky portfolio, we first need to determine the active portfolio. Using the Treynor-Black technique, we construct the active portfolio

	$\dfrac{\alpha}{\sigma_e^2}$	$\dfrac{\alpha / \sigma_e^2}{\Sigma \alpha / \sigma_e^2}$
A	.000476	−.6142
B	−.000873	1.1265
C	.000944	−1.2181
D	−.001322	1.7058
Total	−.000775	1.0000

Do not be disturbed by the fact that the positive alpha stocks get negative weights and vice versa. The entire position in the active portfolio will turn out to be negative, returning everything to good order. With these weights, the forecast for the active portfolio is:

$$\alpha = -.6142 \times 1.6 + 1.1265 \times (-4.4) - 1.2181 \times 3.4 + 1.7058 \times (-4.0) = -16.90\%$$

$$\beta = -.6142 \times 1.3 + 1.1265 \times 1.8 - 1.2181 \times .70 + 1.7058 \times 1 = 2.08$$

The high beta (higher than any individual beta) results from the short position in relatively low beta stocks and long position in relatively high beta stocks.

$$\sigma_e^2 = (-.6142)^2 \times 3364 + 1.1265^2 \times 5041 + (-1.2181)^2 \times 3600 + 1.7058^2 \times 3025$$
$$= 21809.6$$
$$\sigma_e = 147.68\%$$

Here, again, the levered position in stock B (with the high σ_e), overcomes the diversification effect, and results in a high residual standard deviation. The optimal risky portfolio has a proportion w^* in the active portfolio as follows:

$$w_0 = \frac{\alpha / \sigma_e^2}{[E(r_M) - r_f] / \sigma_M^2} = \frac{-16.90 / 21809.6}{8 / 23^2} = -.05124$$

The negative position is justified for the reason given earlier.

The adjustment for beta is

$$w^* = \frac{w_0}{1 + (1 - \beta) w_0} = \frac{-.05124}{1 + (1 - 2.08)(-.05124)} = -.0486$$

Because w* is negative, we end up with a positive position in stocks with positive alphas and vice versa. The position in the index portfolio is:

$$1 - (-.0486) = 1.0486$$

28-4

c.   To calculate Sharpe's measure for the optimal risky portfolio we need the appraisal ratio for the active portfolio and Sharpe's measure for the market portfolio. The appraisal ratio of the *active portfolio* is:

$$A = \alpha / \sigma_e = -16.90/147.68 = -.1144$$

and $A^2 = .0131$

Hence, the square of Sharpe's measure, S, of the *optimized risky portfolio* is :

$$S^2 = S_M^2 + A^2 = (\frac{8}{23})^2 + .0131 = .1341$$

and $S = .3662$

Compare this to the market's Sharpe measure,

$$S_M = 8/23 = .3478$$

The difference is .0184.

Note that the only-moderate improvement in performance results from the fact that only a small position is taken in the active portfolio A because of its large residual variance.

We calculate the "Modigliani-squared", or M^2 measure, as follows:

$$E(r_{P*}) = r_f + S_P \sigma_M = 8\% + .3662 \times 23\% = 16.423\%$$

$$M^2 = E(r_{P*}) - E(r_M) = 16.423\% - 16\% = 0.423\%$$

d.   To calculate the exact makeup of the *complete portfolio*, we need the mean excess return of the optimal risky portfolio and its variance. The risky portfolio beta is given by

$$\beta_P = w_M + w_A \times \beta_A = 1.0486 + (-.0486)2.08 = .95$$

$$E(R_P) = \alpha_P + \beta_P E(R_M) = -.0486(-16.90) + .95 \times 8 = 8.42\%$$

$$\sigma_P^2 = \beta_P^2 \sigma_M^2 + \sigma_{e_P}^2 = (.95 \times 23)^2 + (-.0486)^2 \times 21809.6 = 528.94$$

$$\sigma_P = 23.00\%$$

Since A = 2.8, the optimal position in this portfolio is:

$$y = \frac{8.42}{.01 \times 2.8 \times 528.94} = .5685$$

In contrast, with a passive strategy

$$y = \frac{8}{.01 \times 2.8 \times 23^2} = .5401$$

which is a difference of .0284.

The final positions of the complete portfolio are:

Bills	$1 - .5685 =$	43.15%
M:	$.5685 \times 1.0486 =$	59.61
A:	$.5685 \, (-.0486)(-.6142) =$	1.70
B:	$.5685 \, (-.0486)(1.1265) =$	$- 3.11$
C:	$.5685 \, (-.0486)(-1.2181) =$	3.36
D:	$.5685 \, (-.0486)(1.7058) =$	$- 4.71$
		100.00

Note that M may include positive proportions of stocks A through D.

5.   If a manager is not allowed to sell short he will not include stocks with negative alphas in his portfolio, so that A and C are the only ones he will consider.

	α	σ_e^2	$\dfrac{\alpha}{\sigma_e^2}$	$\dfrac{\alpha / \sigma_e^2}{\Sigma \alpha / \sigma_e^2}$
A:	1.6	3364	.000476	.3352
C:	3.4	3600	.000944	.6648
			.001420	1.0000

The forecast for the active portfolio is:

$$\alpha = .3352 \times 1.6 + .6648 \times 3.4 = 2.80\%$$

$$\beta = .3352 \times 1.3 + .6648 \times 0.7 = 0.90$$

$$\sigma_e^2 = .3352^2 \times 3364 + .6648^2 \times 3600 = 1969.03$$

$$\sigma_e = 44.37\%$$

The weight in the active portfolio is:

$$w_0 = \frac{\alpha / \sigma_e^2}{E(R_M) / \sigma_M^2} = \frac{2.80 / 1969.03}{8 / 23^2} = .0940$$

and adjusting for beta

$$w^* = \frac{w_0}{1 + (1 - \beta)w_0} = \frac{.094}{1 + (1 - .90)(.094)} = .0931$$

The appraisal ratio of the active portfolio is

$$A = \alpha / \sigma_e = 2.80 / 44.37 = .0631$$

and hence, the square of Sharpe's measure is:

$$S^2 = (8/23)^2 + .0631^2 = .1250$$

and S = .3535, compared to the market's Sharpe measure S_M = .3478. When short sales were allowed (problem 4), the manager's Sharpe measure was higher, .3662. The reduction in the Sharpe measure is the cost of the short sale restriction.

We calculate the "Modigliani-squared", or M^2 measure, as follows:

$$E(r_{P*}) = r_f + S_P \sigma_M = 8\% + .3535 \times 23\% = 16.1305\%$$

$$M^2 = E(r_{P*}) - E(r_M) = 16.1305\% - 16\% = 0.1305\%$$

versus .423% when short sales were allowed.

The characteristics of the optimal risky portfolio are:

$$\beta_P = w_M + w_A \times \beta_A = 1 - .0931 + .0931 \times .9 = .99$$

$$E(R_P) = \alpha_P + \beta_P E(R_M) = .0931 \times 2.8 + .99 \times 8 = 8.18\%$$

$$\sigma_P^2 = \beta_P^2 \sigma_M^2 + \sigma_{e_P}^2 = (.99 \times 23)^2 + .0931^2 \times 1969.03 = 535.54$$

$$\sigma_P = 23.14\%$$

With A = 2.8, the optimal position in this portfolio is:

$$y = \frac{8.18}{.01 \times 2.8 \times 535.54} = .5455$$

The final positions in each asset are:

Bills	$1 - .5455 =$	45.45%
M:	$.5455 \times (1 - .0931) =$	49.47%
A:	$.5455 \times .0931 \times .3352 =$	1.70%
C:	$.5455 \times .0931 \times .6648 =$	3.38%
		————
		100.00%

b. The mean and variance of the optimized complete portfolios in the unconstrained and short-sales constrained cases, and the passive strategy are:

	$E(R_C)$	σ_C^2
Unconstrained	$.5685 \times 8.42 = 4.79$	$.5685^2 \times 528.93 = 170.95$
Constrained	$.5455 \times 8.18 = 4.46$	$.5455^2 \times 535.54 = 159.36$
Passive	$.5401 \times 8.00 = 4.32$	$.5401^2 \times 529.00 = 154.31$

The utility level, $E(r_C) - .005A\sigma_C^2$ is:

Unconstrained	$8 + 4.79 - .005 \times 2.8 \times 170.95 = 10.40$
Constrained	$8 + 4.46 - .005 \times 2.8 \times 159.36 = 10.23$
Passive	$8 + 4.32 - .005 \times 2.8 \times 154.31 = 10.16$

6. a. The optimal passive portfolio is obtained from equation (8.7) in Chapter 8 on Optimal Risky Portfolios.

$$w_M = \frac{E(R_M)\sigma_H^2 - E(R_H)Cov(r_H, r_M)}{E(R_M)\sigma_H^2 + E(R_H)\sigma_M^2 - [E(R_H) + E(R_M)]Cov(r_H, r_M)}$$

where $E(R_M) = 8\%$, $E(R_H) = 2\%$ and $Cov(r_H, r_M) = \rho\sigma_M\sigma_H = .6 \times 23 \times 18 = 248.4$

$$w_M = \frac{8 \times 18^2 - 2 \times 248.4}{8 \times 18^2 + 2 \times 23^2 - (8 + 2)248.4} = 1.797$$

and
$$w_H = -.797$$

If short sales are not allowed, portfolio H would have to be left out of the passive portfolio because the weight on H is negative.

28-8

b. With short sales allowed,

$$E(R_{passive}) = 1.797 \times 8 + (-.797) \times 2 = 12.78$$

$$\sigma^2_{passive} = (1.797 \times 23)^2 + [(-.797) \times 18]^2 + 2 \times 1.797 \times (-.797) \times 248.4$$

$$= 1202.54$$

$$\sigma_{passive} = 34.68\%$$

Sharpe's measure in this case is:

$$S_{passive} = 12.78 \,/\, 34.68 = .3685$$

compared with the market's Sharpe measure of

$$S_M = 8 \,/\, 23 = .3478$$

c. The improvement in utility for the expanded model of H and M versus a portfolio of M alone is calculated below for A = 2.8.

$$y = \frac{12.78}{.01 \times 2.8 \times 1202.54} = .3796$$

Therefore,

$$U_{passive} = 8 + 12.78 \times .3796 - .005 \times 2.8 \times .3796^2 \times 1202.54 = 10.43$$

which is greater than $U_{passive} = 10.16$ from problem 5.

7. The first step is to find the beta of the stocks relative to the optimized passive portfolio. For any stock i, the covariance with a portfolio is the sum of the covariances with the portfolio components, accounting for the weights of the components. Thus,

$$\beta_i = \frac{Cov(r_i, r_{passive})}{\sigma^2_{passive}}$$

$$= \frac{\beta_{iM} w_M \sigma^2_M + \beta_{iH} w_H \sigma^2_H}{\sigma^2_{passive}}$$

Therefore,

$$\beta_A = \frac{1.2 \times 1.797 \times 23^2 + 1.8 \times (-.797)18^2}{1202.54} = .5621$$

$$\beta_B = \frac{1.4 \times 1.797 \times 23^2 + 1.1 \times (-.797)18^2}{1202.54} = .8705$$

$$\beta_C = \frac{0.5 \times 1.797 \times 23^2 + 1.5 \times (-.797)18^2}{1202.54} = .0731$$

$$\beta_D = \frac{1.0 \times 1.797 \times 23^2 + 0.2 \times (-.797)18^2}{1202.54} = .7476$$

Now the alphas relative to the optimized portfolio are:

$\alpha_i = E(r_i) - r_f - \beta_{i,passive} \times E(R_{passive})$

$\alpha_A = 20 - 8 - .5621 \times 12.78 = 4.82\%$

$\alpha_B = 18 - 8 - .8705 \times 12.78 = -1.12$

$\alpha_C = 17 - 8 - .0731 \times 12.78 = 8.07$

$\alpha_D = 12 - 8 - .7476 \times 12.78 = -5.55$

The residual variances are now obtained from:

$$\sigma_e^2(i:passive) = \sigma_i^2 - \left(\beta_{i:passive}^2 \times \sigma_{passive}^2 \right)$$

where $\sigma_i^2 = \beta_M^2 \sigma_M^2 + \sigma_e^2(i)$ from Problem 4.

$\sigma_e^2(A) = (1.3 \times 23)^2 + 58^2 - (.5621 \times 34.68)^2 = 3878.01$

$\sigma_e^2(B) = (1.8 \times 23)^2 + 71^2 - (.8705 \times 34.68)^2 = 5843.59$

$\sigma_e^2(C) = (0.7 \times 23)^2 + 60^2 - (.0731 \times 34.68)^2 = 3852.78$

$\sigma_e^2(D) = (1.0 \times 23)^2 + 55^2 - (.7476 \times 34.68)^2 = 2881.80$

From this point, the procedure is identical to that of problem 6:

	$\dfrac{\alpha}{\sigma_e^2}$	$\dfrac{\alpha / \sigma_e^2}{\Sigma \alpha / \sigma_e^2}$
A	.001243	1.0189
B	−.000192	−0.1574
C	.002095	1.7172
D	−.001926	−1.5787
Total	.001220	1.0000

The active portfolio parameters are:

$$\alpha = 1.0189 \times 4.82 + (-0.1574)(-1.12) + 1.7172 \times 8.07 + (-1.5787)(-5.55) = 27.71\%$$

$$\beta = 1.0189 \times .5621 + (-0.1574)(.8705) + 1.7172 \times .0731 + (-1.5787)(.7476) = -0.6190$$

$$\begin{aligned}\sigma_e^2 &= 1.0189^2 \times 3878.01 + (-0.1574)^2 \times 5843.59 \\ &\quad + 1.7172^2 \times 3852.78 + (-1.5787)^2 \times 2881.80 = 22{,}714.03\end{aligned}$$

The proportions in the overall risky portfolio can now be determined.

$$w_0 = \frac{\alpha/\sigma_e^2}{E(R_{passive})/\sigma_{passive}^2} = \frac{27.71 / 22{,}714.03}{12.78 / 1202.54} = .1148$$

$$w^* = \frac{.1148}{1 + (1 + 0.6190).1148} = .0968$$

a. Sharpe's measure for the optimal risky portfolio is

$$S^2 = S_{passive}^2 + (\alpha/\sigma_e)^2 = .3685^2 + \frac{27.71^2}{22{,}714.03} = .1696$$

$$S = .4118 \text{ compared to } S_{passive} = .3685$$

The difference in the Sharpe measure is therefore .0433.

b. The beta of the optimal risky portfolio is:

$$\beta_P = w^*\beta_A + (1 - w^*) = .0968(-0.6190) + .9032 = .8433$$

The mean excess return of this portfolio is:

$$E(R) = .0968 \times 27.71 + .8433 \times 12.78 = 13.46\%$$

and its variance and standard deviation are:

$$\sigma^2 = .8433^2 \times 1202.54 + .0968^2 \times 22714.03 = 1068.03$$

$$\sigma = 32.68\%$$

Therefore, the position in it would be:

$$y = \frac{13.46}{.01 \times 2.8 \times 1068.03} = .4501$$

The utility value for this portfolio is:

$$U = 8 + .4501 \times 13.46 - .005 \times 2.8 \times .4501^2 \times 1068.03 = 11.03$$

which is superior to all previous alternatives.

8.   If short sales are not allowed, then the passive portfolio reverts to M, and the solution mimics the solution to problem 5.

9.   All alphas are reduced to .3 times their values in the original case. Therefore, the relative weights of each security in the active portfolio are unchanged, but the alpha of the active portfolio is only .3 times its previous value, $.3 \times 16.90 = 5.07\%$, and the investor will take a smaller position in the active portfolio.

The optimal risky portfolio has a proportion w^* in the active portfolio as follows:

$$w_0 = \frac{\alpha / \sigma_e^2}{[E(r_M)-r_f] / \sigma_M^2} = \frac{-5.07 / 21,809.6}{8 / 23^2} = -.01537$$

The negative position is justified for the reason given earlier.

The adjustment for beta is

$$w^* = \frac{w_0}{1 + (1 - \beta)w_0} = \frac{-.01537}{1 + (1 - 2.08)(-.01537)} = -.0156$$

Because w^* is negative, we end up with a positive position in stocks with positive alphas and vice versa. The position in the index portfolio is:

$$1 - (-.0156) = 1.0156$$

To calculate Sharpe's measure for the optimal risky portfolio we need the appraisal ratio for the active portfolio and Sharpe's measure for the market portfolio. The appraisal ratio of the *active portfolio* is .3 times its previous value:

$$A = \alpha / \sigma_e = -5.07/147.68 = -.0343$$

and $A^2 = .00118$

Hence, the square of Sharpe's measure of the *optimized risky portfolio* is :

$$S^2 = S_M^2 + A^2 = (\frac{8}{23})^2 + .00118 = .1222$$

and $\qquad$ S = .3495

Compare this to the market's Sharpe measure,

$$S_M = 8/23 = .3478$$

The difference is .0017.

Note that the reduction of the forecast alphas by a factor of .3 reduced the squared appraisal ratio and improvement in the squared Sharpe ratio by a factor of $(.3)^2 = .09$.